MW01285492

TEXAS
PATTERN JURY CHARGES

Business • Consumer • Employment

TEXAS

PATTERN JURY CHARGES

Business   Consumer   Employment

Prepared by the

COMMITTEE

on

PATTERN JURY CHARGES

of the

STATE BAR OF TEXAS

Austin   1998

The State Bar of Texas, through its Books & Systems Department, publishes practice books prepared and edited by knowledgeable authors to give practicing lawyers as much assistance as possible. The competence of the authors ensures outstanding professional products, but, of course, neither the State Bar of Texas, the editors, nor the authors make either express or implied warranties in regard to their use. Each lawyer must depend on his or her own knowledge of the law and expertise in the use or modification of these materials.

The use of the masculine gender throughout this publication is purely for literary convenience and should, of course, be understood to include the feminine gender as well.

International Standard Book Number: 0-938160-99-0
Library of Congress Catalog Card Number: 87-62226

Printed in the United States of America

Texas Pattern Jury Charges—Business, Consumer & Employment was formerly titled *Texas Pattern Jury Charges, Volume 4.*

COMMITTEE ON PATTERN JURY CHARGES

Business • Consumer • Employment

1989–1990

MIKE M. TABOR, *Chair*

THOMAS BLACK

JUDGE ANN T. COCHRAN

DON C. DENNIS

MARTIN DIES, JR.

DAVID E. KELTNER

JOHN G. LEWIS

PETER LINZER

PHILIP K. MAXWELL

FRANK W. MITCHELL

RICHARD G. MUNZINGER

DUDLEY OLDHAM

THOMAS H. WATKINS

1991–1992

MIKE M. TABOR, *Chair*

PHILIP K. MAXWELL, *Vice-Chair*

THOMAS BLACK

SAMUEL L. BOYD

DON C. DENNIS

WILLIAM T. HANKINSON

JOHN G. LEWIS

PETER LINZER

MARK E. LOWES

FRANK W. MITCHELL

RICHARD G. MUNZINGER

CARRIN F. PATMAN

CHARLES R. WATSON, JR.

STATE BAR OF TEXAS

1990–1991

JAMES N. PARSONS III, *President*

RICHARD C. HILE, *Chairman of the Board*

ANTONIO ALVARADO, *Chairman, Board PDP Committee*

KAREN R. JOHNSON, *Executive Director*

COMMITTEE ON CONTINUING LEGAL EDUCATION

1990–1991

CHARLES M. WILSON III, *Chair*

ARTHUR R. HINOJOSA, *Vice-Chair*

J. LINDSEY SHORT, JR., *Board Advisor*

JOHN J. SAMPSON, *Books Subcommittee Chair*

BOOKS & SYSTEMS

SUSANNAH R. MILLS, *Director*

RICHARD MASELES, *Project Legal Editor*

DIANE MORRISON, *Senior Production Editor*

MICHAEL AMBROSE, *Production Editor*

JILL HOEFLING, *Production and Editorial Assistant*

ISABELLE LOPEZ, *Production and Editorial Assistant*

CONTENTS

PREFACE

The Pattern Jury Charges (volume 4) Committee has worked for over five years to produce this addition to the Pattern Jury Charges series. During most of that period the Committee met once a month and spent additional time between meetings doing research and writing drafts of the various questions, instructions, and comments that make up this volume.

The Committee gratefully acknowledges the instrumental role of Chief Justice Thomas R. Phillips, who chaired the Committee from 1985–87. It is also grateful for the help and support of five State Bar presidents: Charles L. Smith (1985–86), Bill Whitehurst (1986–87), Joe H. Nagy (1987–88), James B. Sales (1988–89), and Darrell Jordan (1989–90).

In every successful enterprise there can be found a few key people who make things happen. The chair is particularly grateful for the attendance, participation, and hard work of Tom Black, Ann Cochran, Don Dennis, John Lewis, Peter Linzer, Phil Maxwell, Frank Mitchell, Richard Munzinger, and Dudley Oldham. We are also indebted to numerous other lawyers and judges who read the drafts and offered ideas for improvement—ranging from matters of substantive law to those having to do with style, format, and utility.

Our project legal editor, Vickie Tatum, deserves special recognition for her work on this volume. The State Bar Books and Systems staff has provided invaluable support, and we are also grateful for the advice and counsel of J. Hadley Edgar, chairman of the State Bar standing Committee on Pattern Jury Charges.

—Mike Tabor, *Chairman*

PREFACE TO THE 1992 SUPPLEMENT

It is the goal of the Pattern Jury Charges (volume 4) Committee to publish quality jury instructions for commercial, consumer, and business cases. Our goal was partially completed with the publication of the main volume in the fall of 1990 covering contract and consumer cases. We are pleased to publish this supplement with additional sections on fraud and bad faith.

The Committee is blessed to have highly qualified members who are dedicated to the task. The Committee owes a special debt of gratitude to Judge Ann Cochran. Before her resignation this spring, Judge Cochran served as cochair of the Committee for the 1991–92 bar year. During her tenure on the Committee, Judge Cochran was a catalyst in the chemistry of drafting pattern jury charges, and we will miss her leadership and organizational skills and her substantive knowledge.

This supplement is dedicated to the memory of J. Carlisle DeHay, Jr. Carlisle served on various Pattern Jury Charges Committees for more than ten years. He was regular in attendance and always well prepared. His attention to detail and careful analysis of the issues were an inspiration, and his companionship was a treasure.

The publication of this supplement would not have been possible without the diligence of the Committee members, the assistance of the State Bar Books and Systems staff, and the encouragement of lawyers and judges from all corners of the state. The Committee is particularly grateful for the hard work of John Lewis and Bill Hankinson. The sections on good faith and fair dealing were originated by John Lewis, and those on fraud and negligent misrepresentation were originated by Bill Hankinson. Without the first drafts and numerous revisions by John and Bill, the Committee could not have completed the final product.

Special recognition must be given to State Bar Books and Systems staff members Vickie Tatum and Rada Potts. For several years, Vickie has served as our project legal editor, and the Committee is pleased to welcome Rada as our new publications attorney for the project. Vickie and Rada worked jointly in the final stages of this publication, and we look forward to working with Rada on future publications. We are also grateful for the support of State Bar Presidents Jim Parsons (1990–91) and Bob Dunn (1991–92).

—Mike Tabor, *Chair*
—Phil Maxwell, *Vice-Chair*

PREFACE TO THE 1993 SUPPLEMENT

The Pattern Jury Charges (volume 4) Committee has completed its eighth year of work by publishing this supplement, which adds sections on tortious interference and updates other sections. Formed in 1985, the Committee published the main volume, covering contract and consumer cases, in the fall of 1990. The first supplement, adding sections on fraud and bad faith, was published in the fall of 1992.

The Committee acknowledges the contribution of Irene Aldrich to pattern jury charges. Irene has taken part in the production of every volume and supplement since 1975 and has been the chief production editor for the main volume and both supplements to PJC 4. The functionality and quality of pattern jury charges are unsurpassed, thanks to the efforts of dedicated people like Irene Aldrich.

Business, commercial, and consumer cases provide a large quantity of work for the bench and bar. The Committee endeavors to provide jury instructions and questions that will be useful during the decade of the nineties and beyond. Successful bar committees must have a combination of continuity and energy. Members who remain active provide continuity, and new members provide energy.

During the past two years, the Committee has been blessed with highly qualified new members who have been persistent in pressing forward for the publication of this supplement. Prominent among them are Judge Marilyn Aboussie, Sharon E. Callaway, Timothy G. Chovanec, Edwin R. Fleuriet, Rosemary T. Snider, Charles R. Watson, Jr., and Judge Mark L. Whittington. The Committee is grateful to them and particularly to Mark Lowes for producing the first draft of and numerous revisions to the tortious interference sections.

The State Bar Books and Systems staff continues to provide invaluable support to the Committee. We are particularly grateful for the hard work and dedication of our publications attorney for the project, Rada Potts. We also express our appreciation to State Bar Presidents Harriet Miers (1992-93) and Lonny D. Morrison (1993-94). The Committee has also benefited from the advice and counsel of J. Hadley Edgar, chairman of the State Bar standing Committee on Pattern Jury Charges, and Sue Mills, director of the State Bar Books and Systems Department.

—Mike Tabor, *Chair*
—Phil Maxwell, *Vice-Chair*

PREFACE TO THE 1997 EDITION

I don't believe a committee can write a book. There are all kinds of things a committee can do. It can, oh, govern a country, perhaps, but I don't believe it can write a book.

—Arnold Toynbee

This edition of *Texas Pattern Jury Charges—Business, Consumer & Employment* is the result of over three years' hard work by the committee charged with its drafting and revision. Entirely new chapters on employment law, piercing the corporate veil, and civil conspiracy are included. New sections covering proportionate responsibility and exemplary damages have been added, reflecting the work of the 74th Legislature in its 1995 session. Every existing chapter of this book was also reviewed by the Committee, and extensive changes were made as a result.

Every incarnation of this Committee has been a remarkable gathering of trial and appellate lawyers, and the Committee responsible for this book is no exception. This book was formed in crucibles of advocacy and scholarship, tempered by the goodwill and good humor of its members. Every member deserves recognition for his or her contribution, but several merit special recognition: Mark Kincaid, chair of the subcommittee that revised the DTPA/Insurance Code chapter; Rosemary Snider and Skip Watson, initial authors of the piercing and conspiracy chapters, respectively; and Art Brender, Tim Chovanec, Don Dennis, Mark Howell, Andy Kerr, Bob Mace, Keith O'Connell, and Ed Walton, for consistent excellence in their respective contributions. Sharon Callaway, who served both as vice-chair of the Committee and as chair of the subcommittee responsible for the new employment chapter, deserves special recognition as well for her multiple contributions. It has been a special pleasure to share my time on this Committee with my fellow members, who are, uniformly, both exemplary lawyers and fine people. Those qualities also apply to Richard Maseles of the State Bar. Richard brought superb legal and organizational skills to a job Tim Chovanec likened to herding cats.

We recognize the special place that pattern jury charges have in Texas civil jurisprudence, and take our responsibility to bench and bar very seriously. We welcome your comments, suggestions, and criticisms. Richard Maseles acts as a clearinghouse for your feedback. He can be reached at (800) 204-2222, extension 1481. His fax number is (512) 463-1509.

Now we are looking for a country to govern.

—Phil Maxwell, *Chair*

PREFACE TO THE 1998 EDITION

This edition of *Texas Pattern Jury Charges—Business, Consumer & Employment* contains both edits to the existing book necessitated by statutory and common-law changes and one new chapter on fiduciary duty. The small size of the new chapter belies the effort that went into its creation. In 1994, the Committee decided to undertake the topic, and a subcommittee charged with preparing drafts for full Committee consideration worked on it from that time until its final approval in early 1998. Andy Kerr, the chair of that subcommittee, led this effort with impeccable legal scholarship, a light leadership touch, and unfailing good humor. The Committee, and the Bar, is in his debt.

As always, some of the finest (and busiest) lawyers in Texas have given freely of their time, expertise, and experience to make this book both scrupulously accurate and evenhanded. Larry Smith ably led the employment law subcommittee through the revisions necessary because of the U.S. Supreme Court's recent sexual harassment decisions. A special thanks goes to that subcommittee's members Art Brender, Gregg Rosenberg, and Jeff Wray, employment lawyers *par excellence*, for their three years of hard and continuous work to produce the employment chapter published in 1997—which was the result of many hours of debate, including both congenial academic exchange and some hard-fought battles.

For years, the Committee has benefited from the fine legal minds of Skip Watson, Mark Kincaid, Don Dennis, Mark Howell, and Rosemary Snider. Also, this year we reaped the benefits of having sitting judges on the Committee, notably the Honorable Mark Whittington of the Dallas Court of Appeals and the Honorable Frank Montalvo of Bexar County's 288th District Court. Phil Maxwell, our "Chair Emeritus," who has served on this Committee since its inception in 1985 and chaired it from 1993 to 1997, continued to contribute his inimitable wit, his general brilliance, and his irreplaceable knowledge and understanding of Texas jury charge practice. Last, but not least, the Committee wishes to express its thanks, again, to our State Bar staff liaison Richard Maseles, as we bid him farewell. We will miss Richard's painstaking attention to detail, his enviable legal research abilities, and his overall wonderful organizational skills, which have enabled him to "herd this group of cats" for four years.

We commend this volume to you, the bench and bar of Texas. Like you, its creators have spent many late hours researching, analyzing, honing our arguments for the next day, sitting in tension-filled charge conferences, arguing cases both great and small to the juries and judges of this state, or sitting in judgment of those cases. We hope our efforts fulfill your needs.

—Sharon Callaway, *Chair*
—Tim Chovanec, *Vice-Chair*

INTRODUCTION

1. PURPOSE OF PUBLICATION

The purpose of this volume, like those of the others in this series, is to assist the bench and bar in preparing the court's charge in jury cases. It provides definitions, instructions, and questions needed to submit jury charges in the following cases:

- contract cases, both common-law and UCC sale of goods;

- actions under the Texas Deceptive Trade Practices–Consumer Protection Act (DTPA) and the Texas Insurance Code;

- actions against insurers for violation of the duty of good faith and fair dealing;

- breach of fiduciary duty;

- fraud, both common-law and statutory (Tex. Bus. & Com. Code Ann. § 27.01 (Vernon 1987)), and negligent misrepresentation;

- tortious interference with existing contracts and prospective contractual relations;

- employment actions;

- actions to hold shareholders personally liable for the liabilities of a corporation ("piercing the corporate veil"); and

- civil conspiracy.

It also contains questions and comments pertaining to defenses to the above actions and a section on damages.

The pattern charges are suggestions and guides to be used by a trial court if they are applicable and proper in a specific case. The Committee hopes that this volume will prove as worthy as have the earlier *Texas Pattern Jury Charges* volumes.

2. SCOPE OF PATTERN CHARGES

The infinite combinations of possible facts in contract, consumer, employment, and other business cases make it impracticable for the Committee to offer questions suitable for every occasion. The Committee has tried to prepare charges to serve as guides for the usual litigation encountered in these types of cases. However, a charge should conform to the pleadings and evidence of a case, and occasions will arise for the use of questions and instructions not specifically addressed here.

3. USE OF ACCEPTED PRECEDENTS

Like its predecessors, this Committee has avoided recommending changes in the law and has based this material on what it perceives the present law to be. It has attempted to foresee theories and objections that might be made in a variety of circumstances but not to express favor or disfavor for particular positions. In unsettled areas, the Committee generally has not taken a position on the exact form of a charge. However, it has provided guidelines in some areas in which there is no definitive authority. Of course, trial judges and attorneys should recognize that these recommendations may be affected by future appellate decisions and statutory changes.

4. PRINCIPLES OF STYLE

a. *Preference for broad-form questions.* Tex. R. Civ. P. 277 provides that "the court shall, whenever feasible, submit the cause upon broad-form questions." Accordingly, the basic questions are designed to be accompanied with one or more instructions. *See Texas Department of Human Services v. E.B.*, 802 S.W.2d 647 (Tex. 1990).

b. *Simplicity.* The Committee has sought to be as brief as possible and to use language that is simple and easy to understand.

c. *Definitions and instructions.* The Supreme Court of Texas has disapproved the practice of embellishing standard definitions and instructions, *Lemos v. Montez*, 680 S.W.2d 798 (Tex. 1984), or of adding unnecessary instructions, *First International Bank v. Roper Corp.*, 686 S.W.2d 602 (Tex. 1985). The Committee has endeavored to adhere to standard definitions and instructions stated in general terms rather than terms of the particular parties and facts of the case. If an instruction in general terms would be unduly complicated and confusing, however, reference to specific parties and facts is suggested.

d. *Placement of definitions and instructions in the charges.* Definitions and instructions that apply to a number of questions should be given immediately after the general instructions required by Tex. R. Civ. P. 226a. *See Woods v. Crane Carrier Co.*, 693 S.W.2d 377 (Tex. 1985). However, if a definition or instruction applies to only one question or cluster of questions (e.g., damages questions), it should be placed with that question or cluster. Specific guidance for placement of definitions and instructions can be found in the individual PJCs and comments.

e. *Burden of proof.* As authorized by Tex. R. Civ. P. 277, it is recommended that the burden of proof be placed by instruction rather than by inclusion in each question. When the burden is placed by instruction, it is not necessary that each question begin: "Do you find from a preponderance of the evidence that . . . " The admonitory instructions contain the following instruction, applicable to all questions:

> Answer "Yes" or "No" to all questions unless otherwise instructed. A "Yes" answer must be based on a preponderance of the evidence *unless otherwise instructed.* If you do not find that a preponderance of the evidence supports a "Yes" answer, then answer "No." The term "preponderance of the evidence" means the greater weight and degree of credible testimony or evidence introduced before you and admitted in this case. Whenever a question requires an answer other than "Yes" or "No," your answer must be based on a preponderance of the evidence *unless otherwise instructed.*

f. *Hypothetical examples.*   The names of hypothetical parties and facts have been italicized to indicate that the names and facts of the particular case should be substituted. In general, the name *Paul Payne* has been used for the plaintiff and *Don Davis* for the defendant. Some PJCs use other hypothetical parties (see, e.g., PJC 110.32). Their use is explained in the comments.

5. COMMENTS AND CITATIONS OF AUTHORITY

The comments to each PJC provide a ready reference to the law that serves as a foundation for the charge. The primary authority cited is Texas (or, for employment law, federal) case law. In some instances, secondary authority—for example, *Restatement (Second) of Contracts*—is also cited. The Committee wishes to emphasize that secondary authority is cited solely as additional guidance to the reader and not as legal authority for the proposition stated. Some comments also include variations of the recommended forms and additional questions or instructions for special circumstances.

6. USING THE PATTERN CHARGES

Matters on which the evidence is undisputed should not be submitted by either instruction or question. Conversely, questions, instructions, and definitions not included in this book may sometimes become necessary. Finally, preparation of a proper charge requires careful legal analysis and sound judgment.

7. FUTURE REVISIONS

The contents of questions, instructions, and definitions in the court's charge depend on the underlying substantive law relevant to the case. The Committee expects to publish updates as needed to reflect changes and new developments in the law.

CHAPTER 100   ADMONITORY INSTRUCTIONS

PJC 100.1   Instructions to Jury Panel before Voir Dire Examination

LADIES AND GENTLEMEN OF THE JURY PANEL:

The case that is now on trial is *Paul Payne* vs. *Don Davis*. This is a civil action which will be tried before a jury. Your duty as jurors will be to decide the disputed facts. It is the duty of the judge to see that the case is tried in accordance with the rules of law. In this case, as in all cases, the actions of the judge, parties, witnesses, attorneys and jurors must be according to law. The Texas law permits proof of any violation of the rules of proper jury conduct. By this I mean that jurors and others may be called upon to testify in open court about acts of jury misconduct. I instruct you, therefore, to follow carefully all instructions which I am now going to give you, as well as others which you will receive while this case is on trial. If you do not obey the instructions I am about to give you, it may become necessary for another jury to re-try this case with all of the attendant waste of your time here and the expense to the litigants and the taxpayers of this county for another trial. These instructions are as follows:

1. Do not mingle with nor talk to the lawyers, the witnesses, the parties, or any other person who might be connected with or interested in this case, except for casual greetings. They have to follow these same instructions and you will understand it when they do.

2. Do not accept from, nor give to, any of those persons any favors however slight, such as rides, food or refreshments.

3. Do not discuss anything about this case, or even mention it to anyone whomsoever, including your wife or husband, nor permit anyone to mention it in your hearing until you are discharged as jurors or excused from this case. If anyone attempts to discuss the case, report it to me at once.

4. The parties through their attorneys have the right to direct questions to each of you concerning your qualifications, background, experiences and attitudes. In questioning you, they are not meddling in your personal affairs, but are trying to select fair and impartial jurors who are free from any bias or prejudice in this particular case.

    a. Do not conceal information or give answers which are not true. Listen to the questions and give full and complete answers.

    b. If the attorneys ask some questions directed to you as a group which require an answer on your part individually, hold up your hand until you have answered the questions.

Do you understand these instructions? If not, please let me know now.

Whether you are selected as a juror for this case or not, you are performing a significant service which only free people can perform. We shall try the case as fast as possible consistent with justice, which requires a careful and correct trial. If selected on the jury, unless I instruct you differently, you will be permitted to separate at recesses and for meals, and at night.

The attorneys will now proceed with their examination.

COMMENT

When to use. The foregoing oral instructions are prescribed in Tex. R. Civ. P. 226a. The instructions, with such modifications as the circumstances of the particular case may require, are to be given to the jury panel "after they have been sworn as provided in Rule 226 and before the voir dire examination."

PJC 100.2   Instructions to Jury after Jury Selection

[Oral Instructions]

LADIES AND GENTLEMEN:

By the oath which you take as jurors, you become officials of this court and active participants in the public administration of justice. I now give you further instructions which you must obey throughout this trial.

It is your duty to listen to and consider the evidence and to determine fact issues later submitted to you, but I, as judge, will decide matters of the law. You will now receive written instructions which you will observe during this trial, together with such other instructions as I may hereafter give, or as heretofore I have given to you.

*[A copy of the written instructions set out below
shall thereupon be handed to each juror.]*

As you examine the instructions which have just been handed to you, we will go over them briefly together. The first three instructions have previously been stated, and you will continue to observe them throughout the trial. These and the other instructions just handed to you are as follows:

*[The written instructions set out below shall
thereupon be read by the court to the jury.]*

Counsel, you may proceed.

[Written Instructions]

1.   Do not mingle with nor talk to the lawyers, the witnesses, the parties, or any other person who might be connected with or interested in this case, except for casual greetings. They have to follow these same instructions and you will understand it when they do.

2.   Do not accept from, nor give to, any of those persons any favors however slight, such as rides, food or refreshments.

3.   Do not discuss anything about this case, or even mention it to anyone whomsoever, including your wife or husband, nor permit anyone to mention it in your hearing until you are discharged as jurors or excused from this case. If anyone attempts to discuss the case, report it to me at once.

4.   Do not even discuss this case among yourselves until after you have heard all of the evidence, the court's charge, the attorneys' arguments and until I have sent you to the jury room to consider your verdict.

5.   Do not make any investigation about the facts of this case. Occasionally we have a juror who privately seeks out information about a case on trial. This is improper. All evidence must be presented in open court so that each side may question the witnesses and make proper objection. This avoids a trial based upon secret evidence. These rules apply to jurors the same as they apply to the parties and to me. If you know of, or learn anything about, this case except from the evidence admitted during the course of this trial, you should tell me about it at once. You have just taken an oath that you will render a verdict on the evidence submitted to you under my rulings.

6.   Do not make personal inspections, observations, investigations, or experiments nor personally view premises, things or articles not produced in court. Do not let anyone else do any of these things for you.

7.   Do not tell other jurors your own personal experiences nor those of other persons, nor relate any special information. A juror may have special knowledge of matters such as business, technical or professional matters or he may have expert knowledge or opinions, or he may know what happened in this or some other lawsuit. To tell the other jurors any of this information is a violation of these instructions.

8.   Do not discuss or consider attorney's fees unless evidence about attorney's fees is admitted.

9.   Do not consider, discuss, nor speculate whether or not any party is or is not protected in whole or in part by insurance of any kind.

10. Do not seek information contained in law books, dictionaries, public or private records or elsewhere, which is not admitted in evidence.

At the conclusion of all the evidence, I may submit to you a written charge asking you some specific questions. You will not be asked, and you should not consider, whether one party or the other should win. Since you will need to consider all of the evidence admitted by me, it is important that you pay close attention to the evidence as it is presented.

The Texas law permits proof of any violation of the rules of proper jury conduct. By this I mean that jurors and others may be called upon to testify in open court about acts of jury misconduct. I instruct you, therefore, to follow carefully all instructions which I have given you, as well as others which you later receive while this case is on trial.

You may keep these instructions and review them as the case proceeds. A violation of these instructions should be reported to me.

COMMENT

When to use. The foregoing instructions are prescribed in Tex. R. Civ. P. 226a. The instructions, with such modifications as the circumstances of the particular case may require, are to be given to the jury "immediately after the jurors are selected for the case."

If no tort claim is involved. Item 9 should be deleted from the foregoing instructions unless a tort claim is involved in the case.

PJC 100.3   Charge of the Court

LADIES AND GENTLEMEN OF THE JURY:

This case is submitted to you by asking questions about the facts, which you must decide from the evidence you have heard in this trial. You are the sole judges of the credibility of the witnesses and the weight to be given their testimony, but in matters of law, you must be governed by the instructions in this charge. In discharging your responsibility on this jury, you will observe all the instructions which have previously been given you. I shall now give you additional instructions which you should carefully and strictly follow during your deliberations.

1.   Do not let bias, prejudice or sympathy play any part in your deliberations.

2.   In arriving at your answers, consider only the evidence introduced here under oath and such exhibits, if any, as have been introduced for your consideration under the rulings of the court, that is, what you have seen and heard in this courtroom, together with the law as given you by the court. In your deliberations, you will not consider or discuss anything that is not represented by the evidence in this case.

3.   Since every answer that is required by the charge is important, no juror should state or consider that any required answer is not important.

4.   You must not decide who you think should win, and then try to answer the questions accordingly. Simply answer the questions, and do not discuss nor concern yourselves with the effect of your answers.

5.   You will not decide the answer to a question by lot or by drawing straws, or by any other method of chance. Do not return a quotient verdict. A quotient verdict means that the jurors agree to abide by the result to be reached by adding together each juror's figures and dividing by the number of jurors to get an average. Do not do any trading on your answers; that is, one juror should not agree to answer a certain question one way if others will agree to answer another question another way.

6.   You may render your verdict upon the vote of ten or more members of the jury. The same ten or more of you must agree upon all of the answers made and to the entire verdict. You will not, therefore, enter into an agreement to be bound by a majority or any other vote of less than ten jurors. If the verdict and all of the answers therein are reached by unanimous agreement, the presiding juror shall sign the verdict for the entire jury. If any juror disagrees as to any answer made by the verdict, those jurors who agree to all findings shall each sign the verdict.

These instructions are given you because your conduct is subject to review the same as that of the witnesses, parties, attorneys and the judge. If it should be found that you have disregarded any of these instructions, it will be jury misconduct and it may require another trial by another jury; then all of our time will have been wasted.

The presiding juror or any other who observes a violation of the court's instructions shall immediately warn the one who is violating the same and caution the juror not to do so again.

When words are used in this charge in a sense that varies from the meaning commonly understood, you are given a proper legal definition, which you are bound to accept in place of any other meaning.

Answer "Yes" or "No" to all questions unless otherwise instructed. A "Yes" answer must be based on a preponderance of the evidence *unless otherwise instructed*. If you do not find that a preponderance of the evidence supports a "Yes" answer, then answer "No." The term "preponderance of the evidence" means the greater weight and degree of credible testimony or evidence introduced before you and admitted in this case. Whenever a question requires an answer other than "Yes" or "No," your answer must be based on a preponderance of the evidence *unless otherwise instructed*.

*[Definitions, questions, and special instructions
given to the jury will be transcribed here.]*

After you retire to the jury room, you will select your own presiding juror. The first thing the presiding juror will do is to have this complete charge read aloud and then you will deliberate upon your answers to the questions asked.

It is the duty of the presiding juror—

1. to preside during your deliberations,

2. to see that your deliberations are conducted in an orderly manner and in accordance with the instructions in this charge,

3. to write out and hand to the bailiff any communications concerning the case that you desire to have delivered to the judge,

4. to vote on the questions,

5. to write your answers to the questions in the spaces provided, and

6. to certify to your verdict in the space provided for the presiding juror's signature or to obtain the signatures of all the jurors who agree with the verdict if your verdict is less than unanimous.

You should not discuss the case with anyone, not even with other members of the jury, unless all of you are present and assembled in the jury room. Should anyone attempt to talk to you about the case before the verdict is returned, whether at the courthouse, at your home, or elsewhere, please inform the judge of this fact.

When you have answered all the questions you are required to answer under the instructions of the judge and your presiding juror has placed your answers in the spaces provided and signed the verdict as presiding juror or obtained the signatures, you will inform the bailiff at the door of the jury room that you have reached a verdict, and then you will return into court with your verdict.

_____

JUDGE PRESIDING

Certificate

We, the jury, have answered the above and foregoing questions as herein indicated, and herewith return same into court as our verdict.

(To be signed by the presiding juror if unanimous.)

_____

PRESIDING JUROR

(To be signed by those rendering the verdict if not unanimous.)

_____   _____

_____   _____

_____   _____

_____   _____

_____   _____

_____

COMMENT

When to use.   The above charge of the court includes the written instructions required by Tex. R. Civ. P. 226a to "be given by the court to the jury as part of the charge." The paragraph beginning with "Answer 'Yes' or 'No' " has been added to the form prescribed in rule 226a and is necessary to place the burden of proof by instruction. The paragraph beginning with "When words are used in this charge" and all the language from "It is the duty of the presiding juror" to the end of the charge have also been added to the form prescribed in rule 226a. It is the Committee's view that these additional instructions are desirable.

PJC 100.4   Additional Instruction for Bifurcated Trial

LADIES AND GENTLEMEN OF THE JURY:

In discharging your responsibility on this jury, you will observe all the instructions that have been previously given you. I shall now give you additional instructions that you should carefully and strictly follow during your deliberations.

All jurors have the right and the responsibility to deliberate on [*this*] [*these*] Question[*s*], but at least ten of those who agreed to the verdict in the first phase of this trial must agree to this answer and sign this verdict accordingly. If your first verdict was unanimous, this second verdict may be rendered by the vote of at least ten of you.

_____
JUDGE PRESIDING

Certificate

We, the jury, have answered the above and foregoing question[*s*] as herein indicated, and herewith return same into court as our verdict.

(To be signed by the presiding juror if unanimous.)

_____
PRESIDING JUROR

(To be signed by those rendering the verdict if not unanimous.)

_____   _____

_____   _____

_____   _____

_____   _____

_____   _____

_____

COMMENT

When to use.   PJC 100.4 should be used as an instruction for the second phase of a bifurcated trial pursuant to *Transportation Insurance Co. v. Moriel*, 879 S.W.2d 10, 29–30 (Tex. 1994), or Tex. Civ. Prac. & Rem. Code Ann. § 41.009 (Vernon 1997).

Source of instruction.   The instruction with regard to the less-than-unanimous verdict is derived from *Hyman Farm Service, Inc. v. Earth Oil & Gas Co.*, 920 S.W.2d 452 (Tex. App.—Amarillo 1996, no writ); *see also* Tex. R. Civ. P. 292.

PJC 100.5   **Instructions to Jury after Verdict**

The court has previously instructed you that you should observe strict secrecy during the trial and during your deliberations, and that you should not discuss this case with anyone except other jurors during your deliberations. I am now about to discharge you. After your discharge, you are released from your secrecy. You will then be free to discuss the case and your deliberations with anyone. However, you are also free to decline to discuss the case and your deliberations if you wish.

After you are discharged, it is lawful for the attorneys or other persons to question you to determine whether any of the standards for jury conduct which I have given you in the course of this trial were violated and to ask you to give an affidavit to that effect. You are free to discuss or not to discuss these matters and to give or not to give an affidavit.

COMMENT

When to use.   The foregoing instructions are prescribed in Tex. R. Civ. P. 226a. The instructions are to be given orally to the jury "after the verdict has been accepted by the court and before the jurors are discharged."

PJC 100.6   Instruction to Jury If Permitted to Separate

You are again instructed that it is your duty not to converse with, or permit yourselves to be addressed by, any other person on any subject connected with this trial.

COMMENT

When to use.   The foregoing instruction is required by Tex. R. Civ. P. 284, which states, "If permitted to separate, either during the trial or after the case is submitted to them, the jury shall be admonished by the court that it is their duty not to converse with, or permit themselves to be addressed by any other person, on any subject connected with the trial."

PJC 100.7   **Instruction If Jury Disagrees about Testimony**

MEMBERS OF THE JURY:

You have made the following request in writing:

[Insert copy of request.]

Your request is governed by the following rule:

"If the jury disagree as to the statement of any witness, they may, upon applying to the court, have read to them from the court reporter's notes that part of such witness' testimony on the point in dispute. . . ."

If you report that you disagree concerning the statement of a witness and specify the point on which you disagree, the court reporter will search his notes and read to you the testimony of the witness on the point.

_____

JUDGE PRESIDING

COMMENT

When to use.   This written instruction is based on Tex. R. Civ. P. 287 and is to be used if the jurors request that testimony from the court reporter's notes be read to them.

PJC 100.8   Circumstantial Evidence

A fact may be established by direct evidence or by circumstantial evidence or both. A fact is established by direct evidence when proved by documentary evidence or by witnesses who saw the act done or heard the words spoken. A fact is established by circumstantial evidence when it may be fairly and reasonably inferred from other facts proved.

COMMENT

When to use.   PJC 100.8 may be used if there is circumstantial evidence in the case. It would be placed in the charge of the court (PJC 100.3) after the instruction on preponderance of the evidence and immediately before the definitions, questions, and special instructions. It is not error to give or to refuse an instruction on circumstantial evidence. *Larson v. Ellison*, 217 S.W.2d 420 (Tex. 1949); *Johnson v. Zurich General Accident & Liability Insurance Co.*, 205 S.W.2d 353 (Tex. 1947).

PJC 100.9   Proximate Cause

"Proximate cause" means that cause which, in a natural and continuous sequence, produces an event, and without which cause such event would not have occurred. In order to be a proximate cause, the act or omission complained of must be such that a person using the degree of care required of him would have foreseen that the event, or some similar event, might reasonably result therefrom. There may be more than one proximate cause of an event.

COMMENT

When to use.   PJC 100.9 should be used in every case in which a finding of proximate cause is required. It is based on the definition approved by the court in *Rudes v. Gottschalk*, 324 S.W.2d 201, 207 (Tex. 1959). For a discussion of the element of "foreseeability," see *Motsenbocker v. Wyatt*, 369 S.W.2d 319, 323 (Tex. 1963); *Carey v. Pure Distributing Corp.*, 124 S.W.2d 847, 849 (Tex. 1939).

PJC 100.10   Instructions to Deadlocked Jury

I have your note that you are deadlocked. In the interest of justice, if you could end this litigation by your verdict, you should do so.

I do not mean to say that any individual juror should yield his or her own conscience and positive conviction, but I do mean that when you are in the jury room, you should discuss this matter carefully, listen to each other, and try, if you can, to reach a conclusion on the questions. It is your duty as a juror to keep your mind open and free to every reasonable argument that may be presented by your fellow jurors so that this jury may arrive at a verdict that justly answers the consciences of the individuals making up this jury. You should not have any pride of opinion and should avoid hastily forming or expressing an opinion. At the same time, you should not surrender any conscientious views founded on the evidence unless convinced of your error by your fellow jurors.

If you fail to reach a verdict, this case may have to be tried before another jury. Then all of our time will have been wasted.

Accordingly, I return you to your deliberations.

COMMENT

Source.   The foregoing instructions are modeled on the charge in *Stevens v. Travelers Insurance Co.*, 563 S.W.2d 223 (Tex. 1978), and on Tex. R. Civ. P. 226a.

PJC 100.11   Instructions on Jurors' Note-Taking (Comment)

A number of trial judges permit jurors to take notes during the presentation of evidence. *See Manges v. Willoughby*, 505 S.W.2d 379 (Tex. Civ. App.—San Antonio 1974, writ ref'd n.r.e.). The Committee expresses no opinion on this practice. If, however, jurors are allowed to take notes during the trial, they should be instructed, both after jury selection and before retiring to deliberate, on how the notes are to be taken and used. Some of the points a judge may wish to cover are contained in the following sample instructions.

[*To be included in PJC 100.2 (instructions to jury after jury selection):*]

During trial, if taking notes will help focus your attention on the evidence, you may take notes. If taking notes will distract your attention from the evidence, you should not take notes. Any notes you take are for your own personal use, and you may not share them with other jurors. Your personal recollection of the evidence takes precedence over any notes you have taken. A juror may not rely on the notes of another juror.

[*To be included in PJC 100.3 (charge of the court):*]

During trial it was permissible for you to take notes. You may carry those notes to the jury room for your personal use during deliberation on the court's charge. You may not share these notes with other jurors. Your personal recollection of the evidence takes precedence over any notes you have taken. A juror may not rely on the notes of another juror. If you disagree about the evidence, the presiding juror may apply to the court and have the court reporter's notes read to the jury.

PJC 101.1   Basic Question—Existence

QUESTION _____

Did *Paul Payne* and *Don Davis* agree [*insert all disputed terms*]?

[*Insert instructions, if appropriate.*]

Answer: _____

COMMENT

When to use.   PJC 101.1 submits the issue of the existence of an agreement. It should be used if there is a dispute about the existence of an agreement or its terms and a specific factual finding is necessary to determine whether the agreement constitutes a legally binding contract. (See the discussion of consideration and essential terms below.) Usually PJC 101.1 will apply in cases involving oral agreements, oral modification of written agreements, and agreements based on several written instruments.

Broad form mandated by rule 277.   The broad form of this question follows the mandate of Tex. R. Civ. P. 277, which states: "In all jury cases the court shall, whenever feasible, submit the cause upon broad-form questions."

In some cases an even broader question that combines issues of both existence and breach of an agreement may be appropriate. For example:

Did *Don Davis* fail to comply with the agreement, if any?

In such a case, however, care should be taken that the submission does not ask the jury to decide questions of law, which must be determined by the court alone. *Lone Star Steel Co. v. Scott*, 759 S.W.2d 144, 157 (Tex. App.—Texarkana 1988, writ denied) (whether agreement constitutes binding contract and interpretation of that contract are questions of law).

Accompanying instructions.   In cases involving straightforward factual disputes about the existence of an agreement, no definition of "agreement" is required. *Texaco, Inc. v. Pennzoil Co.*, 729 S.W.2d 768, 814 (Tex. App.—Houston [1st Dist.] 1987, writ ref'd n.r.e.), *cert. dismissed*, 108 S. Ct. 1305 (1988) (applying New York law); *Mann v. Fender*, 587 S.W.2d 188, 199 (Tex. Civ. App.—Waco 1979, writ ref'd n.r.e.); *West Texas State Bank v. Tri-Service Drilling Co.*, 339 S.W.2d 249, 256 (Tex. Civ. App.—Eastland 1960, writ ref'd n.r.e.). If, however, questions relating to contract formation are involved, additional instructions will be required. See PJC 101.3.

Essential terms.   To form a valid contract, the parties must have the same understanding of the subject matter of the contract and all its essential terms. *Smulcer v. Rogers*, 256 S.W.2d 120 (Tex. Civ. App.—Fort Worth 1953, writ ref'd n.r.e.). To be enforceable, a contract must be reasonably definite and certain. *T.O. Stanley Boot Co. v. Bank of El Paso*, 847 S.W.2d 218, 221 (Tex. 1992); *Kirkwood & Morgan, Inc. v. Roach*, 360 S.W.2d 173 (Tex.

Civ. App.—San Antonio 1962, writ ref'd n.r.e.). Failure to agree on or include an essential term renders a contract unenforceable. *T.O. Stanley Boot Co.*, 847 S.W.2d at 221; *Wheeler v. White*, 398 S.W.2d 93 (Tex. 1965); *Weitzman v. Steinberg*, 638 S.W.2d 171, 175 (Tex. App.—Dallas 1982, no writ); *Estate of Eberling v. Fair*, 546 S.W.2d 329, 333–34 (Tex. Civ. App.—Dallas 1976, writ ref'd n.r.e.). The court should include in PJC 101.1, therefore, all disputed terms essential to create an enforceable agreement. A disputed nonessential term should also be included if it is the basis of the plaintiff's claim for damages.

Some omitted terms supplied by law.   Some omitted terms, however, will be supplied by application of law, and the failure to include those terms will not render the agreement invalid. See, e.g., PJCs 101.10 (instruction on time of compliance) and 101.13 (instruction on price). In such cases it is not necessary to secure a jury finding on the parties' agreement to those terms, and they should not be included in PJC 101.1 unless their absence will be confusing to the jury. The circumstances of each case will determine whether it is appropriate to include instructions such as those contemplated by PJCs 101.10 and .13.

Agreement contemplating further negotiations or writings.   During negotiations, the parties may agree to some terms of the agreement with the expectation that other terms are to be agreed on later. Such an expectation does not prevent the agreement already made from being an enforceable agreement. *Scott v. Ingle Bros. Pacific, Inc.*, 489 S.W.2d 554, 555 (Tex. 1972); *see also Simmons & Simmons Construction Co. v. Rea*, 286 S.W.2d 415 (Tex. 1955). In such a case, the basic issue submitted in PJC 101.1 should be modified to inquire whether the parties intended to bind themselves to an agreement that includes the terms initially agreed on. *Scott*, 489 S.W.2d at 555. Case law suggests the following question:

> Did *Paul Payne* and *Don Davis* intend to bind themselves to an agreement that included the following terms:
>
> [*Insert disputed terms.*]

Scott, 489 S.W.2d at 555; *see also Texaco, Inc.*, 729 S.W.2d at 812.

A similar issue is presented if the parties reach preliminary agreement on certain material terms yet also contemplate a future written document. Whether the parties intended to be bound in the absence of execution of the final written document is a question of fact. *Foreca, S.A. v. GRD Development Co.*, 758 S.W.2d 744 (Tex. 1988). The *Foreca* opinion approves the following submission in such a case:

> Do you find that the writings of *September 2, 1983,* and *October 19, 1983,* constituted an agreement whereby [*insert disputed terms*]?

The court cited comment c to section 27 of the *Restatement (Second) of Contracts* (1981) as setting forth circumstances that may be helpful in determining whether a contract has been formed. *Foreca, S.A.*, 758 S.W.2d at 746 n.2. The court, however, did not make it clear whether these considerations should be included in the jury instructions.

PJC 101.2   Basic Question—Compliance

QUESTION _____

Did *Don Davis* fail to comply with *the agreement*?

> [*Insert instructions, if appropriate.*]

Answer: _____

COMMENT

When to use.   If breach is the only issue in dispute, no predicate is required. Otherwise, PJC 101.2 should be submitted predicated on an affirmative answer to PJC 101.1.

Broad form mandated by rule 277.   Tex. R. Civ. P. 277 mandates broad-form submission whenever feasible. *See Ryan Mortgage Investors v. Fleming-Wood*, 650 S.W.2d 928, 932–33 (Tex. App.—Fort Worth 1983, writ ref'd n.r.e.) (approving broad question in written contract case); *Jon-T Farms, Inc. v. Goodpasture, Inc.*, 554 S.W.2d 743, 750–51 (Tex. Civ. App.—Amarillo 1977, writ ref'd n.r.e.) (approving broad question in UCC sale-of-goods case). When a broad-form submission is not feasible, the cause may be submitted on more limited fact-specific questions, such as—

> Did *Don Davis* fail [*insert alleged failure*]?

Integrated written document.   If the dispute arises from an integrated written document, a phrase identifying the agreement should be substituted for the words *the agreement*. *See Ryan Mortgage Investors*, 650 S.W.2d at 932–33.

Implied terms.   If the alleged breach involves an omitted term, such as time of compliance, an additional instruction is necessary. See, e.g., PJCs 101.10 and .13.

Interpretation.   Construction of an unambiguous term is an issue for the court. If appropriate, an instruction should be included giving the jury the correct interpretation of that term. See PJC 101.7. If the court determines that a particular provision is ambiguous, an instruction on resolving that ambiguity should be included. See PJC 101.8.

Caveat.   Care must be taken to ensure that the question is appropriate under the facts of the particular case. Many contract disputes focus entirely on issues such as defenses, damages, promissory estoppel, quantum meruit, or agency, which are addressed in other parts of this volume. In such cases the parties may not need any form of PJC 101.2. If the only jury question is the validity of a defense, PJC 101.2 is not appropriate, and the instruction appropriate to that defense (e.g., PJCs 101.21–.33) may be rewritten as the question.

UCC good-faith obligation.   Every contract or duty governed by the Uniform Commercial Code imposes an obligation of good faith in its performance of enforcement. Tex. Bus. & Com. Code Ann. § 1.203 (Tex. UCC) (Vernon 1994); *Printing Center of Texas, Inc.*

v. Supermind Publishing Co., 669 S.W.2d 779, 784 (Tex. App.—Houston [14th Dist.] 1984, no writ); *see Adolph Coors Co. v. Rodriguez*, 780 S.W.2d 477, 482 (Tex. App.—Corpus Christi 1989, writ denied) (to be actionable as a breach of contract under Tex. UCC § 1.203, bad-faith conduct must relate to some aspect of performance under terms of contract).

There are two definitions of good faith under the Code. The general definition, which applies to all transactions subject to the Code, reads: " 'Good faith' means honesty in fact in the conduct or transaction concerned." Tex. UCC § 1.201(19). The definition specifically applying to transactions in goods subject to article 2 of the Code states that "unless the context otherwise requires . . . '[g]ood faith' in the case of a merchant means honesty in fact and the observance of reasonable commercial standards of fair dealing in the trade." Tex. UCC § 2.103(a)(2). The Code defines "merchant" at Tex. UCC § 2.104(a).

If the transaction is covered by the Code and is one not involving a merchant, the following instruction would be appropriate to submit with the basic question:

> In addition to the language of the agreement, the law imposes on a party to a contract a duty to [*perform*] [*enforce*] [*perform or enforce*] the contract in good faith. In that connection, good faith means honesty in fact in the conduct or transaction concerned.

In the case of a sale of goods involving a merchant under article 2 of the Code, the following instruction would be appropriate:

> In addition to the language of the agreement, the law imposes on a merchant the duty to [*perform*] [*enforce*] [*perform or enforce*] the contract with honesty in fact and to observe the reasonable commercial standards of fair dealing in the trade.

Depending on the pleadings and evidence in the particular case, the court may instruct on performance or enforcement or both.

If a party contends that the agreement defines the standards for good-faith performance, the jury should be instructed as follows:

> The parties to the agreement may by agreement determine the standards by which the performance of the obligation of good faith is to be measured if such standards are not manifestly unreasonable.

Tex. UCC § 1.102(c). The committee is not aware of any Texas case supporting a departure from the language of section 1.102(c).

Good and workmanlike manner.   In cases involving construction, repairs, and at least some services, there is an obligation to perform in a good and workmanlike manner. For instructions and comments, see PJC 102.12.

PJC 101.3   Instruction on Formation of Agreement

In deciding whether the parties reached an agreement, you may consider what they said and did in light of the surrounding circumstances, including any earlier course of dealing. You may not consider the parties' unexpressed thoughts or intentions.

COMMENT

When to use.   If appropriate, PJC 101.3 should be submitted with the question of the existence of a contract (PJC 101.1) to confine the jury's deliberations on the issue of contract formation to legally appropriate factors.

Source of instruction.   Only the parties' objective manifestations of intent may be considered. *Adams v. Petrade International, Inc.*, 754 S.W.2d 696, 717 (Tex. App.—Houston [1st Dist.] 1988, writ denied); *Slade v. Phelps*, 446 S.W.2d 931, 933 (Tex. Civ. App.—Tyler 1969, no writ). An agreement may be implied from and evidenced by the parties' conduct in the light of the surrounding circumstances, including any earlier course of dealing. *Haws & Garrett General Contractors v. Gorbett Bros. Welding Co.*, 480 S.W.2d 607, 609–10 (Tex. 1972); *Calvin V. Koltermann, Inc. v. Underream Piling Co.*, 563 S.W.2d 950, 956 (Tex. Civ. App.—San Antonio 1977, writ ref'd n.r.e.).

UCC article 2 cases.   Tex. Bus. & Com. Code Ann. § 1.201(3) (Tex. UCC) (Vernon 1994) defines "agreement" and includes those factors that may be considered in determining the existence of an agreement. *See also* Tex. UCC § 1.205 (course of dealing and usage of trade), § 2.202 (final written expression: parol evidence), § 2.204 (formation in general), § 2.208 (course of performance or practical construction).

PJC 101.4   Instruction on Authority

A party's conduct includes the conduct of another who acts with the party's authority or apparent authority.

Authority for another to act for a party must arise from the party's agreement that the other act on behalf and for the benefit of the party. If a party so authorizes another to perform an act, that other party is also authorized to do whatever else is proper, usual, and necessary to perform the act expressly authorized.

Apparent authority exists if a party (1) knowingly permits another to hold himself out as having authority or, (2) through lack of ordinary care, bestows on another such indications of authority that lead a reasonably prudent person to rely on the apparent existence of authority to his detriment. Only the acts of the party sought to be charged with responsibility for the conduct of another may be considered in determining whether apparent authority exists.

COMMENT

When to use.   PJC 101.4 may be appropriate if the evidence raises a question of express, implied, or apparent authority. It is only to be used to determine whether a party is contractually bound by the conduct of another. In common-law tort and statutory actions, where the issue is a party's vicarious liability for the wrongful conduct of another, different rules of law may apply. For the rules relating to deceptive trade practices and insurance actions, see the comments titled "Vicarious liability" at PJCs 102.1, .7, .8, and .14.

Express authority.   Express authority arises from the principal's agreement that the agent act on the principal's behalf and for his benefit. *Clark's-Gamble, Inc. v. State*, 486 S.W.2d 840, 845 (Tex. Civ. App.—Amarillo 1972, writ ref'd n.r.e.).

Implied authority.   Implied authority arises by implication from a grant of express authority. A grant of express authority implies authority to do those acts proper, usual, and necessary to perform the act expressly authorized. *Employers Casualty Co. v. Winslow*, 356 S.W.2d 160, 168 (Tex. Civ. App.—El Paso 1962, writ ref'd n.r.e.).

Apparent authority.   Apparent authority arises if a principal either intentionally or negligently induces parties to believe that a person is the principal's agent even though the principal has conferred no authority on that person. *Roberts v. Capitol City Steel Co.*, 376 S.W.2d 771, 775 (Tex. Civ. App.—Austin 1964, writ ref'd n.r.e.). Apparent authority, which is based partly on estoppel, may arise from two sources: first, from the principal's knowingly allowing an agent to claim authority; and second, from the principal's negligently bestowing on the agent such indications of authority that a reasonably prudent person is led to rely on the existence of that authority. *Ames v. Great Southern Bank*, 672 S.W.2d 447, 450 (Tex. 1984); *Rourke v. Garza*, 530 S.W.2d 794, 802 (Tex. 1975); *Hall v.*

F.A. Halamicek Enterprises, 669 S.W.2d 368, 375 (Tex. App.—Corpus Christi 1984, no writ); *Sorenson v. Shupe Bros. Co.*, 517 S.W.2d 861, 864 (Tex. Civ. App.—Amarillo 1974, no writ).

Because apparent authority is based on estoppel, the principal's conduct must be that which would lead a reasonably prudent person to believe that authority exists. *Douglass v. Panama, Inc.*, 504 S.W.2d 776, 778–79 (Tex. 1974); *Campbell v. C.D. Payne & Geldermann Securities, Inc.*, 894 S.W.2d 411, 422 (Tex. App.—Amarillo 1995, writ denied).

If apparent authority is not an issue, the phrase *or apparent authority* should be deleted from the first paragraph of the instruction, along with the definition of apparent authority.

PJC 101.5   Instruction on Ratification

A party's conduct includes conduct of others that the party has ratified. Ratification may be express or implied.

Implied ratification occurs if a party, though he may have been unaware of unauthorized conduct taken on his behalf at the time it occurred, retains the benefits of the transaction involving the unauthorized conduct after he acquired full knowledge of the unauthorized conduct. Implied ratification results in the ratification of the entire transaction.

COMMENT

When to use.   PJC 101.5 may be appropriate if a party seeks to avoid liability on the basis that the act of a purported agent was unauthorized or if a party seeks to hold another responsible for unauthorized but ratified conduct.

Source of instruction.   The instruction is derived from *Land Title Co. v. F.M. Stigler, Inc.*, 609 S.W.2d 754, 756–58 (Tex. 1980) (ratification occurs if principal retains benefits of transaction after full knowledge of unauthorized acts of person acting on principal's behalf). Ratification, rather than any type of authority, binds the principal in these cases. *Land Title Co.*, 609 S.W.2d at 756–58.

Not applicable to fraud.   PJC 101.5 does not apply in situations involving ratification of fraud.

PJC 101.6   Conditions Precedent (Comment)

Conditions precedent defined.   "A condition precedent may be either a condition to the formation of a contract or to an obligation to perform an existing agreement. Conditions may, therefore, relate either to the formation of contracts or to liability under them." *Hohenberg Bros. Co. v. George E. Gibbons & Co.*, 537 S.W.2d 1, 3 (Tex. 1976).

Conditions precedent to an obligation to perform are acts or events that are to occur after the contract is made and that must occur before there is a right to immediate performance and before there can be a breach of contractual duty. *Hohenberg Bros. Co.*, 537 S.W.2d at 3.

Creation of condition precedent.   Although no particular words are necessary to create a condition, terms such as "if," "provided that," and "on condition that" usually connote a condition rather than a covenant or promise. Absent such a limiting clause, whether a provision represents a condition or a promise must be gathered from the contract as a whole and from the intent of the parties. *Hohenberg Bros. Co.*, 537 S.W.2d at 3.

Conditions not favored.   To prevent forfeitures, courts are inclined to construe provisions as covenants rather than as conditions. *Rogers v. Ricane Enterprises*, 772 S.W.2d 76, 79 (Tex. 1989); *Henshaw v. Texas Natural Resources Foundation*, 216 S.W.2d 566, 570 (Tex. 1949); *Ogilvie v. Hill*, 563 S.W.2d 846, 849 (Tex. Civ. App.—Texarkana 1978, writ ref'd n.r.e.).

**PJC 101.7   Court's Construction of Provision of Agreement
                (Comment)**

Court's construction should be included in charge.   If the construction of a provision of the agreement is in dispute and the court resolves the dispute by interpreting the provision according to the rules of construction, the court should include that interpretation in submitting PJC 101.2.

Court's duty to interpret unambiguous contract.   If an instrument is unambiguous or if it is ambiguous but parol evidence of circumstances is undisputed, construction of the instrument is an issue for the court. *Brown v. Payne*, 176 S.W.2d 306, 308 (Tex. 1943). An instrument is ambiguous if, after application of the pertinent rules of construction, it remains reasonably susceptible of more than one meaning, taking into consideration the circumstances present when the instrument was executed. *Towers of Texas, Inc. v. J & J Systems, Inc.*, 834 S.W.2d 1, 2 (Tex. 1992); *Coker v. Coker*, 650 S.W.2d 391, 393–94 (Tex. 1983).

PJC 101.8 Instruction on Ambiguous Provisions

It is your duty to interpret the following language of the agreement:

[*Insert ambiguous language.*]

You must decide its meaning by determining the intent of the parties at the time of the agreement. Consider all the facts and circumstances surrounding the making of the agreement, the interpretation placed on the agreement by the parties, and the conduct of the parties.

COMMENT

When to use. If the court determines that the contract contains ambiguous language, PJC 101.8 should accompany PJC 101.1.

Rules of construction. If an instrument is unambiguous or if it is ambiguous but parol evidence of circumstances is undisputed, construction of the instrument is an issue for the court. *Friendswood Development Co. v. McDade + Co.*, 926 S.W.2d 280, 282 (Tex. 1996); *Brown v. Payne*, 176 S.W.2d 306, 308 (Tex. 1943). If the court determines that the contract is ambiguous, establishing its terms becomes a task for the jury. *Reilly v. Rangers Management, Inc.*, 727 S.W.2d 527 (Tex. 1987). The jury may not construe the legal effect of a contract, but it may resolve ambiguous intent of the parties. *Trinity Universal Insurance Co. v. Ponsford Bros.*, 423 S.W.2d 571, 575 (Tex. 1968).

Intent must be understandable. Parties to a contract must express their intentions understandably. To be enforceable, a contract must be sufficiently certain to enable the court to determine the legal obligations of the parties. *T.O. Stanley Boot Co. v. Bank of El Paso*, 847 S.W.2d 218, 221 (Tex. 1992); *Bendalin v. Delgado*, 406 S.W.2d 897, 899 (Tex. 1966).

Parties' interpretation given great weight. The most significant rule of contractual interpretation is that great, if not controlling, weight should be given to the parties' interpretation. The court and the jury should assume that parties to a contract are in the best position to know what they intended by the language used. *James Stewart & Co. v. Law*, 233 S.W.2d 558, 561 (Tex. 1950); *see also Trinity Universal Insurance Co.*, 423 S.W.2d at 575. One factor to be considered in determining the parties' interpretation is their conduct. *Consolidated Engineering Co. v. Southern Steel Co.*, 699 S.W.2d 188, 192–93 (Tex. 1985).

PJC 101.9   Trade Custom (Comment)

Instruction may be appropriate.   Texas law is not clear on whether trade custom is merely evidentiary and not appropriate for jury instruction, or whether it may in fact form the basis for a proper instruction. Such an instruction would be used to augment or modify PJC 101.1 or .2. It could inquire whether a particular custom or usage existed and, if it existed, whether the parties intended that it would affect a contract term. *Lambert v. H. Molsen & Co.*, 551 S.W.2d 151, 154 (Tex. Civ. App.—Waco 1977, writ ref'd n.r.e.) ("The [trial] court instructed the jury . . . that if it found . . . that the custom and usage actually existed, then it could be considered by the jury toward determining the parties' contractual intent."). The court in *Lambert* did not expressly approve the instruction used by the trial court, but the opinion does provide an example of the form of a trade-custom instruction. *See also Tennell v. Esteve Cotton Co.*, 546 S.W.2d 346 (Tex. Civ. App.—Amarillo 1976, writ ref'd n.r.e.); *Englebrecht v. W.D. Brannan & Sons*, 501 S.W.2d 707 (Tex. Civ. App.— Amarillo 1973, no writ) (discussing submission of instructions on custom).

Evidence of trade custom may aid interpretation of ambiguous contract.   Evidence of custom may be admitted to aid in the interpretation of a contract if the contract is ambiguous, imprecise, incomplete, or inconsistent, but such evidence is not admissible to contradict, restrict, or enlarge what otherwise needs no explanation. *Miller v. Gray*, 149 S.W.2d 582 (Tex. 1941); *PGP Gas Products, Inc. v. Reserve Equipment, Inc.*, 667 S.W.2d 604, 607–08 (Tex. App.—Austin 1984, writ ref'd n.r.e.).

UCC article 2 cases.   Trade custom, course of dealing, and course of performance are relevant in determining the meaning of the agreement. *See* Tex. Bus. & Com. Code Ann. §§ 1.205, 2.208 (Tex. UCC) (Vernon 1994).

PJC 101.10   Instruction on Time of Compliance

Compliance with an agreement must occur within a reasonable time under the circumstances unless the parties agreed that compliance must occur within a specified time and the parties intended compliance within such time to be an essential part of the agreement.

In determining whether the parties intended time of compliance to be an essential part of the agreement, you may consider the nature and purpose of the agreement and the facts and circumstances surrounding its making.

COMMENT

When to use.   PJC 101.10 is appropriate if a party contends that failure to comply by the date specified in the agreement constitutes a material breach, even though the agreement itself does not expressly state that time is of the essence. *See Siderius, Inc. v. Wallace Co.*, 583 S.W.2d 852, 863–64 (Tex. Civ. App.—Tyler 1979, no writ); *Laredo Hides Co. v. H & H Meat Products Co.*, 513 S.W.2d 210, 216–18 (Tex. Civ. App.—Corpus Christi 1974, writ ref'd n.r.e.).

UCC article 2 cases.   If the time for delivery or shipment is not specified in the contract, the time shall be reasonable. Tex. Bus. & Com. Code Ann. § 2.309(a) (Tex. UCC) (Vernon 1994). What is a reasonable time for taking any action depends on the nature, purpose, and circumstance of that action and any prior dealing between the parties. Tex. UCC §§ 1.204(b), 1.204 cmt. 2; *see also* Tex. UCC §§ 2.504, 2.601, 2.612.

PJC 101.11 Instruction on Offer and Acceptance

In attempting to reach an agreement, one party may specifically prescribe the time, manner, or other requirements for the other party's acceptance of the offer. If the offer is not accepted as prescribed, there is no agreement.

COMMENT

When to use. PJC 101.11 submits a common offer-and-acceptance instruction and may be used in an appropriate case with PJC 101.1.

Waiver. The offeror can waive limitations on manner of acceptance, and the above instruction should be modified to incorporate waiver in an appropriate case. *See Town of Lindsay v. Cooke County Electric Cooperative Ass'n*, 502 S.W.2d 117 (Tex. 1973).

Acceptance by performance. The supreme court has adopted sections 32 and 62 of the *Restatement (Second) of Contracts* (1981). These sections state that under some circumstances performance of an act that the offeree is requested to promise to perform may constitute a valid acceptance. *United Concrete Pipe Corp. v. Spin-Line Co.*, 430 S.W.2d 360, 364 (Tex. 1968) (citing 1964 tentative draft, with different section numbers).

Time for acceptance. If no time for acceptance of an offer is specified, the law implies a reasonable time. *Moore v. Dodge*, 603 S.W.2d 236, 239 (Tex. Civ. App.—El Paso 1980, writ ref'd n.r.e.).

PJC 101.12   Instruction on Withdrawal or Revocation of Offer

There is no agreement unless the party to whom an offer is made accepts it before knowing that the offer has been withdrawn.

COMMENT

When to use.   PJC 101.12 should be included with PJC 101.1 only if one party claims the offer was withdrawn before it was accepted.

Acceptance by performance.   The supreme court has adopted sections 32 and 62 of the *Restatement (Second) of Contracts* (1981). These sections state that under some circumstances performance of an act that the offeree is requested to promise to perform may constitute a valid acceptance. *United Concrete Pipe Corp. v. Spin-Line Co.*, 430 S.W.2d 360, 364 (Tex. 1968) (citing 1964 tentative draft, with different section numbers).

Revocable offers.   Ordinarily, the party making an offer may revoke it any time before the offeree accepts it in the manner prescribed. *See Bowles v. Fickas*, 167 S.W.2d 741, 743 (Tex. 1943). The offeror can effectively revoke an offer by doing some act inconsistent with the offer, but the offeree must have actual knowledge of the revocation. *Antwine v. Reed*, 199 S.W.2d 482, 485 (Tex. 1947). After making an irrevocable offer, however, the offeror cannot unilaterally vary or revoke it. *Wall v. Trinity Sand & Gravel Co.*, 369 S.W.2d 315, 317 (Tex. 1963). A common type of irrevocable offer is an option contract where the offer is supported by independent consideration.

UCC cases.   *See* Tex. Bus. & Com. Code Ann. § 2.206(b) (Tex. UCC) (Vernon 1994).

PJC 101.13   Instruction on Price

If *Paul Payne* and *Don Davis* agreed to other essential terms but failed to specify price, it is presumed a reasonable price was intended.

COMMENT

When to use.   PJC 101.13 should accompany PJC 101.1 or .2 in appropriate cases.

Source of instruction.   The above instruction is derived from *Bendalin v. Delgado*, 406 S.W.2d 897, 900 (Tex. 1966).

UCC cases.   Tex. Bus. & Com. Code Ann. § 2.305(a) (Tex. UCC) (Vernon 1994) states:

> The parties if they so intend can conclude a contract for sale even though the price is not settled. In such a case the price is a reasonable price at the time for delivery if
>
> (1) nothing is said as to price; or
>
> (2) the price is left to be agreed by the parties and they fail to agree; or
>
> (3) the price is to be fixed in terms of some agreed market or other standard as set or recorded by a third person or agency and it is not so set or recorded.

PJC 101.14   Consideration (Comment)

Consideration essential.   Consideration is essential to a contract. *Unthank v. Rippstein*, 386 S.W.2d 134 (Tex. 1964). Whether a particular matter constitutes adequate legal consideration is a question of law for the court. *Williams v. Hill*, 396 S.W.2d 911 (Tex. Civ. App.—Dallas 1965, no writ). The court's determination, however, may be based on facts found by the jury. *See, e.g., Schepps Grocery Co. v. Burroughs Corp.*, 635 S.W.2d 606 (Tex. App.—Houston [14th Dist.] 1982, no writ).

Burden of proof.   In suits on a written contract, the burden of proof rests on the party alleging a lack of consideration. *Simpson v. MBank Dallas, N.A.*, 724 S.W.2d 102, 107 (Tex. App.—Dallas 1987, writ ref'd n.r.e.). In actions on an oral contract, the burden is on the plaintiff to prove the existence of consideration. *Okemah Construction, Inc. v. Barkley-Farmer, Inc.*, 583 S.W.2d 458, 460 (Tex. Civ. App.—Houston [1st Dist.] 1979, no writ) (collecting cases).

Failure of consideration.   The doctrine of failure of consideration does not involve issues relating to contract formation but is usually an affirmative defense based on a claim that the party seeking to recover on the contract has breached it in a manner sufficient to excuse the other party's noncompliance. For appropriate instructions, see PJC 101.22.

[PJCs 101.15–.20 are reserved for expansion.]

PJC 101.21   Defenses—Basic Question

If your answer to Question _____ [*101.1*] is "Yes," then answer the following question. Otherwise, do not answer the following question.

QUESTION _____

Was *Don Davis*'s failure to comply excused?

[*Insert instructions; see PJCs 101.22–.33.*]

Answer: _____

COMMENT

When to use.   PJC 101.21 poses the controlling question for cases where a defendant asserts one or more defenses to a contract suit.

Broad form mandated by rule 277.   The broad form of this question follows the mandate of Tex. R. Civ. P. 277. When feasible, the courts are urged to submit the controlling issues of a case in broad terms in order to simplify the charge. *Island Recreational Development Corp. v. Republic of Texas Savings Ass'n*, 710 S.W.2d 551, 555 (Tex. 1986). A single broad question may include one or more independent grounds. *Island Recreational Development Corp.*, 710 S.W.2d at 554–55. The dissenting opinions agree but would require instructions referring to the grounds. *Island Recreational Development Corp.*, 710 S.W.2d at 557–58, 561.

Instructions on grounds of defense required.   In the absence of one or more independent grounds of defense, the jury is not permitted to excuse the defendant from complying with the agreement. Standing alone, PJC 101.21 does not encompass any grounds of defense, so it is mandatory that grounds raised by the pleadings and evidence be submitted by including instructions such as PJCs 101.22–.33. *See, e.g., Traeger v. Lorenz*, 749 S.W.2d 249 (Tex. App.—San Antonio 1988, no writ) (separate grounds of waiver and abandonment should have been submitted in deed restriction case).

**PJC 101.22   Defenses—Instruction on Plaintiff's Material Breach
(Failure of Consideration)**

Failure to comply by *Don Davis* is excused by *Paul Payne*'s previous failure to comply with a material obligation of the same agreement.

COMMENT

When to use.   PJC 101.22 may accompany PJC 101.1 if the defendant raises the affirmative defense of plaintiff's material breach of the agreement. A party in default on a contract cannot maintain a suit for its breach. *Dobbins v. Redden*, 785 S.W.2d 377 (Tex. 1990).

Form of instruction.   The instruction is suggested by *Huff v. Speer*, 554 S.W.2d 259, 262 (Tex. Civ. App.—Houston [1st Dist.] 1977, writ ref'd n.r.e.), and *King Title Co. v. Croft*, 562 S.W.2d 536, 537 (Tex. Civ. App.—El Paso 1978, no writ).

If the alleged failure to comply by the complaining party involves timeliness of performance and if no date for completion is specified in the agreement, the following instruction should be added to PJC 101.22:

Delay in compliance beyond a reasonable period is a failure to comply.

See *Cannan v. Varn*, 591 S.W.2d 583 (Tex. Civ. App.—Corpus Christi 1979, writ ref'd n.r.e.).

Material breach versus failure of consideration.   Although designated here as plaintiff's material breach, the issue is commonly referred to as failure or partial failure of consideration. The Committee considers the latter designation inappropriate and confusing, however, because it suggests issues relating to contract formation. See PJC 101.3. The facts involved usually pertain instead to the affirmative defense that the party seeking to recover on a contract has breached it in a manner sufficient to excuse the defendant's noncompliance. *See National Bank of Commerce v. Williams*, 84 S.W.2d 691, 692 (Tex. 1935); *Austin Lake Estates, Inc. v. Meyer*, 557 S.W.2d 380 (Tex. Civ. App.—Austin 1977, no writ).

Failure to comply with provisions of a bilateral contract may be excused by the unjustifiable failure of the other party to comply with provisions binding on him. *Jordan Drilling Co. v. Starr*, 232 S.W.2d 149, 159 (Tex. Civ. App.—El Paso 1949, writ ref'd n.r.e.). The breach need not be total for rescission to be proper; a partial breach is sufficient if it affects a material part of the agreement. *Hausler v. Harding-Gill Co.*, 15 S.W.2d 548, 549 (Tex. Comm'n App. 1929, judgm't adopted); *Ennis v. Interstate Distributors, Inc.*, 598 S.W.2d 903, 906 (Tex. Civ. App.—Dallas 1980, no writ). Partial failure of consideration involves breach of a nonmaterial provision of the contract and does not support rescission but merely damages. *Gensco, Inc. v. Transformaciones Metalurgicias Especiales, S.A.*, 666 S.W.2d 549, 553 (Tex. App.—Houston [14th Dist.] 1984, writ dism'd).

Whether a breach is so material as to support this defense is a question of fact for the jury. *Hudson v. Wakefield*, 645 S.W.2d 427, 430 (Tex. 1983).

PJC 101.23 Defenses—Instruction on Anticipatory Repudiation

Failure to comply by *Don Davis* is excused by *Paul Payne*'s prior repudiation of the same agreement.

A party repudiates an agreement when *he* indicates, by *his* words or actions, that *he* is not going to perform *his* obligations under the agreement in the future, showing a fixed intention to abandon, renounce, and refuse to perform the agreement.

COMMENT

When to use. PJC 101.23 submits the doctrine of anticipatory repudiation as a defensive measure. It may also be appropriate, in slightly different form, as an element of the plaintiff's cause of action for recovery of the present value of payments or other consideration that would have been received from the wrongdoer in the future if the contract had been performed.

Source of instruction. The elements in the instruction are adapted from the discussion of the doctrine in *Group Life & Health Insurance Co. v. Turner*, 620 S.W.2d 670, 672–73 (Tex. Civ. App.—Dallas 1981, no writ).

"Without just excuse." To excuse a failure to comply, the repudiation must have been without just excuse. *Group Life & Health Insurance Co.*, 620 S.W.2d at 672–73.

PJC 101.24   Defenses—Instruction on Waiver

Failure to comply by *Don Davis* is excused if compliance is waived by *Paul Payne*.

Waiver is an intentional surrender of a known right or intentional conduct inconsistent with claiming the right.

COMMENT

When to use.   PJC 101.24 is appropriate to submit the affirmative defense of waiver. It may also be appropriate, in slightly different form, as an element of the plaintiff's cause of action, because waiver is an independent ground of recovery. *See Middle States Petroleum Corp. v. Messenger*, 368 S.W.2d 645, 654 (Tex. Civ. App.—Dallas 1963, writ ref'd n.r.e.). The Committee believes that an instruction on waiver should be submitted if the issue is raised by the evidence. *But see Island Recreational Development Corp. v. Republic of Texas Savings Ass'n*, 710 S.W.2d 551 (Tex. 1986) (affirming judgment notwithstanding lack of submission of waiver).

Source of definition.   The definition is adapted from *United States Fidelity & Guaranty Co. v. Bimco Iron & Metal Corp.*, 464 S.W.2d 353, 357 (Tex. 1971); *see also Gage v. Langford*, 582 S.W.2d 203, 207 (Tex. Civ. App.—Eastland 1979, writ ref'd n.r.e.) (definition of waiver incorrectly omitted "intentionally" from phrase "give up, relinquish or surrender some known right").

Distinguished from estoppel.   The supreme court has emphasized the unilateral character of waiver and distinguished it from estoppel:

> [W]aiver is essentially unilateral in its character; it results as a legal consequence from some act or conduct of the party against whom it operates; no act of the party in whose favor it is made is necessary to complete it. It need not be founded upon a new agreement or be supported by consideration, nor is it essential that it be based upon an estoppel.

Massachusetts Bonding & Insurance Co. v. Orkin Exterminating Co., 416 S.W.2d 396, 401 (Tex. 1967).

UCC article 2 cases.   A waiver affecting an executory portion of the agreement may be retracted on reasonable notification that strict performance will be required. Tex. Bus. & Com. Code Ann. § 2.209(e) (Tex. UCC) (Vernon 1994).

PJC 101.25 **Defenses—Instruction on Equitable Estoppel**

Failure to comply by *Don Davis* is excused if all the following circumstances occurred:

1. *Paul Payne*

    a. by words or conduct made a false representation or concealed material facts,

    b. with knowledge of the facts or with knowledge or information that would lead a reasonable person to discover the facts, and

    c. with the intention that *Don Davis* would rely on the false representation or concealment in acting or deciding not to act; and

2. *Don Davis*

    a. did not know and had no means of knowing the real facts and

    b. relied to *his* detriment on the false representation or concealment of material facts.

COMMENT

When to use. PJC 101.25 submits the affirmative defense of equitable estoppel.

Source of definition. The elements of estoppel are adapted from *Gulbenkian v. Penn*, 252 S.W.2d 929, 932 (Tex. 1952); *see also Nelson v. Jordan*, 663 S.W.2d 82, 87 (Tex. App.—Austin 1983, writ ref'd n.r.e.) (listing elements). For a general discussion of equitable estoppel, see *Barfield v. Howard M. Smith Co.*, 426 S.W.2d 834 (Tex. 1968).

Equitable estoppel distinguished from other types of estoppel. Equitable estoppel differs from other types of estoppel because it requires some deception practiced on a party who was misled to his injury. *Bocanegra v. Aetna Life Insurance Co.*, 605 S.W.2d 848, 851 (Tex. 1980). That party, however, must show his justifiable reliance on the representation. *Kuehne v. Denson*, 219 S.W.2d 1006, 1008–09 (Tex. 1949).

Estoppel based on silence. Estoppel may also be based on silence or inaction, rather than on affirmative misrepresentations, if one under a duty to speak or act has by his silence or inaction misled the opposing party to his detriment. *Smith v. National Resort Communities, Inc.*, 585 S.W.2d 655, 658 (Tex. 1979); *Scott v. Vandor*, 671 S.W.2d 79, 87 (Tex. App.—Houston [1st Dist.] 1984, writ ref'd n.r.e.). If estoppel is based on something other than affirmative misrepresentations, a different instruction should be substituted for PJC 101.25.

PJC 101.26   Defenses—Instruction on Duress

Failure to comply by *Don Davis* is excused if the agreement was made under duress caused by *Paul Payne*.

Duress is the mental, physical, or economic coercion of another, causing that party to act contrary to his free will and interest.

COMMENT

When to use.   PJC 101.26 is appropriate if one party claims the agreement is voidable because it was made under duress. It may also be used in slightly different language to submit an affirmative claim for rescission. As a general rule, a party seeking cancellation or rescission must do equity by restoring the other party to his original status. *Texas Co. v. State*, 281 S.W.2d 83, 91 (Tex. 1955); *Freyer v. Michels*, 360 S.W.2d 559, 562 (Tex. Civ. App.—Dallas 1962, writ dism'd). It is not clear whether this rule applies if the doctrine is asserted as a defense.

Source of definition.   The definition is derived from *Black Lake Pipe Line Co. v. Union Construction Co.*, 538 S.W.2d 80, 85 (Tex. 1976), *overruled on other grounds by Sterner v. Marathon Oil Co.*, 767 S.W.2d 686 (Tex. 1989); *Brooks v. Taylor*, 359 S.W.2d 539, 542 (Tex. Civ. App.—Amarillo 1962, writ ref'd n.r.e.); and *Housing Authority of Dallas v. Hubbell*, 325 S.W.2d 880, 905 (Tex. Civ. App.—Dallas 1959, writ ref'd n.r.e.).

Caveat.   Unless the alleged coercion can legally constitute duress, PJC 101.26 should not be submitted. It is never duress to threaten to do that which a party has a legal right to do. *Ulmer v. Ulmer*, 162 S.W.2d 944 (Tex. 1942). Filing or threatening to file a civil suit cannot, as a matter of law, constitute duress. *Continental Casualty Co. v. Huizar*, 740 S.W.2d 429, 430 (Tex. 1987). The vice arises only if extortive measures are employed or if improper demands are made in bad faith. *Matthews v. Matthews*, 725 S.W.2d 275 (Tex. App.—Houston [1st Dist.] 1986, writ ref'd n.r.e.); *Mitchell v. C.C. Sanitation Co.*, 430 S.W.2d 933 (Tex. Civ. App.—Houston [14th Dist.] 1968, writ ref'd n.r.e.); *Sanders v. Republic National Bank*, 389 S.W.2d 551, 555 (Tex. Civ. App.—Tyler 1965, no writ). Also see *State National Bank v. Farah Manufacturing Co.*, 678 S.W.2d 661 (Tex. App.—El Paso 1984, writ dism'd by agr.) for a general overview of this topic. A threat to file criminal prosecution may constitute duress even if the threatened party is guilty of the crime. *Eggleston v. Humble Pipe Line Co.*, 482 S.W.2d 909, 916 (Tex. Civ. App.—Houston [14th Dist.] 1972, writ ref'd n.r.e.); *Pierce v. Estate of Haverlah*, 428 S.W.2d 422, 425 (Tex. Civ. App.—Tyler 1968, writ ref'd n.r.e.).

Economic duress.   If economic duress is alleged, this instruction should be submitted only if the party against whom duress is charged was responsible for the other party's financial distress. *Simpson v. MBank Dallas, N.A.*, 724 S.W.2d 102 (Tex. App.—Dallas 1987, writ ref'd n.r.e.); *Griffith v. Geffen & Jacobsen, P.C.*, 693 S.W.2d 724 (Tex. App.—Dallas 1985, no writ).

Imminence of harm.   The threat of harm must be imminent, and the threatened party must have no present means of protection. It must cause the threatened person to do what there was no legal obligation to do. *Dale v. Simon*, 267 S.W. 467, 470 (Tex. Comm'n App. 1924, judgm't adopted); *Creative Manufacturing, Inc. v. Unik, Inc.*, 726 S.W.2d 207, 211 (Tex. App.—Fort Worth 1987, writ ref'd n.r.e.).

PJC 101.27   Defenses—Instruction on Undue Influence

Failure to comply by *Don Davis* is excused if the agreement was made as the result of undue influence by *Paul Payne*.

"Undue influence" means that there was such dominion and control exercised over the mind of the person executing the agreement, under the facts and circumstances then existing, as to overcome his free will. In effect, the will of the party exerting undue influence was substituted for that of the party entering the agreement, preventing him from exercising his own discretion and causing him to do what he would not have done but for such dominion and control.

COMMENT

When to use.   PJC 101.27 is appropriate when one party disputes existence of the agreement because it was made under undue influence. As a general rule, a party seeking cancellation or rescission must do equity by restoring the other party to his original status. *Texas Co. v. State*, 281 S.W.2d 83, 91 (Tex. 1955); *Freyer v. Michels*, 360 S.W.2d 559, 562 (Tex. Civ. App.—Dallas 1962, writ dism'd). It is not clear whether this rule applies if the doctrine is asserted as a defense.

Source of definition.   The definition is adapted from *Rothermel v. Duncan*, 369 S.W.2d 917, 922 (Tex. 1963). Although that case concerns a will contest, it is often cited in contract cases. *See, e.g., Sheffield v. Sheffield*, 675 S.W.2d 799, 800–01 (Tex. App.—Beaumont 1984, writ ref'd n.r.e.); *B.A.L. v. Edna Gladney Home*, 677 S.W.2d 826, 831 (Tex. App.—Fort Worth 1984, writ ref'd n.r.e.).

"Undue influence."   Not every influence exerted on the will of another is undue. *Rothermel*, 369 S.W.2d at 922. The exertion of undue influence is usually a subtle thing involving an extended course of dealings and circumstances, and it may be proved by circumstantial as well as direct evidence. *Rothermel*, 369 S.W.2d at 922. Influence is not undue merely because it is persuasive and effective, and the law does not condemn all persuasion, entreaty, importunity, or intercession. *B.A.L.*, 677 S.W.2d at 830.

PJC 101.28   Defenses—Instruction on Mutual Mistake of Fact

Failure to comply is excused if the agreement was made as the result of a mutual mistake.

A mutual mistake results from a mistake of fact common to both parties if both parties had the same misconception concerning the fact in question. A mistake by one party but not the other is not a mutual mistake.

COMMENT

When to use.   PJC 101.28 is appropriate when a party disputes terms of the agreement on the basis that they were established by mutual mistake of fact. See PJC 101.29 for an instruction on mutual mistake due to a scrivener's error.

Mistake must relate to same subject matter.   To prove a mutual mistake, evidence must show that both parties had the same misunderstanding of the same material fact. *A.L.G. Enterprises v. Huffman*, 660 S.W.2d 603, 606 (Tex. App.—Corpus Christi 1983), *aff'd & remanded for mutual mistake issue only*, 672 S.W.2d 230 (Tex. 1984).

Excuses failure to perform.   Mutual mistake is an equitable defense that, if proved, excuses a party's failure to perform a contract. *A.L.G. Enterprises*, 660 S.W.2d at 606. The question of mutual mistake is for the jury. *See James T. Taylor & Son v. Arlington Independent School District*, 335 S.W.2d 371, 376 (Tex. 1960); *Durham v. Uvalde Rock Asphalt Co.*, 599 S.W.2d 866 (Tex. Civ. App.—San Antonio 1980, no writ). This instruction may also be used, in slightly different language, to submit an affirmative claim for rescission.

Caveat: unilateral mistake.   Case law has drawn a distinction between unilateral and mutual mistake. Evidence may give rise to a defense based on one type of mistake but not the other. *See Durham*, 599 S.W.2d at 870. For a discussion of issues involved in cases of unilateral mistake, see *Monarch Marking System Co. v. Reed's Photo Mart*, 485 S.W.2d 905 (Tex. 1972).

**PJC 101.29   Defenses—Instruction on Mutual Mistake—
Scrivener's Error**

Failure to comply is excused if the agreement was made as the result of a mutual mistake.

A mutual mistake arises when parties to an agreement have identical intent and understanding of the terms to be embodied in a proposed written agreement, but, in the effort to reduce the agreement to writing, a mistake is made so that the writing does not present the intended agreement.

COMMENT

When to use.   PJC 101.29 is appropriate if a party disputes terms of the agreement because they resulted from a mutual mistake in recording the agreement. For an instruction on mutual mistake of fact, see PJC 101.28.

True agreement of the parties.   If a scrivener or typist makes a mistake, an instrument may be reformed and modified by a court to reflect the true agreement of the parties if the mistake was a mutual mistake. *Henderson v. Henderson*, 694 S.W.2d 31, 34 (Tex. App.—Corpus Christi 1985, writ ref'd n.r.e.).

Requirements for reformation.   Reformation of an instrument is a proper remedy if two requirements are satisfied: (1) the true agreement of the parties is shown, and (2) the provision erroneously written into the instrument is there by mutual mistake. *Parker v. HNG Oil Co.*, 732 S.W.2d 754 (Tex. App.—Corpus Christi 1987, no writ). Knowledge by one party of another's mistake in the expression of the contract is equal to a mutual mistake. *Goff v. Southmost Savings & Loan Ass'n*, 758 S.W.2d 822, 826 (Tex. App.—Corpus Christi 1988, writ denied).

PJC 101.30   Defenses—Instruction on Novation

Failure to comply with one agreement is excused if the parties agreed that a new agreement would take its place.

COMMENT

When to use.   PJC 101.30 may be used to submit the affirmative defense of novation. Novation occurs when the rights of the parties are determined by a new agreement that extinguishes the previous one. *See Flanagan v. Martin*, 880 S.W.2d 863, 867 (Tex. App.—Waco 1994, writ dism'd w.o.j.); *DoAll Dallas Co. v. Trinity National Bank*, 498 S.W.2d 396 (Tex. Civ. App.—Texarkana 1973, writ ref'd n.r.e.). A novation may also be the substitution of new for old parties to an agreement. *See Russell v. Northeast Bank*, 527 S.W.2d 783, 786 (Tex. Civ. App.—Houston [1st Dist.] 1975, writ ref'd n.r.e.).

If reasonable minds differ on the evidence of a new express agreement, novation is a question of law for the court. Absent an express agreement, novation is a question of fact. *Chastain v. Cooper & Reed*, 257 S.W.2d 422, 424 (Tex. 1953).

Accord and satisfaction distinguished from novation.   The defense of accord and satisfaction "rests upon a new contract, express or implied, in which the parties agree to the discharge of an existing obligation in a manner otherwise than originally agreed." *Harris v. Rowe*, 593 S.W.2d 303, 306 (Tex. 1979).

"An accord and satisfaction may or may not be also a novation, but where the new promise itself is accepted as satisfaction the transaction is more properly termed a novation." *DoAll Dallas Co.*, 498 S.W.2d 396.

PJC 101.31   Defenses—Instruction on Modification

Failure to comply with a term in an agreement is excused if the parties agreed that a new term would take its place.

COMMENT

When to use.   PJC 101.31 is appropriate if the defendant claims he was excused from complying with a term of the agreement because the parties had agreed to modify the agreement by substituting a new term for an old term. *See Mandril v. Kasishke*, 620 S.W.2d 238, 244 (Tex. Civ. App.—Amarillo 1981, writ ref'd n.r.e.) (parties have power to make and modify contracts). The question of whether a modification has taken place is one of fact and depends on the intent of the parties. *Hathaway v. General Mills, Inc.*, 711 S.W.2d 227, 228–29 (Tex. 1986).

UCC article 2 cases.   An agreement modifying a sales contract needs no consideration to be binding, but any modification must meet the test of good faith imposed by the Code. Tex. Bus. & Com. Code Ann. § 2.209 cmt. 2 (Tex. UCC) (Vernon 1994).

Accord and satisfaction and novation.   For instructions on accord and satisfaction and novation, see PJCs 101.32 and .30.

PJC 101.32   Defenses—Instruction on Accord and Satisfaction

Failure to comply with an agreement is excused if a different performance was accepted as full satisfaction of performance of the original obligations of the agreement.

COMMENT

When to use.   PJC 101.32 is appropriate to submit the affirmative defense of accord and satisfaction. This defense is raised by pleading and evidence that the plaintiff agreed to and accepted performance different from that of the original agreement, in full satisfaction of the original obligation. *Jenkins v. Henry C. Beck Co.*, 449 S.W.2d 454, 455 (Tex. 1969); *see also Pileco, Inc. v. HCI, Inc.*, 735 S.W.2d 561 (Tex. App.—Houston [1st Dist.] 1987, writ ref'd n.r.e.). If the plaintiff refuses to accept the differing performance as he has agreed to do, the original obligation is not discharged and the defendant may bring an action against the plaintiff for specific performance of the accord. *Alexander v. Handley*, 146 S.W.2d 740, 743 (Tex. 1941).

If existence of accord is disputed.   If existence of the accord is disputed, the above instruction should be accompanied with an instruction on the elements of agreement, mutual assent, and, if appropriate, other elements of contract formation as suggested in PJCs 101.3–.8.

PJC 101.33 Defenses—Instruction on Mental Capacity

Failure to comply is excused if *Don Davis* lacked sufficient mind and memory to understand the nature and consequences of *his* acts and the business *he* was transacting.

COMMENT

When to use. PJC 101.33 is appropriate if a party defends on the basis of lack of mental capacity. It may also be used, in slightly different language, to submit an affirmative claim for rescission.

Source of instruction. The instruction is derived from *Mandell & Wright v. Thomas*, 441 S.W.2d 841, 845 (Tex. 1969); *see also Bach v. Hudson*, 596 S.W.2d 673, 675–76 (Tex. Civ. App.—Corpus Christi 1980, no writ).

Burden of proof. The burden of proof falls on the party seeking to show lack of mental capacity. *Walker v. Fason*, 643 S.W.2d 390, 391 (Tex. 1982).

[PJCs 101.34–.40 are reserved for expansion.]

PJC 101.41   Question on Promissory Estoppel

QUESTION _____

Did *Paul Payne* substantially rely to *his* detriment on *Don Davis*'s promise, if any, and was this reliance foreseeable by *Don Davis*?

Answer: _____

COMMENT

When to use.   The doctrine of promissory estoppel may be invoked as a cause of action. It is appropriate if a promisee has acted to his detriment in reasonable reliance on an otherwise unenforceable promise. The theory supplies a remedy enabling an injured party to be compensated for "foreseeable, definite and substantial reliance." *Wheeler v. White*, 398 S.W.2d 93, 96–97 (Tex. 1965).

Source of question.   *Wheeler*, 398 S.W.2d at 96–97; *see also Restatement (Second) of Contracts* § 90 (1981); *English v. Fischer*, 660 S.W.2d 521, 524 (Tex. 1983) (requisites of promissory estoppel are (1) a promise, (2) foreseeability of reliance thereon by promisor, and (3) substantial reliance by promisee to his detriment).

Limited remedy.   Recovery under the doctrine of promissory estoppel is limited to restoring the promisee to the position he would have been in had he not acted in reliance on the promise. See PJC 110.2. Lost profits may not be recovered. *Fretz Construction Co. v. Southern National Bank*, 626 S.W.2d 478, 483 (Tex. 1981).

Exception to statute of frauds.   A more limited application of this doctrine has been used as an exception to the statute of frauds. *See "Moore" Burger, Inc. v. Phillips Petroleum Co.*, 492 S.W.2d 934, 937–40 (Tex. 1972). PJC 101.41 is not intended to cover such situations.

PJC 101.42   Question and Instruction on Quantum Meruit

QUESTION _____

Did *Paul Payne* perform compensable work for *Don Davis*?

One party performs compensable work if valuable services are rendered or materials furnished for another party who knowingly accepts and uses them and if the party accepting them should know that the performing party expects to be paid for the work.

Answer: _____

COMMENT

When to use.   If one party receives a benefit by accepting the services of another, the accepting party is obligated by principles of equity to pay the reasonable value of those services. *Colbert v. Dallas Joint Stock Land Bank*, 150 S.W.2d 771, 773 (Tex. 1941). The elements of a quantum meruit claim are set out in *Bashara v. Baptist Memorial Hospital System*, 685 S.W.2d 307, 310 (Tex. 1985). If a valid express contract covering the subject matter exists, recovery on quantum meruit generally is not allowed under Texas law. *Truly v. Austin*, 744 S.W.2d 934, 936 (Tex. 1988); *see also Woodard v. Southwest States, Inc.*, 384 S.W.2d 674, 675 (Tex. 1964). Recovery in quantum meruit is allowed for partial performance of a contract if (1) the defendant's breach prevents the plaintiff's completion, (2) the contract is unilateral and requires no performance by the plaintiff, or (3) the contract involves building or construction. *Truly*, 744 S.W.2d at 936–37. See PJC 110.6 for a question on quantum meruit recovery.

Construction contracts.   The existence of an express contract does not, however, preclude recovery in quantum meruit for the reasonable value of work performed and accepted but not covered by the contract. *Black Lake Pipe Line Co. v. Union Construction Co.*, 538 S.W.2d 80, 86 (Tex. 1976), *overruled on other grounds by Sterner v. Marathon Oil Co.*, 767 S.W.2d 686 (Tex. 1989). The right to recover in quantum meruit is based on a promise implied by law to pay for beneficial services rendered and knowingly accepted. *Davidson v. Clearman*, 391 S.W.2d 48, 50 (Tex. 1965).

A building contractor who has not substantially performed his contract may have quantum meruit as an alternate ground of recovery. *Dobbins v. Redden*, 785 S.W.2d 377 (Tex. 1990); *Truly*, 744 S.W.2d at 936; *see also Beeman v. Worrell*, 612 S.W.2d 953, 956 (Tex. Civ. App.—Dallas 1981, no writ); *Coon v. Schoeneman*, 476 S.W.2d 439, 442 (Tex. Civ. App.—Dallas 1972, writ ref'd n.r.e.). For a further discussion on construction contracts, see PJC 101.46.

Construction contract and quantum meruit issues may be submitted in the same charge. *City of Galveston v. Heffernan*, 155 S.W.2d 912 (Tex. 1941) (dispute concerned both subject matter of express contract and additional work done outside confines of contract); *see Chapa v. Reilly*, 733 S.W.2d 236, 237 (Tex. App.—Corpus Christi 1986, writ ref'd n.r.e.).

[*PJCs 101.43–.45 are reserved for expansion.*]

PJC 101.46   Construction Contracts Distinguished from Ordinary Contracts (Comment)

Doctrine of substantial performance.   In ordinary contract cases, a party who is himself in default cannot maintain a suit for its breach. *Gulf Pipe Line Co. v. Nearen*, 138 S.W.2d 1065, 1068 (Tex. 1940). This strict rule has been relaxed in the law of construction contracts by the doctrine of substantial performance, which allows recovery to a building contractor who has breached but substantially performed his contract. *Dobbins v. Redden*, 785 S.W.2d 377 (Tex. 1990); *Vance v. My Apartment Steak House of San Antonio, Inc.*, 677 S.W.2d 480, 481 (Tex. 1984); *Atkinson v. Jackson Bros.*, 270 S.W. 848, 850 (Tex. Comm'n App. 1925, holding approved).

Quantum meruit as alternate ground.   A building contractor who has not substantially performed may have quantum meruit as an alternate ground of recovery. *Dobbins*, 785 S.W.2d at 378; *Truly v. Austin*, 744 S.W.2d 934, 937 (Tex. 1988); *see also Beeman v. Worrell*, 612 S.W.2d 953, 956 (Tex. Civ. App.—Dallas 1981, no writ); *Coon v. Schoeneman*, 476 S.W.2d 439, 442 (Tex. Civ. App.—Dallas 1972, writ ref'd n.r.e.). For questions on quantum meruit, see PJCs 101.42 and 110.6.

Construction contracts and quantum meruit questions may be submitted in the same charge. *City of Galveston v. Heffernan*, 155 S.W.2d 912 (Tex. 1941) (dispute concerned both subject matter of express contract and additional work done outside contract); *see also Chapa v. Reilly*, 733 S.W.2d 236, 237 (Tex. App.—Corpus Christi 1986, writ ref'd n.r.e.).

Recovery.   A contractor who has substantially performed may recover the contract price less the cost of completion and remedying any defects. *Vance*, 677 S.W.2d at 481.

The doctrine of substantial performance also comes into play when the owner sues the contractor. If the contractor has substantially performed, the owner can recover the cost of completion less the unpaid balance on the contract price, known as the remedial measure of damages. If the contractor has not substantially performed, the measure of the owner's damages is the difference between the value of the building as constructed and its value had it been constructed in accordance with the contract. *Turner, Collie & Braden, Inc. v. Brookhollow, Inc.*, 642 S.W.2d 160, 164 (Tex. 1982).

Jury submissions in these suits are complicated if both the owner and the contractor seek affirmative recovery. *See, e.g., Greene v. Bearden Enterprises, Inc.*, 598 S.W.2d 649 (Tex. Civ. App.—Fort Worth 1980, writ ref'd n.r.e.); *Fidelity & Deposit Co. of Maryland v. Stool*, 607 S.W.2d 17 (Tex. Civ. App.—Tyler 1980, no writ).

Property Code requirement for suits filed after September 1, 1989.   Chapter 27 of the Texas Property Code adds new defenses, notice requirements, and opportunities to cure or settle in suits over residential construction defects filed after September 1, 1989. Tex. Prop. Code Ann. ch. 27 (Vernon Supp. 1998).

PJC 102.1   Question and Instruction on False, Misleading, or Deceptive Act or Practice (DTPA § 17.46(b))

QUESTION _____

Did *Don Davis* engage in any false, misleading, or deceptive act or practice that *Paul Payne* relied on to *his* detriment and that was a producing cause of damages to *Paul Payne*?

> "Producing cause" means an efficient, exciting, or contributing cause that, in a natural sequence, produced the damages, if any. There may be more than one producing cause.

> "False, misleading, or deceptive act or practice" means any of the following:

> > [*Insert appropriate instructions.*]

Answer: _____

COMMENT

When to use.   PJC 102.1 is a basic question that should be appropriate in most cases brought under section 17.46(b) of the Texas Deceptive Trade Practices–Consumer Protection Act (Tex. Bus. & Com. Code Ann. §§ 17.41–.63 (Vernon 1987 & Supp. 1998)) (DTPA). Questions for other causes of action based on the DTPA or the Insurance Code may be found at PJCs 102.7 (unconscionable action), 102.8 (warranty), 102.14 (Insurance Code), and 102.21 (knowing or intentional conduct).

Accompanying instructions.   Instructions to accompany PJC 102.1, informing the jury what type of conduct should be considered under the question, are at PJCs 102.2–.6. If more than one instruction is used, each must be separated by the word *or*, because a finding of any one of the acts or practices defined in the instructions would support recovery under the DTPA.

"Producing cause."   A consumer may maintain an action where any act or omission violating the DTPA constitutes a *producing cause* of actual damages. *See* DTPA § 17.50(a) (Supp. 1998). The definition of "producing cause" is from *Rourke v. Garza*, 530 S.W.2d 794, 801 (Tex. 1975).

Broad form preferred.   PJC 102.1 is a broad-form question designed to be accompanied with one or more appropriate instructions. Tex. R. Civ. P. 277 requires that "the court shall, whenever feasible, submit the cause upon broad-form questions." *See also Brown v. American Transfer & Storage Co.*, 601 S.W.2d 931, 937 (Tex. 1980) (approving broad question in deceptive trade practice case).

Knowing or intentional conduct.   If the defendant is found to have knowingly or intentionally engaged in any false, misleading, or deceptive conduct, the DTPA provides for additional damages. DTPA § 17.50(b)(1). See PJC 102.21 for a question on knowing or intentional conduct and PJC 110.11 for a question on additional damages.

Pre-1995 suits.   The 1995 amendments to the DTPA added a requirement that the false, misleading, or deceptive act or practice be "relied on by a consumer to the consumer's detriment." DTPA § 17.50(a)(1)(B). The amendments apply to all causes of action that accrue on or after September 1, 1995, and to all suits filed on or after September 1, 1996. In suits governed by the prior law, the question should read:

> Did *Don Davis* engage in any false, misleading, or deceptive act or practice that was a producing cause of damages to *Paul Payne*?

Vicarious liability.   If the issue is the vicarious liability of one for another's conduct, see *Celtic Life Insurance Co. v. Coats*, 885 S.W.2d 96, 98–99 (Tex. 1994); *Royal Globe Insurance Co. v. Bar Consultants, Inc.*, 577 S.W.2d 688, 693–95 (Tex. 1979) (discussing principal's liability for acts of agent in DTPA and Insurance Code case); and *Southwestern Bell Telephone Co. v. Wilson*, 768 S.W.2d 755, 759 (Tex. App.—Corpus Christi 1988, writ denied) (company liable for unreasonable collection efforts of outside attorneys because they "were committed for the purpose of accomplishing the mission entrusted to the attorneys"). In cases involving insurance, the following statutory and regulatory provisions should be consulted: Tex. Ins. Code Ann. art. 21.02 (Vernon Supp. 1998) (who are agents for insurance companies); art. 21.04 (solicitor deemed company's agent); art. 21.14(2) ("local recording agent" and "solicitor" defined); 28 Tex. Admin. Code § 21.1 (West 1998) (unfair conduct in insurance business unlawful "whether done directly or indirectly"); § 21.2 ("meanings given to the provisions, terms, and words" of unfair insurance practice regulation "are not to be limited to the common law meaning . . . but . . . interpreted to accomplish the purpose of these sections").

PJC 102.2   **Description of Goods or Services or Affiliation of Persons (DTPA § 17.46(b)(5))**

Representing that *goods* [*or services*] had or would have *characteristics* that they did not have [*or*]

COMMENT

When to use.   PJC 102.2 is designed to accompany the question in PJC 102.1 to submit a cause of action based on Tex. Bus. & Com. Code Ann. § 17.46(b)(5) (Vernon Supp. 1998) (DTPA).

Use of "or."   If used with other instructions (see PJCs 102.3–.6), PJC 102.2 must be followed by the word *or*, because a finding of any one of the acts or practices defined in the instructions would support recovery under the DTPA.

Source of instruction.   DTPA § 17.46(b)(5) prohibits "representing that goods or services have sponsorship, approval, characteristics, ingredients, uses, benefits, or quantities which they do not have or that a person has a sponsorship, approval, status, affiliation, or connection which he does not."

Use of statutory language.   The supreme court has held that jury submissions of section 17.46(b) cases should follow the language of the statute as closely as possible but may be altered somewhat to conform to the evidence of the case. *Spencer v. Eagle Star Insurance Co. of America*, 876 S.W.2d 154, 157 (Tex. 1994); *Brown v. American Transfer & Storage Co.*, 601 S.W.2d 931, 937 (Tex. 1980). Thus, if appropriate, the word *characteristics* may be replaced with the words *sponsorship*, *approval*, *ingredients*, *uses*, *benefits*, or *quantities*. *Brown*, 601 S.W.2d at 937; DTPA § 17.46(b)(5). Material terms, however, should not be omitted or substituted. *See Transportation Insurance Co. v. Faircloth*, 898 S.W.2d 269, 273 (Tex. 1995) (construing DTPA § 17.46(b)(23)).

Affiliation of person.   If deception regarding a person's affiliation is claimed, PJC 102.2 may be reworded as follows:

Representing that a *person* had or would have *a sponsorship* that the *person* does not or will not have.

A. *Substitutions for "a sponsorship."*   In an appropriate case, the words *a sponsorship* may be replaced with the words *a status*, *an affiliation*, or *a connection*. *See* DTPA § 17.46(b)(5).

B. *"Person" includes business entity.*   Under the DTPA, the word *person* includes a business entity. DTPA § 17.45(3) (1987). In a case in which a business entity is involved, however, it may be advisable either to include the statutory definition in the charge or to substitute the name of the entity for the word *person*.

"Goods" includes real estate.   The use of the word *goods* in PJC 102.2 is intended to cover real property. DTPA § 17.45(1). If real estate is involved, however, it may be advisable either to include the statutory definition in the charge or to substitute a reference to the real estate in question for the word *goods*.

Misrepresentations about future characteristics, uses, or benefits.   Although not appearing in the statute, the words *would have* are used in PJC 102.2. The Committee believes this use to be appropriate under *Brown*, 601 S.W.2d at 937, and *Smith v. Baldwin*, 611 S.W.2d 611, 614–16 (Tex. 1980) (representation need not be untrue when made: DTPA § 17.46(b) applies to misrepresentations about the future as well as about the present).

PJC 102.3   Quality of Goods or Services (DTPA § 17.46(b)(7))

Representing that *goods* [*or services*] are or will be of a particular *quality* if they were of another [*or*]

COMMENT

When to use.   PJC 102.3 should be used with PJC 102.1 to submit a cause of action under Tex. Bus. & Com. Code Ann. § 17.46(b)(7) (Vernon Supp. 1998) (DTPA).

Use of "or."   If used with other instructions (see PJCs 102.2 and .4–.6), PJC 102.3 must be followed by the word *or*, because a finding of any one of the acts or practices defined in the instructions would support recovery under the DTPA.

Source of instruction.   DTPA § 17.46(b)(7) prohibits "representing that goods or services are of a particular standard, quality, or grade, or that goods are of a particular style or model, if they are of another."

Use of statutory language.   The supreme court has held that jury submissions of section 17.46(b) cases should follow the language of the statute as closely as possible but may be altered somewhat to conform to the evidence of the case. *Spencer v. Eagle Star Insurance Co. of America*, 876 S.W.2d 154, 157 (Tex. 1994); *Brown v. American Transfer & Storage Co.*, 601 S.W.2d 931, 937 (Tex. 1980). Thus, if appropriate, the word *quality* may be replaced with the words *standard* or *grade*, and, if only goods and not services are involved, the words *style* or *model* may replace the word *quality*. *Brown*, 601 S.W.2d at 937; DTPA § 17.46(b)(7). Material terms, however, should not be omitted or substituted. *See Transportation Insurance Co. v. Faircloth*, 898 S.W.2d 269, 273 (Tex. 1995) (construing DTPA § 17.46(b)(23)).

"Goods" includes real estate.   The use of the word *goods* in PJC 102.3 is intended to cover real property. DTPA § 17.45(1) (1987). If real estate is involved, however, it may be advisable either to include the statutory definition in the charge or to substitute a reference to the real estate in question for the word *goods*.

Misrepresentations about future quality.   Although not appearing in the statute, the words *will be* are used in PJC 102.3. The Committee believes this use to be appropriate under *Brown*, 601 S.W.2d at 937, and *Smith v. Baldwin*, 611 S.W.2d 611, 614–16 (Tex. 1980) (representation need not be untrue when made: DTPA § 17.46(b) applies to misrepresentations concerning both present and future quality of goods or services).

**PJC 102.4   Misrepresented and Unlawful Agreements
(DTPA § 17.46(b)(12))**

Representing that an agreement confers or involves *rights* that it did not have or involve [*or*]

COMMENT

When to use.   PJC 102.4 should be used with PJC 102.1 to submit a cause of action under Tex. Bus. & Com. Code Ann. § 17.46(b)(12) (Vernon Supp. 1998) (DTPA).

Use of "or."   If used with other instructions (see PJCs 102.2–.3 and .5–.6), PJC 102.4 must be followed by the word *or*, because a finding of any one of the acts or practices defined in the instructions would support recovery under the DTPA.

Source of instruction.   DTPA § 17.46(b)(12) prohibits "representing that an agreement confers or involves rights, remedies, or obligations which it does not have or involve, or which are prohibited by law."

Use of statutory language.   The supreme court has held that jury submissions of section 17.46(b) cases should follow the language of the statute as closely as possible but may be altered somewhat to conform to the evidence of the case. *Spencer v. Eagle Star Insurance Co. of America*, 876 S.W.2d 154, 157 (Tex. 1994); *Brown v. American Transfer & Storage Co.*, 601 S.W.2d 931, 937 (Tex. 1980). In an appropriate case, the words *remedies* and/or *obligations* may be added to or substituted for the word *rights* in the above instruction. *Brown*, 601 S.W.2d at 937; DTPA § 17.46(b)(12). Material terms, however, should not be omitted or substituted. *See Transportation Insurance Co. v. Faircloth*, 898 S.W.2d 269, 273 (Tex. 1995) (construing DTPA § 17.46(b)(23)).

Misrepresentations about the future.   A representation need not be untrue when made. Because DTPA § 17.46(b) applies to misrepresentations about the future as well as about the present, misrepresentations of present and future rights are covered by this instruction. *See Smith v. Baldwin*, 611 S.W.2d 611, 614–16 (Tex. 1980).

Unlawful agreement.   DTPA § 17.46(b)(12) also prohibits representing that an agreement has terms that are "prohibited by law." Because the Committee believes that the question of what is prohibited by law would be for the court, the jury would only be asked whether the representation occurred. In such a case, the question might include:

Representing that an agreement confers or involves [*insert particular right, remedy, or obligation found to be unlawful*].

PJC 102.5   Failure to Disclose Information (DTPA § 17.46(b)(23))

Failing to disclose information about *goods [or services]* that was known at the time of the transaction with the intention to induce *Paul Payne* into a transaction *he* otherwise would not have entered into if the information had been disclosed [*or*]

COMMENT

When to use.   PJC 102.5 should be used with PJC 102.1 to submit a cause of action under Tex. Bus. & Com. Code Ann. § 17.46(b)(23) (Vernon Supp. 1998) (DTPA).

Use of "or."   If used with other instructions (see PJCs 102.2–.4 and .6), PJC 102.5 must be followed by the word *or*, because a finding of any one of the acts or practices defined in the instructions would support recovery under the DTPA.

Source of instruction.   DTPA § 17.46(b)(23) makes it a deceptive trade practice to fail "to disclose information concerning goods or services which was known at the time of the transaction if such failure to disclose such information was intended to induce the consumer into a transaction into which the consumer would not have entered had the information been disclosed."

Use of statutory language.   The supreme court has held that jury submissions of section 17.46(b) cases should follow the language of the statute as closely as possible but may be altered somewhat to conform to the evidence of the case. *Spencer v. Eagle Star Insurance Co. of America*, 876 S.W.2d 154, 157 (Tex. 1994); *Brown v. American Transfer & Storage Co.*, 601 S.W.2d 931, 937 (Tex. 1980). Material terms, however, should not be omitted or substituted. *See Transportation Insurance Co. v. Faircloth*, 898 S.W.2d 269, 273 (Tex. 1995) (construing DTPA § 17.46(b)(23)).

"Goods" includes real estate.   The use of the word *goods* in PJC 102.5 is intended to cover real property. DTPA § 17.45(1) (1987). If real estate is involved, however, it may be advisable either to include the statutory definition in the charge or to substitute a reference to the real estate in question for the word *goods*.

PJC 102.6   Other "Laundry List" Violations (DTPA § 17.46(b)) (Comment)

PJCs 102.2–.5 provide patterns for submitting the most frequently litigated claims under section 17.46(b). *See* Tex. Bus. & Com. Code Ann. § 17.46(b)(5), (7), (12), (23) (Vernon Supp. 1998) (DTPA). However, a claim arising under any other subsection of section 17.46(b) may be handled in the same manner—for example, by adapting the statutory language to the facts of the case in the form of an instruction to be submitted with PJC 102.1.

PJC 102.7   Question and Instruction on Unconscionable Action or Course of Action (DTPA §§ 17.50(a)(3) and 17.45(5))

QUESTION _____

Did *Don Davis* engage in any unconscionable action or course of action that was a producing cause of damages to *Paul Payne*?

"Producing cause" means an efficient, exciting, or contributing cause that, in a natural sequence, produced the damages, if any. There may be more than one producing cause.

An unconscionable action or course of action is an act or practice that, to a consumer's detriment, takes advantage of the lack of knowledge, ability, experience, or capacity of the consumer to a grossly unfair degree.

Answer: _____

COMMENT

When to use. PJC 102.7 is to be used with PJC 102.1 to submit a claim based on Tex. Bus. & Com. Code Ann. § 17.50(a)(3) (Vernon Supp. 1998) (DTPA). This statute gives a consumer a cause of action for "any unconscionable action or course of action by any person." The definition of "unconscionable action or course of action" is derived from DTPA § 17.45(5). Questions for other causes of action based on the DTPA or the Insurance Code may be found at PJCs 102.1 (false, misleading, or deceptive act), 102.8 (warranty), 102.14 (Insurance Code), and 102.21 (knowing or intentional conduct).

1995 amendments. The 1995 amendments to the DTPA deleted the "gross disparity" language from the definition and changed the reference from "person" to "consumer." The amendments apply to all causes of action accruing on or after September 1, 1995, and to all suits filed on or after September 1, 1996. In suits governed by the prior law, the definition of "unconscionable action or course of action" should read:

An unconscionable action or course of action is an act or practice that, to a person's detriment, either—

(a) takes advantage of the lack of knowledge, ability, experience, or capacity of a person to a grossly unfair degree or

(b) results in a gross disparity between value received and consideration paid in a transaction involving transfer of consideration.

Act of May 6, 1977, 65th Leg., R.S., ch. 216, § 1, 1977 Tex. Gen. Laws 600.

"Producing cause."   Under section 17.50(a) of the DTPA, a "consumer may maintain an action where any of the following constitute a *producing cause*" of actual damages. DTPA § 17.50(a) (emphasis added). The definition of "producing cause" is from *Rourke v. Garza*, 530 S.W.2d 794, 801 (Tex. 1975).

Broad form preferred.   PJC 102.7 is a broad-form question designed to be accompanied with one or more appropriate instructions. Tex. R. Civ. P. 277 requires that "the court shall, whenever feasible, submit the cause upon broad-form questions." *See also Brown v. American Transfer & Storage Co.*, 601 S.W.2d 931, 937 (Tex. 1980) (approving broad question in deceptive trade practice case).

Knowing or intentional conduct.   If the defendant is found to have knowingly or intentionally engaged in any false, misleading, or deceptive conduct, the DTPA provides for additional damages. DTPA § 17.50(b)(1). See PJC 102.21 for a question on knowing or intentional conduct and PJC 110.11 for a question on additional damages.

Vicarious liability.   If the issue is the vicarious liability of one for another's conduct, see *Celtic Life Insurance Co. v. Coats*, 885 S.W.2d 96, 98–99 (Tex. 1994); *Royal Globe Insurance Co. v. Bar Consultants, Inc.*, 577 S.W.2d 688, 693–95 (Tex. 1979) (discussing principal's liability for acts of agent in DTPA and Insurance Code case); and *Southwestern Bell Telephone Co. v. Wilson*, 768 S.W.2d 755, 759 (Tex. App.—Corpus Christi 1988, writ denied) (company liable for unreasonable collection efforts of outside attorneys because they "were committed for the purpose of accomplishing the mission entrusted to the attorneys"). In cases involving insurance, the following statutory and regulatory provisions should be consulted: Tex. Ins. Code Ann. art. 21.02 (Vernon Supp. 1998) (who are agents for insurance companies); art. 21.04 (solicitor deemed company's agent); art. 21.14(2) ("local recording agent" and "solicitor" defined); 28 Tex. Admin. Code § 21.1 (West 1998) (unfair conduct in insurance business unlawful "whether done directly or indirectly"); § 21.2 ("meanings given to the provisions, terms, and words" of unfair insurance practice regulation "are not to be limited to the common law meaning . . . but . . . interpreted to accomplish the purpose of these sections").

PJC 102.8   Question and Instruction on Warranty (DTPA § 17.50(a); Tex. UCC §§ 2.313–.315)

QUESTION _____

Was the failure, if any, of *Don Davis* to comply with a warranty a producing cause of damages to *Paul Payne*?

> "Producing cause" means an efficient, exciting, or contributing cause that, in a natural sequence, produced the damages, if any. There may be more than one producing cause.

> "Failure to comply with a warranty" means any of the following:

> *[Insert appropriate instructions.]*

Answer: _____

COMMENT

When to use. PJC 102.8 is a basic question that should be appropriate in most cases brought under Tex. Bus. & Com. Code Ann. § 17.50(a)(2) (Vernon Supp. 1998) (DTPA); *see also* Tex. Bus. & Com. Code Ann. §§ 2.313–.315 (Tex. UCC) (1994). Questions for other causes of action based on the DTPA or the Insurance Code may be found at PJCs 102.1 (false, misleading, or deceptive act), 102.7 (unconscionable action), 102.14 (Insurance Code), and 102.21 (knowing or intentional conduct).

Creation of warranty. The DTPA does not define "warranty." Nor does it create any warranties; therefore, any warranty must be established independently of the Act. *La Sara Grain Co. v. First National Bank*, 673 S.W.2d 558, 565 (Tex. 1984).

"Producing cause." Under section 17.50(a) of the DTPA, a "consumer may maintain an action where any of the following constitute a *producing cause*" of actual damages. DTPA § 17.50(a) (emphasis added). The definition of "producing cause" is from *Rourke v. Garza*, 530 S.W.2d 794, 801 (Tex. 1975).

Accompanying instructions. Instructions to accompany PJC 102.8, informing the jury what type of conduct should be considered under the question, are at PJCs 102.9–.13. If more than one instruction is used, each must be separated by the word *or*, because a finding of any one of the acts or practices defined in the instructions would support recovery under the DTPA.

Broad form preferred. PJC 102.8 is a broad-form question designed to be accompanied with one or more appropriate instructions. Tex. R. Civ. P. 277 requires that "the court shall, whenever feasible, submit the cause upon broad-form questions." *See also Brown v.*

American Transfer & Storage Co., 601 S.W.2d 931, 937 (Tex. 1980) (approving broad question in deceptive trade practice case).

Knowing or intentional conduct. If the defendant is found to have knowingly or intentionally engaged in any false, misleading, or deceptive conduct, the DTPA provides for additional damages. DTPA § 17.50(b)(1). See PJC 102.21 for a question on knowing or intentional conduct and PJC 110.11 for a question on additional damages.

Vicarious liability. If the issue is the vicarious liability of one for another's conduct, see *Celtic Life Insurance Co. v. Coats*, 885 S.W.2d 96, 98–99 (Tex. 1994); *Royal Globe Insurance Co. v. Bar Consultants, Inc.*, 577 S.W.2d 688, 693–95 (Tex. 1979) (discussing principal's liability for acts of agent in DTPA and Insurance Code case); and *Southwestern Bell Telephone Co. v. Wilson*, 768 S.W.2d 755, 759 (Tex. App.—Corpus Christi 1988, writ denied) (company liable for unreasonable collection efforts of outside attorneys because they "were committed for the purpose of accomplishing the mission entrusted to the attorneys"). In cases involving insurance, the following statutory and regulatory provisions should be consulted: Tex. Ins. Code Ann. art. 21.02 (Vernon Supp. 1998) (who are agents for insurance companies); art. 21.04 (solicitor deemed company's agent); art. 21.14(2) ("local recording agent" and "solicitor" defined); 28 Tex. Admin. Code § 21.1 (West 1998) (unfair conduct in insurance business unlawful "whether done directly or indirectly"); § 21.2 ("meanings given to the provisions, terms, and words" of unfair insurance practice regulation "are not to be limited to the common law meaning . . . but . . . interpreted to accomplish the purpose of these sections").

**PJC 102.9   Express Warranty—Goods or Services
                     (DTPA § 17.50(a)(2); Tex. UCC § 2.313)**

Failing to comply with an express warranty.

An express warranty is any affirmation of fact or promise made by *Don
Davis* that relates to the [*describe particular goods*] and becomes part of
the basis of the bargain. It is not necessary that formal words such as
"warrant" or "guarantee" be used or that there be a specific intent to make
a warranty.

[*or*]

COMMENT

When to use.   PJC 102.9 may be used with PJC 102.8 to submit a claim of breach of
express warranty involving the sale of goods. *See* Tex. Bus. & Com. Code Ann.
§ 17.50(a)(2) (Vernon Supp. 1998) (DTPA); *see also* Tex. Bus. & Com. Code Ann. § 2.313
(Tex. UCC) (1994) (creation of express warranty).

Use of "or."   If used with other instructions (see PJCs 102.10–.13), PJC 102.9 must be
followed by the word *or*, because a finding of any one of the acts or practices defined in the
instructions would support recovery under the DTPA.

Creation of warranty.   The DTPA does not define "warranty." Nor does it create any
warranties; therefore, any warranty must be established independently of the Act. *La Sara
Grain Co. v. First National Bank*, 673 S.W.2d 558, 565 (Tex. 1984).

Goods or services.   The Uniform Commercial Code defines and creates warranties in
the sale of goods. Tex. UCC § 2.313. It defines "goods" as "all things . . . movable at the
time of identification to the contract for sale . . . [and] the unborn young of animals and
growing crops and other identified things attached to realty." Tex. UCC § 2.105. The
DTPA, however, has a broader definition of "goods" in that it includes real estate. DTPA
§ 17.45(1) (1987) ("goods" means tangible chattels or real property purchased or leased for
use). The DTPA also includes services. DTPA § 17.45(2).

There are no decisions compelling the use of the UCC definition of express warranty set
forth in PJC 102.9 in a nongoods case. In *Southwestern Bell Telephone Co. v. FDP Corp.*,
811 S.W.2d 572 (Tex. 1991), the supreme court stated that because "sale of advertising is
predominantly a service transaction, not a sale of goods, the warranty provisions of Article
Two of the [UCC] do not explicitly govern this case." 811 S.W.2d at 574. The court also
stated that "although the case at bar involves a service transaction, reference to the Code is
instructive." 811 S.W.2d at 575. The Committee expresses no opinion on whether the above
definition should be used in nongoods cases.

Affirmation merely of value of goods. A mere affirmation of the value of the goods or a statement purporting to be merely the seller's opinion or commendation of the goods does not create a warranty. Tex. UCC § 2.313 (1994).

Superior knowledge. If, however, the seller has knowledge superior to that of the consumer, such an affirmation may create a warranty. *Valley Datsun v. Martinez*, 578 S.W.2d 485, 490 (Tex. Civ. App.—Corpus Christi 1979, no writ) (seller's knowledge, in conjunction with buyer's ignorance, operated to "make the slightest divergence from mere praise into representations of fact" and created warranty). In a case in which the issue is in dispute, the jury might be asked whether the defendant *had* such knowledge:

> Did *Don Davis* have, or purport to have, superior knowledge of the subject matter of any misrepresentation that you have found was a producing cause of *Paul Payne*'s damages?

> *Don Davis* had superior knowledge of the subject matter if *his* knowledge or information regarding that subject matter was superior to that possessed by *Paul Payne* and *Paul Payne* did not have equal access to such knowledge or information.

> *Don Davis* purported to have superior knowledge if *he* had the appearance of having such knowledge or implied, professed outwardly, or claimed that *he* had such knowledge regarding a matter that was not equally open to *Paul Payne*.

For discussions of the "superior knowledge" rule, see *Trenholm v. Ratcliff*, 646 S.W.2d 927, 930 (Tex. 1983); *Valley Datsun*, 578 S.W.2d at 490; *General Supply & Equipment Co. v. Phillips*, 490 S.W.2d 913, 917 (Tex. Civ. App.—Tyler 1972, writ ref'd n.r.e.); *see also United States Pipe & Foundry Co. v. City of Waco*, 108 S.W.2d 432, 435–37 (Tex.), *cert. denied*, 58 S. Ct. 266 (1937).

PJC 102.10   Implied Warranty of Merchantability—Goods
(DTPA § 17.50(a)(2); Tex. UCC § 2.314)

Furnishing goods that, because of a lack of something necessary for adequacy, were not fit for the ordinary purposes for which such goods are used [*or*]

COMMENT

When to use.   PJC 102.10 may be used with PJC 102.8 to submit a cause of action for breach of an implied warranty of merchantability under Tex. Bus. & Com. Code Ann. § 2.314(b)(3) (Tex. UCC) (Vernon 1994). *See also* Tex. Bus. & Com. Code § 17.50(a)(2) (Supp. 1998) (DTPA); *Plas-Tex, Inc. v. U.S. Steel Corp.*, 772 S.W.2d 442 (Tex. 1989).

Caveat.   Note that the above instruction is appropriate *only* for a case brought under Tex. UCC § 2.314(b)(3) (1994). *See Plas-Tex*, 772 S.W.2d at 445. *Plas-Tex* defined "defect" as "a condition of the goods that renders them unfit for the ordinary purposes for which they are used because of a lack of something necessary for adequacy." *Plas-Tex*, 772 S.W.2d at 444. For simplicity and clarity, the Committee has included only the definition itself in the above instruction. The Committee expresses no opinion about the above definition's applicability if the evidence shows a *presence*, rather than a *lack*, of something that makes the goods unfit.

Other elements of merchantability.   For cases involving other elements of merchantability, the instruction should be modified to delete the reference to "defect" and to include the relevant elements raised by the evidence. The elements are as follows:

Furnishing fungible goods not of fair average quality within the description;

Furnishing goods that did not run, within the variations permitted by the agreement, of even kind, quality, and quantity within each unit and among all units involved;

Furnishing goods that were not adequately contained, packaged, and labeled as the agreement required;

Furnishing goods that did not conform to the promises or affirmations of fact made on the container or label.

Tex. UCC § 2.314(b)(1)–(2), (4)–(6).

Use of "or."   If used with other instructions (see PJCs 102.9 and .11–.13), PJC 102.10 must be followed by the word *or*, because a finding of any one of the acts or practices defined in the instructions would support recovery under the DTPA.

Seller must be merchant.   The implied warranty only arises if the seller is a "merchant" as defined in Tex. UCC § 2.104(a). Whether the seller is subject to the statute has been held to be a jury issue. *Nelson v. Union Equity Co-operative Exchange*, 536 S.W.2d 635, 641 (Tex. Civ. App.—Fort Worth 1976), *aff'd on other grounds*, 548 S.W.2d 352 (Tex. 1977).

PJC 102.11 Implied Warranty of Fitness for Particular Purpose— Goods (DTPA § 17.50(a)(2); Tex. UCC § 2.315)

Furnishing or selecting goods that were not suitable for a particular purpose if *Don Davis* had reason to know the purpose and also had reason to know that *Paul Payne* was relying on *Don Davis*'s skill or judgment to furnish or select suitable goods [*or*]

COMMENT

When to use. PJC 102.11 may be used with PJC 102.8 to submit a claim of breach of an implied warranty of fitness for a particular purpose. *See* Tex. Bus. & Com. Code Ann. § 17.50(a)(2) (Vernon Supp. 1998) (DTPA); Tex. Bus. & Com. Code Ann. § 2.315 (Tex. UCC) (1994).

Use of "or." If used with other instructions (see PJCs 102.10 and .12–.13), PJC 102.11 must be followed by the word *or*, because a finding of any one of the acts or practices defined in the instructions would support recovery under the DTPA.

Defendant need not be merchant. Note that this warranty does not require the defendant to be a "merchant," as does the implied warranty of merchantability in Tex. UCC § 2.314. See PJC 102.10.

PJC 102.12   Implied Warranty of Good and Workmanlike Performance—Services (DTPA § 17.50(a)(2))

Failing to perform services in a good and workmanlike manner.

A good and workmanlike manner is that quality of work performed by one who has the knowledge, training, or experience necessary for the successful practice of a trade or occupation and performed in a manner generally considered proficient by those capable of judging such work.

[*or*]

COMMENT

When to use.   PJC 102.12, when used with PJC 102.8, submits the claim of a breach of an implied warranty to perform services in a good and workmanlike manner. *See* Tex. Bus. & Com. Code Ann. § 17.50(a)(2) (Vernon Supp. 1998) (DTPA); *Melody Home Manufacturing Co. v. Barnes*, 741 S.W.2d 349, 354 (Tex. 1987) (implied warranty to repair or modify goods or property in good and workmanlike manner); *Humber v. Morton*, 426 S.W.2d 554 (Tex. 1968) (implied warranty of construction of new home in good and workmanlike manner). In *Parkway Co. v. Woodruff*, 901 S.W.2d 434, 439 (Tex. 1995), the supreme court announced that this service warranty (1) "will not be judicially imposed unless there is a demonstrated need for it"; and (2) "extends only to services provided to remedy defects existing at the time of the relevant consumer transaction."

Use of "or."   If used with other instructions (see PJCs 102.9–.11 and .13), PJC 102.12 must be followed by the word *or,* because a finding of any one of the acts or practices defined in the instructions would support recovery under the DTPA.

Source of instruction.   The above instruction is from *Melody Home Manufacturing Co.*, 741 S.W.2d at 354.

Independent of warranty of habitability.   The warranty covered by PJC 102.12 is independent of the implied warranty of habitability. *Evans v. J. Stiles, Inc.*, 689 S.W.2d 399, 400 (Tex. 1985). There is no need for additional language in the instruction, such as "and suitable for human habitation." *Cocke v. White*, 697 S.W.2d 739, 744 (Tex. App.—Corpus Christi 1985, writ ref'd n.r.e.). See PJC 102.13 for the implied warranty of habitability.

PJC 102.13   Implied Warranty of Habitability (DTPA § 17.50(a)(2))

Selling a home that was not suitable for human habitation [*or*]

COMMENT

When to use.   PJC 102.13 may be used with PJC 102.8 to submit a claim of breach of implied warranty of habitability. *See* Tex. Bus. & Com. Code Ann. § 17.50(a)(2) (Vernon Supp. 1998) (DTPA); *Humber v. Morton*, 426 S.W.2d 554 (Tex. 1968) (implied warranty of habitability in new home construction); *see also Gupta v. Ritter Homes, Inc.*, 646 S.W.2d 168, 169 (Tex. 1983) (warranty extends to all subsequent purchasers).

Use of "or."   If used with other instructions (see PJCs 102.9–.12), PJC 102.13 must be followed by the word *or*, because a finding of any one of the acts or practices defined in the instructions would support recovery under the DTPA.

Habitability in residential leases.   In *Kamarath v. Bennett*, 568 S.W.2d 658, 660–61 (Tex. 1978), the court found an implied warranty of habitability applicable to a rented apartment. However, legislation has since been passed setting forth the specific duties of a landlord "to repair and remedy" residential premises. Tex. Prop. Code Ann. § 92.052 (Vernon 1995). These duties are in lieu of existing common-law and statutory warranties. Tex. Prop. Code § 92.061.

Suitability in commercial leases.   In *Davidow v. Inwood North Professional Group—Phase I*, 747 S.W.2d 373, 377 (Tex. 1988), the court held that an implied warranty of suitability had been breached in the commercial lease of a doctor's office. In an appropriate case, the language of PJC 102.13 may be adapted to cover the breach of this warranty.

Distinguished from "good and workmanlike" warranty.   The *Humber* warranty contains two distinct elements: (1) warranty of good and workmanlike manner of construction of a new home and (2) warranty of habitability. *Evans v. J. Stiles, Inc.*, 689 S.W.2d 399, 400 (Tex. 1985). For the warranty of good and workmanlike manner of construction, see PJC 102.12.

PJC 102.14   Question on Insurance Code Article 21.21

QUESTION _____

Did *Don Davis* engage in any unfair or deceptive act or practice that caused damages to *Paul Payne*?

"Unfair or deceptive act or practice" means any of the following:

[*Insert appropriate instructions.*]

Answer: _____

COMMENT

When to use.   PJC 102.14 is a basic question that should be appropriate in most cases brought under Tex. Ins. Code Ann. art. 21.21 (Vernon 1981 & Supp. 1998). Section 1 of article 21.21, however, also prohibits "unfair methods of competition," and in such a case PJC 102.14 should be modified as appropriate. Questions for causes of action based on the DTPA may be found at PJCs 102.1 (false, misleading, or deceptive act), 102.7 (unconscionable action), and 102.8 (warranty). See also PJC 102.21 (knowing or intentional conduct).

Accompanying instructions.   Instructions to accompany PJC 102.14, informing the jury what type of conduct should be considered under the question, are at PJCs 102.15–.19. If more than one instruction is used, each must be separated by the word *or*, because a finding of any one of the acts or practices defined in the instructions would support recovery under the DTPA. Failure to instruct is error. *Spencer v. Eagle Star Insurance Co. of America*, 876 S.W.2d 154, 157 (Tex. 1994).

Broad form preferred.   PJC 102.14 is a broad-form question designed to be accompanied with one or more appropriate instructions. Tex. R. Civ. P. 277 requires that "the court shall, whenever feasible, submit the cause upon broad-form questions." *See also Brown v. American Transfer & Storage Co.*, 601 S.W.2d 931, 937 (Tex. 1980) (approving broad question in deceptive trade practice case).

Knowing conduct.   If the defendant is found to have knowingly engaged in an unfair or deceptive act or practice, the Insurance Code provides for additional damages. Tex. Ins. Code art. 21.21, § 16(b)(1) (Supp. 1998). See PJC 102.21 for a question on knowing conduct and PJC 110.11 for a question on additional damages.

Treble damages.   Recovery of treble damages under Tex. Ins. Code art. 21.21 varies, depending on which version of the statute applies. Treble damages are mandatory and automatic in causes of action arising in whole or in part before April 4, 1985. *State Farm Fire & Casualty Co. v. Gros*, 818 S.W.2d 908, 917 (Tex. App.—Austin 1991, no writ); *Rainey-Mapes v. Queen Charters, Inc.*, 729 S.W.2d 907, 915 (Tex. App.—San Antonio 1987, writ granted, dism'd as moot). In these cases, a finding of liability alone was enough to support recovery of treble damages.

After the 1985 amendments, but before the 1995 amendments, treble damages were mandatory, but only if the jury found the defendant acted "knowingly." Act of March 13, 1985, 69th Leg., R.S., ch. 22, § 3, 1985 Tex. Gen. Laws 71, 72, *amended by* Act of May 19, 1995, 74th Leg., R.S., ch. 414, § 13, 1995 Tex. Gen. Laws 2988, 3000. See PJC 102.21 for a question on knowing conduct.

The 1995 amendments to article 21.21 make additional damages discretionary with the trier of fact, if the defendant acted knowingly. The amendments apply to all causes of action that accrue on or after September 1, 1995, and to all suits filed on or after September 1, 1996. Tex. Ins. Code art. 21.21, § 16(b). In suits subject to the 1995 amendments, the plaintiff should submit the question on knowing conduct as in PJC 102.21 and then should ask the jury to determine the amount of additional damages as in PJC 110.11.

Under each of these versions, recovery of treble damages is the same whether the claim is brought directly under article 21.21 or is brought through Tex. Bus. & Com. Code Ann. § 17.50(a)(4) (Vernon Supp. 1998) (DTPA). The supreme court has held that this DTPA section "incorporates article 21.21 . . . in its entirety," including the treble damages provision in article 21.21, section 16. *Vail v. Texas Farm Bureau Mutual Insurance Co.*, 754 S.W.2d 129, 137 (Tex. 1988).

Causation.   Unlike the DTPA questions (PJCs 102.1, .7, and .8), PJC 102.14 does not contain the term "producing cause," because neither pre-1995 nor post-1995 versions of article 21.21, section 16, refer to "producing cause" as an element. *See* Act of March 19, 1985, 69th Leg., R.S., ch. 22, § 3, 1985 Tex. Gen. Laws 395, *amended by* Act of May 19, 1995, 74th Leg., R.S., ch. 414, § 13, 1995 Tex. Gen. Laws 2988, 3000. The Committee believes that "producing cause" need not be submitted to obtain actual damages as long as the damages question inquires about damages that resulted from the prohibited conduct. See PJC 110.13, the insurance damages question, which contains such an inquiry. For a discussion of the special causation issues relating to recovery of policy benefits as damages, see the Comment to PJC 110.13.

The 1995 amendments to article 21.21 change the causation standard by granting a cause of action to a person who has sustained actual damages "caused by" another's engaging in a prohibited act. The amendments apply to all causes of action accruing on or after September 1, 1995, and to all suits filed on or after September 1, 1996.

In suits governed by the prior law, the question should read:

Did *Don Davis* engage in any unfair or deceptive act or practice?

The Committee expresses no opinion on whether "caused by" is a lower or different threshold of causation.

Vicarious liability.   If the issue is the vicarious liability of one for another's conduct, see *Celtic Life Insurance Co. v. Coats*, 885 S.W.2d 96, 98–99 (Tex. 1994); *Royal Globe Insurance Co. v. Bar Consultants, Inc.*, 577 S.W.2d 688, 693–95 (Tex. 1979) (discussing principal's liability for acts of agent in DTPA and Insurance Code case); and *Southwestern*

Bell Telephone Co. v. Wilson, 768 S.W.2d 755, 759 (Tex. App.—Corpus Christi 1988, writ denied) (company liable for unreasonable collection efforts of outside attorneys because they "were committed for the purpose of accomplishing the mission entrusted to the attorneys"). In cases involving insurance, the following statutory and regulatory provisions should be consulted: Tex. Ins. Code art. 21.02 (who are agents for insurance companies); art. 21.04 (solicitor deemed company's agent); art. 21.14(2) ("local recording agent" and "solicitor" defined); 28 Tex. Admin. Code § 21.1 (West 1998) (unfair conduct in insurance business unlawful "whether done directly or indirectly"); § 21.2 ("meanings given to the provisions, terms, and words" of unfair insurance practice regulation "are not to be limited to the common law meaning . . . but . . . interpreted to accomplish the purpose of these sections").

PJC 102.15   **False, Misleading, or Deceptive Acts or Practices—Insurance (DTPA § 17.46(a); Tex. Ins. Code art. 21.21, § 16)**

Engaging in any false, misleading, or deceptive acts or practices.

"False, misleading, or deceptive act or practice" means an act or series of acts that have the tendency to deceive an average ordinary person, even though that person may have been ignorant, unthinking, or gullible.

[*or*]

COMMENT

When to use.   PJC 102.15 may be used with PJC 102.14 to submit an act or practice claimed to violate Tex. Bus. & Com. Code Ann. § 17.46 (Vernon Supp. 1998) (DTPA) but that is not specifically listed in section 17.46(b). *Compare Vail v. Texas Farm Bureau Mutual Insurance Co.*, 754 S.W.2d 129, 135 (Tex. 1988) (Insurance Code article 21.21, section 16, incorporates DTPA § 17.46, which "encompasses any type of business activity that deceives consumers" and is not limited to practices specifically listed in DTPA § 17.46(b)), *with Allstate Insurance Co. v. Watson*, 876 S.W.2d 145, 149 (Tex. 1994) (third-party claimant has no article 21.21 cause of action for unfair claim practices against tortfeasor's liability carrier because, *inter alia*, such practices are not "listed" in DTPA § 17.46; but *Vail* remains the law as to claims for alleged unfair claim settlement practices brought by insureds against their insurers). Section 16 of article 21.21 also incorporates the practices listed in DTPA § 17.46(b). *Aetna Casualty & Surety Co. v. Marshall*, 724 S.W.2d 770, 772 (Tex. 1987). Submission of these acts is covered in PJCs 102.2–.6.

In light of *Watson*, lower courts have split on the issue of whether there is a viable cause of action under DTPA § 17.46(a). *Compare Crum & Forster, Inc. v. Monsanto Co.*, 887 S.W.2d 103, 116–18 (Tex. App.—Texarkana 1994, no writ) (holding that there is a cause of action), *with Hart v. Berko, Inc.*, 881 S.W.2d 502, 508–09 (Tex. App.—El Paso 1994, writ denied) (holding that there is not).

This uncertainty has been resolved for cases governed by the 1995 amendments, because the statute now limits the cause of action under DTPA § 17.46 to only those practices "specifically enumerated in a subdivision of Section 17.46(b)." The amendments apply to all causes of action that accrue on or after September 1, 1995, and to all suits filed on or after September 1, 1996. Tex. Ins. Code Ann. art. 21.21, § 16(a) (Vernon Supp. 1998).

Use of "or."   If used with other instructions (see PJCs 102.16–.19), PJC 102.15 must be followed by the word *or*, because a finding of any one of the acts or practices defined in the instructions would support recovery under the DTPA.

Source of instruction.   The instruction is from *Spradling v. Williams*, 566 S.W.2d 561, 562 (Tex. 1978), which was cited with approval in *Vail*, 754 S.W.2d at 135.

PJC 102.16   Misrepresentations or False Advertising of Policy Contracts—Insurance (Tex. Ins. Code art. 21.21, § 4(1))

Making or causing to be made any statement misrepresenting the terms, benefits, or advantages of an insurance policy [*or*]

COMMENT

When to use.   PJC 102.16 may be used with PJC 102.14 to submit a claim of misrepresentation or false advertising of an insurance policy. *See* Tex. Ins. Code Ann. art. 21.21, § 4(1) (Vernon Supp. 1998); *Royal Globe Insurance Co. v. Bar Consultants, Inc.*, 577 S.W.2d 688 (Tex. 1979). A claim may also be brought under Tex. Bus. & Com. Code Ann. § 17.50(a)(4) (Vernon Supp. 1998) (DTPA).

Use of "or."   If used with other instructions (see PJCs 102.15 and .17–.19), PJC 102.16 must be followed by the word *or*, because a finding of any one of the acts or practices defined in the instructions would support recovery.

Adapt instruction for other claims.   Other kinds of conduct are outlawed by Tex. Ins. Code art. 21.21, § 4(1), and the instruction should be adapted to include the kind involved in the case. Also, section 4 contains other prohibitions, all of which are actionable under DTPA § 17.50(a)(4) and Tex. Ins. Code art. 21.21, § 16. For sample instructions submitting claims under sections 4(2), 4(10), and 4(11), see PJCs 102.17–.19. For conduct prohibited by other subparts of section 4, instructions may be drafted using the forms at PJCs 102.16–.19.

**PJC 102.17   False Information or Advertising—Insurance
(Tex. Ins. Code art. 21.21, § 4(2))**

Making, or directly or indirectly causing to be made, an assertion, representation, or statement with respect to insurance that was untrue, deceptive, or misleading [*or*]

COMMENT

When to use.   PJC 102.17 should be used with PJC 102.14 to submit a claim under Tex. Ins. Code Ann. art. 21.21, § 4(2) (Vernon Supp. 1998), which prohibits false information in advertising generally. *See Royal Globe Insurance Co. v. Bar Consultants, Inc.*, 577 S.W.2d 688 (Tex. 1979). A claim may also be brought under Tex. Bus. & Com. Code Ann. § 17.50(a)(4) (Vernon Supp. 1998) (DTPA).

Use of "or."   If used with other instructions (see PJCs 102.15–.16 and .18–.19), PJC 102.17 must be followed by the word *or*, because a finding of any one of the acts or practices defined in the instructions would support recovery.

Adapt instruction for other claims.   Other kinds of conduct are outlawed by Tex. Ins. Code art. 21.21, § 4(2), and the above instruction should be adapted to include the kind involved in the case. Also, section 4 contains other prohibitions, all of which are actionable under DTPA § 17.50(a)(4) and Tex. Ins. Code art. 21.21, § 16. *See, e.g.*, Tex. Ins. Code art. 21.21, § 4(4) ("Boycott, Coercion and Intimidation"). Instructions submitting claims under these other subsections may be drafted using the form above. For sample instructions submitting claims under sections 4(1), 4(10), or 4(11), see PJC 102.16, .18, or .19. For conduct prohibited by other subparts of section 4, instructions may be drafted using the forms at PJCs 102.16–.19.

PJC 102.18   Unfair Insurance Settlement Practices
(Tex. Ins. Code art. 21.21, § 4(10))

Misrepresenting to a claimant a material fact or policy provision relating to the coverage at issue [*or*]

Failing to attempt in good faith to effectuate a prompt, fair, and equitable settlement of a claim when the insurer's liability has become reasonably clear [*or*]

Failing to attempt in good faith to effectuate a prompt, fair, and equitable settlement under one part of a policy, when the insurer's liability has become reasonably clear, if the failure to settle was in order to influence *Paul Payne* to settle an additional claim under another part of the policy [*or*]

Failing to provide promptly to *Paul Payne* a reasonable explanation of the factual and legal basis in the policy for an insurer's denial of the claim [or the insurer's offer of a compromise settlement of the claim] [*or*]

Failing to affirm or deny coverage of a claim within a reasonable time [*or*]

Failing to submit a reservation of rights letter to *Paul Payne* within a reasonable time [*or*]

Refusing [failing or unreasonably delaying] a settlement offer under *Paul Payne*'s policy, because other coverage may have been available, [or because other parties may be responsible for the damages *Paul Payne* suffered] [*or*]

Trying to enforce a full and final release of a claim by *Paul Payne*, when only a partial payment had been made, unless the release was for a doubtful or disputed claim [*or*]

Refusing to pay a claim without conducting a reasonable investigation of the claim [*or*]

Delaying [or refusing] to settle *Paul Payne*'s claim solely because there was other insurance available to satisfy all or any part of the loss that formed the basis of *his* claim [*or*]

Requiring that *Paul Payne* produce *his* federal income tax returns for inspection or investigation, as a condition of settling *his* claim.

COMMENT

When to use.   PJC 102.18 may be used with PJC 102.14 to submit a cause of action for unfair settlement practices under Tex. Ins. Code Ann. art. 21.21, § 4(10) (Vernon Supp.

1998). This language was added by the 1995 amendments to article 21.21 and applies to claims accruing on or after September 1, 1995, and all suits filed on or after September 1, 1996. Use only the subpart(s) raised by the pleadings and the evidence.

Source of instruction.   PJC 102.18 is based on Tex. Ins. Code art. 21.21, § 4(10), which prohibits unfair settlement practices. Before the 1995 amendments to the DTPA and Insurance Code article 21.21, those statutes provided a private cause of action for conduct declared unfair in rules and regulations of the Texas Department of Insurance. *See Vail v. Texas Farm Bureau Mutual Insurance Co.*, 754 S.W.2d 129, 133–34 (Tex. 1988). The 1995 amendments to article 21.21 removed rules and regulations from the Administrative Code as a source of prohibitions, but the language of the regulations was codified in section 4(10) of article 21.21. PJC 102.18 can be used to submit claims under the rules and regulations, or the amended statute, as appropriate.

Use of "or."   If used with other instructions (see PJCs 102.15–.17 and .19), or if more than one subpart is used, each subpart used from PJC 102.18 must be followed by the word *or*, because a finding of any one of the acts or practices defined in the instructions would support recovery.

Use of statutory language.   The supreme court has held that jury submission in this type of case should follow the statutory language as closely as possible but may be altered somewhat to conform to the evidence of the case. *Spencer v. Eagle Star Insurance Co. of America*, 876 S.W.2d 154, 157 (Tex. 1994); *Brown v. American Transfer & Storage Co.*, 601 S.W.2d 931, 937 (Tex. 1980). Material terms, however, should not be omitted or substituted. *See Transportation Insurance Co. v. Faircloth*, 898 S.W.2d 269, 273 (Tex. 1995). Several of the subsections in Tex. Ins. Code art. 21.21, § 4(10), contain additional terms that may be added to the instruction or that may preclude submission of a particular practice.

**PJC 102.19   Misrepresentation—Insurance
(Tex. Ins. Code art. 21.21, § 4(11))**

Making any misrepresentation relating to an insurance policy by:

a.   making any untrue statement of a material fact; or

b.   failing to state a material fact that is necessary to make other statements not misleading, considering the circumstances under which the statements are made; or

c.   making any statement in such a manner as to mislead a reasonably prudent person to a false conclusion of a material fact; or

d.   stating that [*insert any misstatement of law*]; or

e.   failing to disclose [*insert matters required by law to be disclosed*].

[*or*]

COMMENT

When to use.   PJC 102.19 may be used with PJC 102.14 to submit a cause of action for any misrepresentation relating to an insurance policy. *See* Tex. Ins. Code Ann. art. 21.21, § 4(11) (Vernon Supp. 1998); Tex. Bus. & Com. Code Ann. § 17.50(a)(4) (Vernon Supp. 1998) (DTPA).

Source of instruction.   PJC 102.19 is based on Tex. Ins. Code art. 21.21, § 4(11), which prohibits unfair settlement practices. The language was added by the 1995 amendments to article 21.21 and applies to claims accruing on or after September 1, 1995, and all suits filed on or after September 1, 1996.

Before the 1995 amendments to the DTPA and Insurance Code article 21.21, former DTPA § 17.50(a)(4) provided a private cause of action for conduct deemed unfair in sections 21.3 to 21.4 of title 28 of the Texas Administrative Code. The 1995 amendments to article 21.21 removed the Texas Administrative Code rules and regulations as a source of prohibitions, but the language of those rules and regulations was codified in section 4(11) of article 21.21. PJC 102.19 can be used to submit claims under the rules and regulations, or the amended statute, as appropriate.

Use of "or."   If used with other instructions (see PJCs 102.15–.18), PJC 102.19 must be followed by the word *or*, because a finding of any one of the acts or practices defined in the instructions would support recovery.

Use of statutory language. The supreme court has held that jury submission in this type of case should follow the statutory language as closely as possible but may be altered somewhat to conform to the evidence of the case. *Spencer v. Eagle Star Insurance Co. of America*, 876 S.W.2d 154, 157 (Tex. 1994); *Brown v. American Transfer & Storage Co.*, 601 S.W.2d 931, 937 (Tex. 1980). Material terms, however, should not be omitted or substituted. *See Transportation Insurance Co. v. Faircloth*, 898 S.W.2d 269, 273 (Tex. 1995). Subparts *d* and *e* of PJC 102.19 submit questions relating to misstatements of law and failures to disclose information required by law. It is the Committee's opinion that these prohibitions require a preliminary determination by the trial court about whether the conduct was a misstatement of law or nondisclosure of information required by law to be disclosed, before the jury decides whether the conduct occurred. Therefore, the instruction should be adapted to conform to the specific conduct found by the trial court.

[PJC 102.20 is reserved for expansion.]

PJC 102.21   Question and Instruction on Knowing or Intentional Conduct

If your answer to Question _____ [*102.1, .7, .8, or .14*] is "Yes," then answer the following question. Otherwise, do not answer the following question.

QUESTION _____

Did *Don Davis* engage in any such conduct *knowingly* [*intentionally*]?

"Knowingly" means actual awareness, at the time of the conduct, of the falsity, deception, or unfairness of the conduct in question or actual awareness of the conduct constituting a failure to comply with a warranty. Actual awareness may be inferred where objective manifestations indicate that a person acted with actual awareness.

[or insert definition of "intentionally"]

In answering this question, consider only the conduct that you have found *was a producing cause of* damages to *Paul Payne*.

Answer: _____

COMMENT

When to use.   PJC 102.21 is to be used if there is evidence that the defendant knowingly or intentionally engaged in conduct that resulted in a violation of the DTPA or Insurance Code. *See* Tex. Bus. & Com. Code Ann. § 17.50(b)(1) (Vernon Supp. 1998) (DTPA); Tex. Ins. Code Ann. art. 21.21, § 16(b)(1) (Vernon Supp. 1998).

1995 amendments.   Under the pre-1995 DTPA, a finding that the defendant acted knowingly allows the fact finder to award discretionary additional damages up to three times the amount of actual damages. Act of June 13, 1979, 66th Leg., R.S., ch. 603, § 4, 1979 Tex. Gen. Laws 1327, 1329, *amended by* Act of May 19, 1995, 74th Leg., R.S., ch. 414, § 5, 1995 Tex. Gen. Laws 2988, 2992. Under the pre-1995 article 21.21, a finding of knowing conduct results in an automatic trebling of the plaintiff's actual damages. Act of May 10, 1973, 63rd Leg., R.S., ch. 143, 1973 Tex. Gen. Laws 322, 338, *amended by* Act of May 19, 1995, 74th Leg., R.S., ch. 414, § 13, 1995 Tex. Gen. Laws 2988, 3000. The 1995 amendments to article 21.21 make treble damages discretionary, similar to the pre-1995 DTPA. Tex. Ins. Code art. 21.21, § 16(b). The 1995 DTPA amendments distinguish between economic and mental anguish damages. A finding that the defendant acted knowingly allows discretionary trebling of the plaintiff's economic damages. Discretionary trebling of mental anguish damages is allowed only if the defendant acted intentionally. DTPA § 17.50(b).

Definition of "knowingly." The definition of "knowingly" comes from the pre-1995 DTPA § 17.45(9). Act of May 16, 1979, 66th Leg., R.S., ch. 603, § 2, 1979 Tex. Gen. Laws 1327, 1328. The same definition is also found in Tex. Ins. Code art. 21.21, § 2(c).

The 1995 amendments changed the definition of "knowingly" under the DTPA, but not under article 21.21. The amendments apply to all causes of action accruing on or after September 1, 1995, and to all suits filed on or after September 1, 1996. Therefore, in DTPA suits governed by the prior law, the definition should read:

> "Knowingly" means actual awareness of the falsity, deception, or unfairness of the conduct in question or actual awareness of the conduct constituting a failure to comply with a warranty. Actual awareness may be inferred where objective manifestations indicate that a person acted with actual awareness.

DTPA § 17.45(9). Because the definition was not changed in Tex. Ins. Code art. 21.21, § 2(c), insurance cases will continue to use the old definition.

Definition and use of "intentionally." The difference between "knowledge" and "intent" is that under "intent" the defendant specifically intended that the consumer act in detrimental reliance. *Compare* DTPA § 17.45(9) *with* § 17.45(13). A finding that the defendant acted knowingly only allows discretionary trebling of economic damages under the 1995 amendments, whereas a finding of intentional conduct allows discretionary trebling of both economic and mental anguish damages. DTPA § 17.50(b)(1). If both economic damages and mental anguish damages are sought, the consumer may choose to submit separate questions on the defendant's knowledge and intent, or a single question on intent.

If the defendant's intent is submitted, the following definition should be used in addition to, or instead of, the definition of "knowingly":

> "Intentionally" means actual awareness of the falsity, deception, or unfairness of the conduct in question or actual awareness of the conduct constituting a failure to comply with a warranty, coupled with the specific intent that the consumer act in detrimental reliance on the falsity or deception [or *detrimental ignorance of the unfairness*]. Specific intent may be inferred where objective manifestations indicate that a person acted intentionally [or *may be inferred from facts showing that the person acted with such flagrant disregard of prudent and fair business practices that the person should be treated as having acted intentionally*].

DTPA § 17.45(13). The bracketed language should be added or substituted to conform to the evidence in the case. *See Spencer v. Eagle Star Insurance Co. of America*, 876 S.W.2d 154, 157 (Tex. 1994); *Brown v. American Transfer & Storage Co.*, 601 S.W.2d 931, 937 (Tex. 1980).

Treble damages under Insurance Code article 21.21. Recovery of treble damages under article 21.21 varies, depending on which version of the statute applies. Treble damages are mandatory and automatic in causes of action arising in whole or in part before

April 4, 1985. *State Farm Fire & Casualty Co. v. Gros*, 818 S.W.2d 908, 917 (Tex. App.— Austin 1991, no writ); *Rainey-Mapes v. Queen Charters, Inc.*, 729 S.W.2d 907, 915 (Tex. App.—San Antonio 1987, writ granted, dism'd as moot). In these cases, a finding of liability alone was enough to support recovery of treble damages.

After the 1985 amendments, but before the 1995 amendments, treble damages were mandatory, but only if the jury found the defendant acted "knowingly." Act of March 13, 1985, 69th Leg., R.S., ch. 22, § 3, 1985 Tex. Gen. Laws 71, 72, *amended by* Act of May 19, 1995, 74th Leg., R.S., ch. 414, § 13, 1995 Tex. Gen. Laws 2988, 3000.

The 1995 amendments to article 21.21 make additional damages discretionary with the trier of fact, if the defendant acted knowingly. The amendments apply to all causes of action that accrue on or after September 1, 1995, and to all suits filed on or after September 1, 1996. Tex. Ins. Code art. 21.21, § 16(b). In suits subject to the 1995 amendments, the plaintiff should submit the question of knowing conduct as in PJC 102.21 and then should ask the jury to determine the amount of additional damages as in PJC 110.11.

Under each of these versions, recovery of treble damages is the same whether the claim is brought directly under article 21.21 or is brought through DTPA § 17.50(a)(4). The supreme court has held that this DTPA section "incorporates article 21.21 . . . in its entirety," including the treble damages provision in article 21.21, section 16. *Vail v. Texas Farm Bureau Mutual Insurance Co.*, 754 S.W.2d 129, 137 (Tex. 1988).

Additional damages for knowing or intentional conduct.   See PJC 110.11 for a question on additional damages that may be used if PJC 102.21 is answered "Yes."

Actual awareness of failure to comply with a warranty.   If the case does not involve a breach of warranty, the phrase *or actual awareness of the conduct constituting a failure to comply with a warranty* should be deleted from the above definition of "knowingly." If the case does involve a breach of warranty and is brought under the 1995 amendments, the words *condition, defect,* or *failure* may be substituted for the word *conduct* in the definition. DTPA § 17.45(9).

Producing cause.   For cases brought under Tex. Ins. Code art. 21.21, the phrase *resulted in* should be substituted for the phrase *was a producing cause of* in the limiting instruction above. Tex. Ins. Code art. 21.21, § 16.

PJC 102.22   Defenses to Deceptive Trade Practices Act and Insurance Code Article 21.21 Claims (Comment)

Common-law defenses.   A primary purpose of the enactment of the DTPA was to provide consumers a cause of action for deceptive trade practices without the burden of proof and numerous defenses encountered in a common-law fraud or breach-of-warranty suit. *Smith v. Baldwin*, 611 S.W.2d 611, 614 (Tex. 1980) (common-law defense of "substantial performance" no defense to DTPA action); *see also Alvarado v. Bolton*, 749 S.W.2d 47, 48 (Tex. 1988) (doctrine of merger not applicable in warranty suit brought under DTPA); *Ojeda de Toca v. Wise*, 748 S.W.2d 449 (Tex. 1988) (imputed notice under real property recording statute not a defense to DTPA action for damages); *Weitzel v. Barnes*, 691 S.W.2d 598, 600 (Tex. 1985) (parol evidence rule will not bar proof of violation of DTPA section 17.46(b)). Thus it is generally true that common-law defenses are unavailable in a DTPA suit.

The above reasoning has been extended to Insurance Code suits. *See Frank B. Hall & Co. v. Beach, Inc.*, 733 S.W.2d 251, 264 (Tex. App.—Corpus Christi 1987, writ ref'd n.r.e.) (contributory negligence could not defeat recovery on Insurance Code claims).

For cases discussing the applicability of "as is" language to the DTPA, see *Prudential Insurance Co. of America v. Jefferson Associates*, 896 S.W.2d 156 (Tex. 1995), and *Smith v. Levine*, 911 S.W.2d 427 (Tex. App.—San Antonio 1995, writ denied).

Statutory defenses.

A. *Third-party information.*   A defendant's reliance on third-party information in making the false representation may be a defense to a claim brought under DTPA section 17.50. Tex. Bus. & Com. Code Ann. § 17.506(a)–(c) (Vernon 1987) (DTPA).

B. *Complete tender.*   The defense of complete tender may apply if the defendant proves that he tendered to the plaintiff, within thirty days after receiving written notice of the complaint, the amount of actual damages claimed and the expenses, including attorney's fees, if any, reasonably incurred by the plaintiff in asserting his claim. DTPA § 17.506(d) (Supp. 1998).

C. *Waiver.*   The availability and requirements of the affirmative defense of waiver depend on when the suit was filed, when the cause of action accrued, or both.

Actions commenced before September 1, 1989.   Waiver is not applicable. *See Metro Ford Truck Sales, Inc. v. Davis*, 709 S.W.2d 785, 789 (Tex. App.—Ft. Worth 1986, writ ref'd n.r.e.).

Actions commenced between September 1, 1989, and September 1, 1996, unless the cause of action accrued on or after September 1, 1995.   The defendant must prove that the consumer (1) was not in a "significantly disparate" bargaining position, (2) was represented by legal counsel, (3) did not lease or purchase a family residence, (4) paid more than $500,000, and (5) expressly waived the DTPA in a written contract signed by both consumer and legal counsel. Act of May 29, 1989, 71st Leg., R.S., ch. 380, § 1, 1989 Tex. Gen. Laws 1490, *amended by* Act of May 19, 1995, 74th Leg., R.S., ch. 414, § 1, 1995 Tex. Gen. Laws 2988.

Causes of action accruing on or after September 1, 1995, and all actions commenced on or after September 1, 1996.   The following elements must be proved: (1) the waiver was in writing, signed by the consumer, and in the form prescribed by DTPA § 17.42(c); (2) the consumer was not in a significantly disparate bargaining position; and (3) in seeking or acquiring the goods or services, the consumer was represented by legal counsel who was not directly or indirectly identified, suggested, or selected by the defendant or an agent of the defendant. DTPA § 17.42(a).

D. *Comparative or proportionate responsibility.*

Pre-1989 DTPA and pre-1995 Insurance Code claims.   DTPA claims filed before September 1, 1989, and Insurance Code claims filed before September 1, 1996 (unless the cause of action accrued on or after September 1, 1995), are not subject to comparative or proportionate responsibility.

1989–1995 DTPA claims.   In claims commenced between September 1, 1989, and September 1, 1996 (unless the cause of action arose on or after September 1, 1995), the defense of comparative responsibility applies to DTPA actions for death, personal injury (other than mental anguish associated with a DTPA claim), and damage to property other than goods acquired in the consumer transaction if the damage arises out of an occurrence involving death or bodily injury. Act of May 29, 1989, 71st Leg., R.S., ch. 380, § 2, 1989 Tex. Gen. Laws 1490, 1491, *amended by* Act of May 19, 1995, 74th Leg., R.S., ch. 414, § 5, 1995 Tex. Gen. Laws 2988, 2992.

DTPA and Insurance Code claims covered by the 1995 amendments.   All DTPA and Insurance Code claims arising on or after September 1, 1995, and all suits filed on or after September 1, 1996, may be subject to the proportionate responsibility provisions of chapter 33 of the Texas Civil Practice & Remedies Code. *See* Tex. Civ. Prac. & Rem. Code Ann. § 33.002 (Vernon Supp. 1998). Insurance Code claims are not mentioned. For a discussion and a sample submission of a proportionate responsibility claim, see PJC 110.32.

E. *Notice and tender of settlement under DTPA.*   Though technically not a "defense," the presuit notice provisions of the DTPA can defeat or delay a DTPA suit if the plaintiff fails to comply with them. *See* DTPA § 17.505. The notice must state the "specific complaint" and the amount of actual damages and expenses incurred. The defendant then has a statutorily prescribed time to tender a written settlement offer, which, if rejected by the consumer, may be filed with the court. At trial, if the court finds the offer is "substantially the same" as the actual damages found, the consumer may not recover any amount greater than that of the offer or the amount of actual damages. DTPA § 17.5052 (recodified in 1995 from former section 17.505(d)). Note that, pursuant to statute, issues pertaining to notice and tender are to be decided by the court, not by the jury, so no submission is necessary. DTPA § 17.5052(g); *see also Hines v. Hash*, 843 S.W.2d 464, 467 (Tex. 1992). Provisions applicable to specific actions, depending on when the suit was filed, when the cause of action accrued, or both, are as follows:

Actions commenced before September 1, 1989.   The notice period is thirty days. Act of May 10, 1977, 65th Leg., R.S., ch. 216, § 5, 1977 Tex. Gen. Laws 600, 604, *amended by* Act of May 29, 1989, 71st Leg., R.S., ch. 380, § 2, 1989 Tex. Gen. Laws 1490, 1491.

Actions commenced between September 1, 1989, and September 1, 1996, unless the cause of action accrued on or after September 1, 1995. The notice must be given "in reasonable detail," and the notice period is extended from thirty to sixty days, during which period the defendant may request an inspection. If the consumer unreasonably refuses the request, the court shall not award mandatory trebling of the first $1,000 of damages as allowed by DTPA § 17.50(b)(1). Also, any tender of settlement by the defendant is not admissible in evidence. DTPA § 17.5052(k) (recodified in 1995 from former section 17.505(e)). Finally, the consumer recovers the lesser of the amount tendered or the actual damages found by the jury, if the amount tendered is the same as, more than, or substantially the same as the damages found by the jury. DTPA § 17.5052(g) (recodified in 1995 from former section 17.505(d)).

Causes of action accruing on or after September 1, 1995, and all suits filed on or after September 1, 1996. In addition to the notice and tender rules set out immediately above, the defendant also has an opportunity to tender a settlement offer within certain specified times after suit is filed. *See* DTPA § 17.5052(b)–(g). Procedures for comparing the settlement offer to the amount awarded for damages and fees are also clarified.

For the requirements of the notice, the timeliness and the method of objection to lack of notice, and the court action required when no notice has been given, see *Hines*, 843 S.W.2d at 467.

F. *Notice and tender under Insurance Code.* Actions brought under Insurance Code article 21.21 also require notice. The notice must state the "specific complaint" and the amount of actual damages and expenses incurred. Tex. Ins. Code Ann. art. 21.21, § 16(e) (Vernon Supp. 1998). As with the DTPA, the defendant has a statutorily prescribed time in which to tender a written offer of settlement. For causes of action accruing on or after September 1, 1995, and all suits filed on or after September 1, 1996, the defendant has sixty days in which to make the settlement offer; for all other cases, the time limit is thirty days. Act of March 13, 1985, 69th Leg., R.S., ch. 22, § 3, 1985 Tex. Gen. Laws 71, 72, *amended by* Act of May 19, 1995, 74th Leg., R.S., ch. 414, § 13, 1995 Tex. Gen. Laws 2988, 3000. As with DTPA actions, the defendant may file a rejected offer of settlement with the court, and if the court finds the offer is "substantially the same" as the actual damages found, the consumer may not recover any amount greater than that of the offer or the amount of actual damages. Tex. Ins. Code art. 21.21, § 16A.

G. *Warranty defenses under UCC.* The supreme court has stated that section 17.42 of the DTPA makes invalid a limitation or waiver of liability for violations of section 17.46 but does not do so to warranty disclaimers authorized by the UCC or common law. *Southwestern Bell Telephone Co. v. FDP Corp.*, 811 S.W.2d 572, 576–77 (Tex. 1991). If the consumer pleads a DTPA cause of action alleging violation of warranties arising under UCC article 2, several statutory defenses based on article 2 have been held to apply, including—

- buyer's waiver of implied warranties. *FDP Corp.*, 811 S.W.2d at 576–77; *Mercedes-Benz of North America, Inc. v. Dickenson*, 720 S.W.2d 844, 852 (Tex. App.—Fort Worth 1986, no writ).

- buyer's failure to give notice to seller of breach of warranty as required by Tex. Bus. & Com. Code § 2.607(c)(1) (Tex. UCC) (1994). *Import Motors, Inc. v. Matthews*, 557 S.W.2d 807, 809 (Tex. Civ. App.—Austin 1977, writ ref'd n.r.e.).

- contractual limitation of damages in an express warranty. *Rinehart v. Sonitrol of Dallas, Inc.*, 620 S.W.2d 660, 663–64 (Tex. Civ. App.—Dallas 1981, writ ref'd n.r.e.).

H. *Professional services exemption.* The 1995 amendments to the DTPA exempt certain claims for damages based on professional services, the essence of which is the providing of advice, judgment, opinion, or similar professional skill. This exemption does not apply to—

1. an express misrepresentation of a material fact that cannot be characterized as advice, judgment, or opinion;

2. a failure to disclose information in violation of DTPA § 17.46(b)(23);

3. an unconscionable action or course of action that cannot be characterized as advice, judgment, or opinion; or

4. breach of an express warranty that cannot be characterized as advice, judgment, or opinion.

DTPA § 17.49(c). The term "professional services" is not defined in the statute. This exemption applies to causes of action accruing on or after September 1, 1995, and all suits filed on or after September 1, 1996.

I. *Negotiated contract exemption.* The 1995 DTPA amendments also exempt claims for damages based on a written contract with a total consideration of $100,000, if in negotiating the contract the consumer is represented by legal counsel not directly identified, suggested, or selected by the defendant or defendant's agent, and the cause of action does not involve a consumer's residence. DTPA § 17.49(f). This exemption applies to causes of action accruing on or after September 1, 1995, and all suits filed on or after September 1, 1996.

J. *Transaction limit.* The 1995 DTPA amendments also exempt causes of action arising from a transaction, project, or a set of transactions relating to the same project, involving a total consideration by the consumer of more than $500,000, other than a cause of action involving the consumer's residence. DTPA § 17.49(g). This exemption applies to causes of action accruing on or after September 1, 1995, and all suits filed on or after September 1, 1996.

K. *Personal injury exemption.* Except as specifically provided in DTPA § 17.50(b), (h), damages for bodily injury or death or for the infliction of mental anguish are exempted from DTPA coverage. This exemption applies to causes of action accruing on or after September 1, 1995, and all suits filed on or after September 1, 1996. DTPA § 17.49(e). See Comment to PJC 110.10 for discussion of personal injury damages in DTPA cases.

**PJC 102.23   Statute of Limitations
(DTPA § 17.565; Tex. Ins. Code art. 21.21, § 16(d))**

If your answer to Question _____ [*102.1, .7, .8, or .14*] is "Yes," then answer the following question. Otherwise, do not answer the following question.

QUESTION _____

By what date should *Paul Payne*, in the exercise of reasonable diligence, have discovered all the *false, misleading, or deceptive acts or practices* of *Don Davis*?

Answer with a date in the blank below.

Answer: _____

COMMENT

When to use.   PJC 102.23 is used to determine if the suit is barred by the statute of limitations. Tex. Bus. & Com. Code Ann. § 17.565 (Vernon 1987) (DTPA) incorporates the "discovery rule." *See Eshleman v. Shield*, 764 S.W.2d 776 (Tex. 1989); *see also* Tex. Ins. Code Ann. art. 21.21, § 16(d) (Vernon Supp. 1998). Even if the act occurred more than two years before suit was filed, the limitations defense will not apply if the plaintiff did not discover or could not reasonably have discovered the act until a date within two years before the suit was filed. To prevail, a plaintiff need only prove one act or practice that is not time-barred. Therefore, the question asks when the plaintiff discovered or should have discovered the latest act that was a producing cause of damages. If the date is within the two-year period, the limitations defense does not apply.

Insurance Code cases.   In cases brought under the Insurance Code, the phrase *unfair or deceptive acts or practices* should be used instead of the phrase *false, misleading, or deceptive acts or practices* in the above question.

Breach-of-warranty cases.   In cases involving a breach of warranty, the phrase *failures to comply with a warranty* should be used in lieu of the phrase *false, misleading, or deceptive acts or practices* in the above question.

Source of question.   The question is derived from *Willis v. Maverick*, 760 S.W.2d 642, 647 (Tex. 1988).

Distinct damages claims.   If the plaintiff has two claims involving distinctly different damages caused by distinctly different conduct and the limitations defense is raised, the Committee recommends that separate liability, damages, and limitations questions be submitted.

Extra 180 days. Both DTPA § 17.565 and Tex. Ins. Code art. 21.21, § 16(d), provide for an extra 180 days to be tacked onto the two-year period if the plaintiff can show he was induced by the defendant to refrain from filing suit. If that exception is raised, the jury would need to be asked:

> Was *Paul Payne*'s failure to file suit by [*insert date two years after date of occurrence or of plaintiff's actual or deemed discovery*] caused by *Don Davis*'s knowingly engaging in conduct solely calculated to induce *Paul Payne* to refrain from or postpone filing suit?

PJC 102.24   Counterclaim—Bad Faith or Harassment (DTPA § 17.50(c); Tex. Ins. Code art. 21.21, § 16) (Comment)

Statutory remedies.   Tex. Bus. & Com. Code Ann. § 17.50(c) (Vernon Supp. 1998) (DTPA) provides that the defendant may recover attorney's fees and court costs from a plaintiff who files a groundless, bad-faith, or harassing lawsuit. The requirements for such a counterclaim depend on when the cause of action accrued, when the suit was filed, or both.

DTPA causes of action accruing before September 1, 1995 (unless the suit is filed on or after September 1, 1996), and all suits brought under Insurance Code article 21.21.   If the court finds that an action under this section was groundless and brought in bad faith, or brought for the purpose of harassment, the court shall award to the defendant reasonable and necessary attorney's fees and court costs. Act of May 10, 1973, 63rd Leg., R.S., ch. 143, § 1, 1973 Tex. Gen. Laws 322, *amended by* Act of May 16, 1979, 66th Leg., R.S., ch. 603, § 4, 1979 Tex. Gen. Laws 1327, 1329. Tex. Ins. Code Ann. art. 21.21, § 16(c) (Vernon Supp. 1998).

DTPA causes of action accruing on or after September 1, 1995 (and all DTPA suits filed on or after September 1, 1996).   If the court finds any of the following: (1) the suit is groundless in fact or law; (2) the suit was brought in bad faith; or (3) the suit was brought for purposes of harassment, the court shall award reasonable and necessary attorney's fees and court costs. DTPA § 17.50(c).

A number of courts of appeals interpreted DTPA § 17.50(c) to mean that the jury determines bad faith and harassment whereas the court determines groundlessness (*see, e.g., Fichtner v. Richardson*, 708 S.W.2d 479 (Tex. App.—Dallas 1986, writ ref'd n.r.e.); *Parks v. McDougall*, 659 S.W.2d 875 (Tex. App.—San Antonio 1983, no writ); *LaChance v. McKown*, 649 S.W.2d 658 (Tex. App.—Texarkana 1983, writ ref'd n.r.e.)). The supreme court held, however, that the court, not the jury, must decide the issues of groundlessness, bad faith, and harassment. *Donwerth v. Preston II Chrysler-Dodge, Inc.*, 775 S.W.2d 634, 637 (Tex. 1989).

PJC 103.1   **Tort Duty of Good Faith and Fair Dealing—**
Question and Instruction on Insurance Claim Denial
or Delay in Payment

QUESTION _____

Did *Don Davis Insurance Company* fail to comply with its duty of good faith and fair dealing to *Paul Payne*?

An insurer fails to comply with its duty of good faith and fair dealing by—

Failing to attempt in good faith to effectuate a prompt, fair, and equitable settlement of a claim when the insurer's liability has become reasonably clear [*or*]

Refusing to pay a claim without conducting a reasonable investigation of the claim [*or*]

Canceling an insurance policy without a reasonable basis.

Answer: _____

COMMENT

When to use.   PJC 103.1 may be used to submit a breach of the common-law duty of good faith and fair dealing by an insurer.

Source of duty.   The supreme court has held, as a matter of law, that a special relationship exists between an insurer and the insured arising out of the parties' unequal bargaining power and the exclusive control that the insurer exercises over the processing of claims and the canceling of insurance contracts. *Union Bankers Insurance Co. v. Shelton*, 889 S.W.2d 278, 283 (Tex. 1994); *Aranda v. Insurance Co. of North America*, 748 S.W.2d 210, 212 (Tex. 1988); *Arnold v. National County Mutual Fire Insurance Co.*, 725 S.W.2d 165, 167 (Tex. 1987).

The supreme court has refused to apply the duty to a liability insurer investigating and defending claims by a third party against its insured. *Maryland Insurance Co. v. Head Industrial Coatings & Services, Inc.*, 938 S.W.2d 27, 28–29 (Tex. 1996).

Source of instruction.   In *Arnold* and *Aranda*, the supreme court held that an insurer breaches its duty by denying a claim without a reasonable basis, or by failing to conduct a reasonable investigation. In *Shelton*, the supreme court extended the duty to include an insurer's unreasonable cancellation of an insurance policy. PJC 103.1 submits each of these elements of the duty. In *Universe Life Insurance Co. v. Giles*, 950 S.W.2d 48 (Tex. 1997), the supreme court revised the common-law duty to track the statutory prohibition on unfair refusal to settle. *Giles*, 950 S.W.2d 48; Tex. Ins. Code Ann. art. 21.21, § 4(10)(a)(ii) (Vernon Supp. 1998). The first definition is taken from this statutory language and parallels PJC 102.18. By extension, the duty of good faith and fair dealing with respect to failing to conduct a reasonable investigation has been recast in the statutory language of Tex. Ins. Code art. 21.21, § 4(10)(a)(viii). This language also parallels the statutory submission in PJC 102.18. The third definition is based on *Shelton*, and has no statutory counterpart.

Causation. A finding of a breach of the common-law duty of good faith and fair dealing entitles a plaintiff to recovery of all damages proximately caused by the wrongful conduct. *Aranda*, 748 S.W.2d at 215; *Chitsey v. National Lloyds Insurance Co.*, 738 S.W.2d 641, 643 (Tex. 1987). Causation is incorporated into the damages instruction. See PJC 110.14.

Exemplary damages. Exemplary damages are allowed for breach of the duty of good faith and fair dealing and are governed by the same principles applicable to other tort actions. *Transportation Insurance Co. v. Moriel*, 879 S.W.2d 10, 23 & n.16 (Tex. 1994); *Arnold*, 725 S.W.2d at 167. Fraud, as well as malice, is a ground for recovery of exemplary damages. Tex. Civ. Prac. & Rem. Code Ann. § 41.003(a)(1) (Vernon 1997). For questions submitting exemplary damages, see PJCs 110.33 and .34, and the Comments accompanying those questions.

Noninusurance cases. The courts have been reluctant to impose a special relationship on parties to an arm's-length business transaction outside the insurance area. *See, e.g., Seymour v. American Engine & Grinding Co.*, 956 S.W.2d 49, 60 (Tex. App.—Houston [14th Dist.] 1996, writ denied) (at-will employment relationship); *Texstar North America v. Ladd Petroleum Corp.*, 809 S.W.2d 672, 678 (Tex. App.—Corpus Christi 1991, writ denied) (working-interest owners/parties to joint operating agreement); *FDIC v. Coleman*, 795 S.W.2d 706, 708–09 (Tex. 1990) (mortgagor/mortgagee); *Nautical Landings Marina, Inc. v. First National Bank*, 791 S.W.2d 293, 299 (Tex. App.—Corpus Christi 1990, writ denied) (lender/borrower); *Adolph Coors Co. v. Rodriguez*, 780 S.W.2d 477, 481 (Tex. App.—Corpus Christi 1989, writ denied) (supplier/distributor); *City of San Antonio v. Forgy*, 769 S.W.2d 293, 296–98 (Tex. App.—San Antonio 1989, writ denied) (city/contractor); *Lovell v. Western National Life Insurance Co.*, 754 S.W.2d 298, 303 (Tex. App.—Amarillo 1988, writ denied) (mortgagor/mortgagee). *But see Sanus/New York Life Health Plan v. Dube- Seybold-Sutherland Management, Inc.*, 837 S.W.2d 191, 199 (Tex. App.—Houston [1st Dist.] 1992, writ denied) (special relationship existed between health maintenance organization and health-care provider).

PJC 103.2   Duty of Good Faith under the Uniform Commercial Code (Comment)

The basic question in PJC 101.2 should be used with one of the appropriate instructions set out in the Comment titled "UCC good-faith obligation."

PJC 103.3   Duty of Good Faith by Express Contract (Comment)

Parties may create a duty of good faith and fair dealing by the express terms of a contract not governed by the Uniform Commercial Code. The basic question in PJC 101.2 should be used to submit all contractual provisions including the express duty of good faith and fair dealing.

CHAPTER 104   FIDUCIARY DUTY

PJC 104.1   Question and Instruction—Existence of Relationship of Trust and Confidence

QUESTION _____

Did a relationship of trust and confidence exist between *Don Davis* and *Paul Payne*?

> A relationship of trust and confidence existed if *Paul Payne* justifiably placed trust and confidence in *Don Davis* to act in *Paul Payne*'s best interest. *Paul Payne*'s subjective trust and feelings alone do not justify transforming arm's-length dealings into a relationship of trust and confidence.

Answer: _____

COMMENT

When to use.   This question and instruction submit the existence of an informal fiduciary relationship, commonly referred to as a "relationship of trust and confidence" or a "confidential relationship." This relationship may arise from moral, social, domestic, or purely personal relationships. *Thigpen v. Locke*, 363 S.W.2d 247, 253 (Tex. 1962); *MacDonald v. Follett*, 180 S.W.2d 334, 337 (Tex. 1944). In this regard, informal fiduciary relationships are distinguished from technical or formal fiduciary relationships such as attorney-client, principal-agent, partner-partner, trustee-cestui que trust, or guardian-ward, which as a matter of law are relationships of trust and confidence. *Thigpen*, 363 S.W.2d at 253. The existence of an informal relationship of trust and confidence is usually a question of fact. *Crim Truck & Tractor Co. v. Navistar International Transportation Corp.*, 823 S.W.2d 591, 594 (Tex. 1992). If the existence of a formal relationship is disputed, a question should be submitted inquiring whether the formal relationship exists and defining its boundaries. *Schiller v. Elick*, 240 S.W.2d 997, 999 (Tex. 1951).

When the issue is a question of law.   Although the existence of an informal relationship of trust and confidence is ordinarily a question of fact, if the issue is one of no evidence, it becomes a question of law. *Crim*, 823 S.W.2d at 594. The supreme court has held that the following situations, for example, do not rise to the level of a relationship of trust and confidence:

- One businessman trusts another and relies on his promise to perform a contract. *Consolidated Gas & Equipment Co. v. Thompson*, 405 S.W.2d 333, 336 (Tex. 1966); *Thigpen*, 363 S.W.2d at 253.

- The relationship has been a cordial one and of long duration. *Thigpen*, 363 S.W.2d at 253.

- People have had prior dealings with each other and one party subjectively trusts the other. *Schlumberger Technology Corp. v. Swanson*, 959 S.W.2d 171, 177 (Tex. 1997); *Consolidated Gas*, 405 S.W.2d at 336; *Thigpen*, 363 S.W.2d at 253.

- The plaintiff has always done everything requested by the defendant. *Crim*, 823 S.W.2d at 596 n.6.

If commencement or termination of relationship is at issue.   If there is a dispute about whether the relationship had begun or had terminated at the time of the alleged breach, the Committee suggests adding to the question the phrases, *on [date]* or *at the time of the [occurrence or transaction]. See Swanson*, 959 S.W.2d at 177; *Consolidated Gas*, 405 S.W.2d at 336 (in a business transaction, the fiduciary relationship must have existed before, and apart from, the agreement made the basis of the suit); *Schiller*, 240 S.W.2d at 1000 (the relationship must not have been terminated before the time of the occurrence or transaction giving rise to the cause of action).

Source of question and instruction.   PJC 104.1 is derived from *Thigpen*, 363 S.W.2d at 253 (confidential relationship exists if beneficiary is justified in placing trust and confidence in fiduciary to act in beneficiary's best interest); *Crim*, 823 S.W.2d at 594; and *Fitz-Gerald v. Hull*, 237 S.W.2d 256, 261 (Tex. 1951) (informal relationship may arise where one person trusts and relies on another).

PJC 104.2   Question and Instruction—Breach of Fiduciary Duty

QUESTION _____

Did *Don Davis* comply with *his* fiduciary duty to *Paul Payne*?

[*Because a relationship of trust and confidence existed between them,*] [*As Paul Payne's attorney,*] [*Because they were partners,*] [*As Paul Payne's agent,*] *Don Davis* owed *Paul Payne* a fiduciary duty. To prove *he* complied with *his* duty, *Don Davis* must show:

a. The transaction[s] in question [was/were] fair and equitable to *Paul Payne*;

b. *Don Davis* made reasonable use of the confidence that *Paul Payne* placed in *him*;

c. *Don Davis* acted in the utmost good faith and exercised the most scrupulous honesty toward *Paul Payne;*

d. *Don Davis* placed the interests of *Paul Payne* before *his* own, did not use the advantage of *his* position to gain any benefit for *himself* at the expense of *Paul Payne*, and did not place *himself* in any position where *his* self-interest might conflict with *his* obligations as a fiduciary; and

e. *Don Davis* fully and fairly disclosed all important information to *Paul Payne* concerning the transaction[s].

Answer: _____

COMMENT

When to use.   PJC 104.2 submits the question of breach of a fiduciary duty, whether the duty is based on a formal or an informal relationship, where it is alleged that the fiduciary has profited or benefited from a transaction with the beneficiary.

If the existence of a formal fiduciary relationship is disputed, a preliminary question should be submitted. *Schiller v. Elick*, 240 S.W.2d 997, 999 (Tex. 1951) (dispute whether defendant was plaintiff's agent). PJC 104.1 submits the existence of an informal fiduciary relationship. PJC 104.2 should be conditioned on an affirmative answer to either PJC 104.1 or the preliminary question asking whether the formal fiduciary relationship exists.

Source of question and instruction.   The question and instruction are derived from *Stephens County Museum, Inc. v. Swenson*, 517 S.W.2d 257, 261 (Tex. 1974) (material issues are whether fiduciary made reasonable use of the trust and confidence placed in him and whether the transactions were ultimately fair and equitable to the beneficiary); *Fitz-Gerald v. Hull*, 237 S.W.2d 256, 264–65 (Tex. 1951) (persons engaged in joint adventure owe to each other the utmost good faith and the most scrupulous honesty); *Crim Truck & Tractor Co. v. Navistar International Transportation Corp.*, 823 S.W.2d 591, 594 (Tex. 1992) (fiduciary duty requires a party to place the interest of the other party before his own); *Slay v. Burnett Trust*, 187 S.W.2d 377, 378–79 (Tex. 1945) (duty of loyalty prohibits trustee from using the advantage of his position to gain any benefit for himself at the expense of his cestui que trust and from placing himself in any position where his self-interest will or may conflict with his obligations as trustee); *Kinzbach Tool Co. v. Corbett-Wallace Corp.*, 160 S.W.2d 509, 512-14 (Tex. 1942) (it is the duty of a fiduciary to deal openly and to make full disclosure to the party with whom he stands in such relationship); *Johnson v. Peckham*, 120 S.W.2d 786, 787 (Tex. 1938) (partners required to make full disclosure of all material facts within their knowledge relating to partnership affairs. It is necessary to make disclosure of all important information.).

Presumption of unfairness.   When a fiduciary profits or benefits in any way from a transaction with the beneficiary, a presumption of unfairness arises that shifts the burden of persuasion to the fiduciary or the party claiming the validity or benefits of the transaction to show that the transaction was fair and equitable to the plaintiff. *Texas Bank & Trust Co. v. Moore*, 595 S.W.2d 502, 509 (Tex. 1980); *Archer v. Griffith*, 390 S.W.2d 735, 739 (Tex. 1964); *Stephens County Museum*, 517 S.W.2d at 260; *International Bankers Life Insurance Co. v. Holloway*, 368 S.W.2d 567, 576-77 (Tex. 1963); *Slay*, 187 S.W.2d at 388.

The presumption may be rebutted by the fiduciary. *Stephens County Museum*, 517 S.W.2d at 261; *see also Texas Bank & Trust*, 595 S.W.2d at 509. Normally, a rebuttable presumption shifts the burden of producing evidence to the party against whom it operates but does not shift the burden of persuasion to that party. *General Motors Corp. v. Saenz*, 873 S.W.2d 353, 359 (Tex. 1993). In fiduciary duty cases, however, the presumption of unfairness operates to shift both the burden of producing evidence and the burden of persuasion to the fiduciary. *Sorrell v. Elsey*, 748 S.W.2d 584, 586 (Tex. App.—San Antonio 1988, writ denied); *Miller v. Miller*, 700 S.W.2d 941, 945-46 (Tex. App.—Dallas 1985, writ ref'd n.r.e.); *Gum v. Schaefer*, 683 S.W.2d 803, 806 (Tex. App.—Corpus Christi 1984, no writ) (per curiam); *Fillion v. Troy*, 656 S.W.2d 912, 914 (Tex. App.—Houston [1st Dist.] 1983, writ ref'd n.r.e.); *Cole v. Plummer*, 559 S.W.2d 87, 89 (Tex. Civ. App.—Eastland 1977, writ ref'd n.r.e.); *see also Johnson*, 120 S.W.2d at 787; *Moore v. Texas Bank & Trust Co.*, 576 S.W.2d 691, 695 (Tex. Civ. App.—Eastland 1979), *rev'd on other grounds*, 595 S.W.2d 502 (Tex. 1980).

If there is no evidence rebutting the presumption, no breach of fiduciary question is necessary. *Texas Bank & Trust Co.*, 595 S.W.2d at 509.

Question where burden does not shift.   In those cases where the presumption of unfairness does not arise and the burden of persuasion does not shift to the fiduciary, the question in PJC 104.2 should be modified to read:

Did *Don Davis* fail to comply with *his* fiduciary duty to *Paul Payne*?

The instruction should also be modified to place the burden of persuasion on *Paul Payne*.

Modification of instruction.   If the fiduciary duty arises from a formal relationship, the instruction in PJC 104.2 may need to be modified to include additional duties imposed by statute or common law on that particular relationship, such as those specifically applicable to partners, trustees, executors, or attorneys.

Caveat.   If the burden of persuasion is on the fiduciary, it is unclear which party bears the burden of requesting the compliance question. *Compare Moore*, 576 S.W.2d at 695 (burden to properly request the issue rests on the plaintiff-beneficiary because "it is an element of the plaintiff's theory of recovery") *with Cole*, 559 S.W.2d at 89 (fiduciary has burden of "securing a finding the confidential relationship was not breached").

Remedies.   See PJC 110.15 regarding equitable remedies and damages for breach of fiduciary duty; PJC 110.16 for a question on the amount of profit disgorgement; PJC 110.17 for a question on the amount of fee forfeiture; and PJC 110.18 for a question on actual damages for breach of fiduciary duty.

PJC 105.1   Question on Common-Law Fraud—Intentional Misrepresentation

QUESTION _____

Did *Don Davis* commit fraud against *Paul Payne*?

[*Insert appropriate instructions.*]

Answer: _____

COMMENT

When to use.   PJC 105.1 is a broad-form question. *See* Tex. R. Civ. P. 277. It should be appropriate in most cases involving claims for fraud and can be used to submit both affirmative claims for damages and affirmative defenses. In some circumstances, it may be necessary to alter the form of the question or include a limiting instruction that, for example, restricts the jury's consideration to a certain transaction or certain parties.

Accompanying instructions and definitions.   PJC 105.1 should be accompanied with appropriate instructions and definitions. See PJCs 105.2–.4 and .8–.9.

Damages.   Damages questions are set out in chapter 110. PJC 110.19 submits direct damages in fraud cases, and PJC 110.20 submits consequential damages in such cases. A party who suffers actual damages as a result of fraud may seek punitive damages. *Spoljaric v. Percival Tours, Inc.*, 708 S.W.2d 432, 436 (Tex. 1986); *Trenholm v. Ratcliff*, 646 S.W.2d 927, 933 (Tex. 1983); *Dennis v. Dial Finance & Thrift Co.*, 401 S.W.2d 803, 805 (Tex. 1966). PJC 110.34 may be used to submit exemplary damages. *See also* Tex. Civ. Prac. & Rem. Code Ann. § 41.003 (Vernon 1997).

PJC 105.2   **Instruction on Common-Law Fraud—Intentional Misrepresentation**

Fraud occurs when—

a.   a party makes a material misrepresentation,

b.   the misrepresentation is made with knowledge of its falsity or made recklessly without any knowledge of the truth and as a positive assertion,

c.   the misrepresentation is made with the intention that it should be acted on by the other party, and

d.   the other party acts in reliance on the misrepresentation and thereby suffers injury.

"Misrepresentation" means:

[*Insert appropriate definitions from PJCs 105.3A–.3E.*]

COMMENT

When to use.   PJC 105.2 should be used in a common-law fraud case if there is a claim of intentional misrepresentation.

Accompanying question, definitions.   PJC 105.2 is designed to follow PJC 105.1 and to be accompanied with one or more of the definitions of misrepresentation at PJCs 105.3A–.3E.

Use of "or."   If more than one definition is used, each must be separated by the word *or*, because a finding of any one type of misrepresentation would support recovery.

Source of instruction.   The elements of actionable fraud have been consistently stated by the Supreme Court of Texas. *Eagle Properties, Ltd. v. Scharbauer*, 807 S.W.2d 714, 723 (Tex. 1990); *Trenholm v. Ratcliff*, 646 S.W.2d 927, 930 (Tex. 1983); *Stone v. Lawyers Title Insurance Corp.*, 554 S.W.2d 183, 185 (Tex. 1977); *Custom Leasing, Inc. v. Texas Bank & Trust Co.*, 516 S.W.2d 138, 143 (Tex. 1974); *Oilwell Division, United States Steel Corp. v. Fryer*, 493 S.W.2d 487, 491 (Tex. 1973) (fraudulent inducement as affirmative defense).

Reliance need not be justifiable.   In *Koral Industries v. Security-Connecticut Life Insurance Co.*, 802 S.W.2d 650, 651 (Tex. 1990), the supreme court rejected the argument that a party's failure to use due diligence barred a claim of fraud. *See also Trenholm*, 646 S.W.2d at 933 (defendant in fraud case cannot complain that plaintiff failed to discover truth through exercise of care). Consequently, the jury should only be asked to consider the plaintiff's reliance and not asked to find whether that reliance was justified.

PJC 105.3   **Definitions of Misrepresentation—Intentional Misrepresentation**

PJC 105.3A   **Factual Misrepresentation**

A false statement of fact [*or*]

COMMENT

When to use.   PJC 105.3A should be used in cases involving an allegation that the defendant made an affirmative statement of fact that was false. *See Trenholm v. Ratcliff,* 646 S.W.2d 927, 930 (Tex. 1983) (false statement of fact actionable as fraud).

Accompanying question and instruction.   PJC 105.3A is designed to accompany the broad-form fraud question at PJC 105.1 and the basic elements of fraud at PJC 105.2. For other definitions of misrepresentation, see PJCs 105.3B–.3E.

Use of "or."   If more than one definition is used, each must be separated by the word *or,* because a finding of any one type of misrepresentation would support recovery.

PJC 105.3B   Promise of Future Action

A promise of future performance made with an intent not to perform as promised [*or*]

COMMENT

When to use. PJC 105.3B should be used if the alleged fraud is a promise made with intent not to perform. *T.O. Stanley Boot Co. v. Bank of El Paso*, 847 S.W.2d 218, 222 (Tex. 1992); *Spoljaric v. Percival Tours, Inc.*, 708 S.W.2d 432, 434–35 (Tex. 1986).

Accompanying question and instruction. PJC 105.3B is designed to accompany the broad-form fraud question at PJC 105.1 and the basic elements of fraud at PJC 105.2. For other definitions of misrepresentation, see PJCs 105.3A and .3C–.3E.

Use of "or." If more than one definition is used, each must be separated by the word *or*, because a finding of any one type of misrepresentation would support recovery.

PJC 105.3C   Opinion Mixed with Fact

A statement of opinion based on a false statement of fact [*or*]

COMMENT

When to use. PJC 105.3C should be used in cases involving an allegation that the defendant represented to the plaintiff an opinion based on a fact that the defendant knew was false. This type of statement constitutes an exception to the general rule that only false statements of fact can be actionable as fraud. *Trenholm v. Ratcliff*, 646 S.W.2d 927, 930 (Tex. 1983).

Accompanying question and instruction. PJC 105.3C is designed to accompany the broad-form fraud question at PJC 105.1 and the basic elements of fraud at PJC 105.2. For other definitions of misrepresentation, see PJCs 105.3A–.3B and .3D –.3E.

Use of "or." If more than one definition is used, each must be separated by the word *or*, because a finding of any one type of misrepresentation would support recovery.

PJC 105.3D   False Statement of Opinion

A statement of opinion that the maker knows to be false [*or*]

COMMENT

When to use.   PJC 105.3D should be used in cases involving an allegation that the defendant represented to the plaintiff an opinion that the defendant knew to be false. This type of statement constitutes an exception to the general rule that only false statements of fact can be actionable as fraud. *Trenholm v. Ratcliff*, 646 S.W.2d 927, 930 (Tex. 1983); *Brooks v. Parr*, 507 S.W.2d 818, 820 (Tex. Civ. App.—Amarillo 1974, no writ); *Texas Industrial Trust, Inc. v. Lusk*, 312 S.W.2d 324, 326–27 (Tex. Civ. App.—San Antonio 1958, writ ref'd).

Accompanying question and instruction.   PJC 105.3D is designed to accompany the broad-form fraud question at PJC 105.1 and the basic elements of fraud at PJC 105.2. For other definitions of misrepresentation, see PJCs 105.3A–.3C and .3E.

Use of "or."   If more than one definition is used, each must be separated by the word *or*, because a finding of any one type of misrepresentation would support recovery.

PJC 105.3E   Opinion Made with Special Knowledge

An expression of opinion that is false, made by one claiming or implying to have special knowledge of the subject matter of the opinion.

"Special knowledge" means knowledge or information superior to that possessed by the other party and to which the other party did not have equal access.

[*or*]

COMMENT

When to use.   PJC 105.3E should be used in cases involving an allegation that the defendant purported to have special knowledge of facts that would occur or exist in the future and represented to the plaintiff an opinion based on that special knowledge. *Trenholm v. Ratcliff*, 646 S.W.2d 927, 930 (Tex. 1983); *see also Eagle Properties, Ltd. v. Scharbauer*, 807 S.W.2d 714, 723 (Tex. 1990); *Fina Supply, Inc. v. Abilene National Bank*, 726 S.W.2d 537, 540 (Tex. 1987); *United States Pipe & Foundry Co. v. City of Waco*, 108 S.W.2d 432, 435–37 (Tex.), *cert. denied*, 58 S. Ct. 266 (1937); *Wright v. Carpenter*, 579 S.W.2d 575, 580 (Tex. Civ. App.—Corpus Christi 1979, writ ref'd n.r.e.); *Bell v. Bradshaw*, 342 S.W.2d 185, 189–90 (Tex. Civ. App.—Dallas 1960, no writ).

Accompanying question and instruction.   PJC 105.3E is designed to accompany the broad-form fraud question at PJC 105.1 and the basic elements of fraud at PJC 105.2. For other definitions of misrepresentation, see PJCs 105.3A–.3D.

Use of "or."   If more than one definition is used, each must be separated by the word *or*, because a finding of any one type of misrepresentation would support recovery.

PJC 105.4   Instruction on Common-Law Fraud—Concealment or Failure to Disclose

Fraud occurs when—

a.   a party conceals or fails to disclose a material fact within the knowledge of that party,

b.   the party knows that the other party is ignorant of the fact and does not have an equal opportunity to discover the truth,

c.   the party intends to induce the other party to take some action by concealing or failing to disclose the fact, and

d.   the other party suffers injury as a result of acting without knowledge of the undisclosed fact.

COMMENT

When to use.   PJC 105.4 should accompany PJC 105.1 if the court finds that failure to disclose is actionable in a particular case. Absent a fiduciary or confidential relationship, ordinarily there is no duty to disclose. Exceptions do exist, however. See the comment below titled "Silence as misrepresentation."

Source of instruction.   PJC 105.4 is based on an instruction approved in *New Process Steel Corp. v. Steel Corp. of Texas*, 703 S.W.2d 209, 214 (Tex. App.—Houston [1st Dist.] 1985, writ ref'd n.r.e.); *see also Custom Leasing, Inc. v. Texas Bank & Trust Co.*, 516 S.W.2d 138, 142 (Tex. 1974).

Silence as misrepresentation.   When the law imposes a duty to speak, silence may be as actionable as a positive misrepresentation of existing facts. This duty to disclose facts exists within fiduciary and other special relationships, *Castillo v. Neely's TBA Dealer Supply*, 776 S.W.2d 290, 295–96 (Tex. App.—Houston [1st Dist.] 1989, writ denied) (analyzing requirements of *Restatement (Second) of Torts* § 551 (1977)); *Tempo Tamers, Inc. v. Crow-Houston Four, Ltd.*, 715 S.W.2d 658, 669 (Tex. App.—Dallas 1986, writ ref'd n.r.e.), and has been recognized in some other situations. *Spoljaric v. Percival Tours, Inc.*, 708 S.W.2d 432, 435 (Tex. 1986) (specific representations about bonus plan gave rise to duty to disclose changes in plan); *State National Bank v. Farah Manufacturing Co.*, 678 S.W.2d 661, 681 (Tex. App.—El Paso 1984, writ dism'd by agr.) (when information voluntarily disclosed, duty to disclose whole truth); *Smith v. National Resort Communities, Inc.*, 585 S.W.2d 655, 658 (Tex. 1979) (seller of real estate has duty to disclose material facts not reasonably discoverable by purchaser); *Corpus Christi Area Teachers Credit Union v. Hernandez*, 814 S.W.2d 195, 202 (Tex. App.—San Antonio 1991, no writ) (party in interest may become liable by mere silent acquiescence in fraudulent misrepresentations of third party); *Hennigan v. Harris County*, 593 S.W.2d 380, 383–84 (Tex. Civ. App.—Waco 1979, writ ref'd n.r.e.) (attorney had duty to disclose that underlying judgment had been satisfied when it rendered pending proceeding moot); *Susanoil, Inc. v. Continental Oil Co.*, 519 S.W.2d 230, 236 n.6 (Tex. Civ. App.—San Antonio 1975, writ ref'd n.r.e.) (person making representation has duty to disclose new information when he is aware new information makes earlier representation untrue or misleading); *International Security Life Insurance Co. v. Finck*, 475 S.W.2d 363, 370 (Tex. Civ. App.—Amarillo 1971) (duty to speak may arise from partial disclosure if false impression conveyed), *rev'd on other grounds*, 496 S.W.2d 544 (Tex. 1973).

Rescission. If rescission is sought, the intent requirement may be lessened. *See Chase, Inc. v. Bostick*, 551 S.W.2d 116, 119 (Tex. Civ. App.—Tyler 1977, writ ref'd n.r.e.); *Calloway v. Manion*, 572 F.2d 1033, 1039 (5th Cir. 1978). Mere failure to disclose material information may give rise to rescission. *Smith*, 585 S.W.2d at 658.

Concealment. Active concealment of material facts may also be as actionable as false statements. *Campbell v. Booth*, 526 S.W.2d 167, 172 (Tex. Civ. App.—Dallas 1975, writ ref'd n.r.e.).

[PJCs 105.5–.7 are reserved for expansion.]

PJC 105.8   Instruction on Statutory Fraud—Factual Misrepresentation

Fraud occurs when—

a.   there is a false representation of a past or existing material fact,

b.   the false representation is made to a person for the purpose of inducing that person to enter into a contract,

c.   the false representation is relied on by that person in entering into that contract, and

d.   that person thereby suffers injury.

COMMENT

When to use.   PJC 105.8 is based on Tex. Bus. & Com. Code Ann. § 27.01(a)(1) (Vernon 1987), which applies only to fraud in a transaction involving real estate or stock in a corporation or joint stock company. If there is a dispute about whether the transaction involves real estate or stock in a corporation or joint stock company, additional instructions may be necessary. PJC 105.8 is designed to accompany the broad-form question at PJC 105.1.

Caveat.   The statute does not require actual awareness of the falsity for the recovery of actual damages. *Kerrville HRH, Inc. v. City of Kerrville*, 803 S.W.2d 377, 384 (Tex. App.—San Antonio 1990, writ denied); *Wright v. Carpenter*, 579 S.W.2d 575, 579 (Tex. Civ. App.—Corpus Christi 1979, writ ref'd n.r.e.); *Speer v. Pool*, 210 S.W.2d 423, 426 (Tex. Civ. App.—El Paso 1947, no writ). *But see Crofford v. Bowden*, 311 S.W.2d 954, 956 (Tex. Civ. App.—Fort Worth 1958, writ ref'd) (requiring scienter under prior statute).

PJC 105.9   Instruction on Statutory Fraud—False Promise

Fraud occurs when—

a.   a party makes a false promise to do an act,

b.   the promise is material,

c.   the promise is made with the intention of not fulfilling it,

d.   the promise is made to a person for the purpose of inducing that person to enter into a contract, and

e.   that person relies on the promise in entering into that contract.

COMMENT

When to use.   PJC 105.9 is based on Tex. Bus. & Com. Code Ann. § 27.01(a)(2) (Vernon 1987), which applies only to fraud in a transaction involving real estate or stock in a corporation or joint stock company. If there is a dispute about whether the transaction involves real estate or stock in a corporation or joint stock company, additional instructions may be necessary. PJC 105.9 is designed to accompany the broad-form question at PJC 105.1 in cases involving an allegation of a false promise to perform an act with the present intent not to perform it.

PJC 105.10   Question and Instruction on Benefiting from Statutory Fraud

If your answer to Question _____ [*105.1 used with 105.8 or .9*] is "Yes," then answer the following question. Otherwise, do not answer the following question.

QUESTION _____

Did *Deborah Dennis* commit fraud against *Paul Payne*?

Fraud occurs when—

    a.   a person has actual awareness of the falsity of a representation or promise made by another person, and

    b.   fails to disclose the falsity of the representation or promise to the person defrauded, and

    c.   benefits from the false representation or promise.

Actual awareness may be inferred where objective manifestations indicate a person acted with actual awareness.

"Representation or promise" means the representation or promise you found to be fraud in response to Question _____ [*105.1 used with 105.8 or .9*].

Answer: _____

COMMENT

When to use. PJC 105.10 submits liability under Tex. Bus. & Com. Code Ann. § 27.01(d) (Vernon 1987) and must be predicated on a finding of fraud by another person under PJC 105.1.

PJC 105.11   **Question and Instruction on Actual Awareness of Statutory Fraud**

If your answer to Question _____ [*105.1 used with 105.8 or .9*] is "Yes," then answer the following question. Otherwise, do not answer the following question.

QUESTION _____

Did *Don Davis* have actual awareness of the falsity of the representation or promise you found to be fraud in Question _____ [*105.1 used with 105.8 or .9*]?

> Actual awareness may be inferred where objective manifestations indicate a person acted with actual awareness.

Answer: _____

COMMENT

When to use.   Tex. Bus. & Com. Code Ann. § 27.01(c) (Vernon 1987) provides for recovery of exemplary damages if the person making the false representation or promise does so with actual awareness of its falsity. For the appropriate question on exemplary damages, see PJC 110.34. PJC 105.11 should not be used in connection with the question or instruction regarding benefiting from statutory fraud at PJC 105.10.

[PJCs 105.12–.15 are reserved for expansion.]

PJC 105.16   **Question and Instruction on Negligent Misrepresentation**

QUESTION _____

Did *Don Davis* make a negligent misrepresentation on which *Paul Payne* justifiably relied?

Negligent misrepresentation occurs when—

a.   a party makes a representation in the course of his business or in a transaction in which he has a pecuniary interest,

b.   the representation supplies false information for the guidance of others in their business, and

c.   the party making the representation did not exercise reasonable care or competence in obtaining or communicating the information.

Answer: _____

COMMENT

When to use.   PJC 105.16 is a broad-form question that should be appropriate in most cases involving a claim of negligent misrepresentation if the court, as a matter of law, or the jury, as a matter of fact, has found that the plaintiff is within the class of persons allowed to bring this cause of action. *See Blue Bell, Inc. v. Peat, Marwick, Mitchell & Co.*, 715 S.W.2d 408 (Tex. App.—Dallas 1986, writ ref'd n.r.e.) (if accounting firm knew or should have known that financial statements would be received and relied on by limited class of persons, firm might be liable for injuries to members of that class); *Cook Consultants, Inc. v. Larson*, 700 S.W.2d 231 (Tex. App.—Dallas 1985, writ ref'd n.r.e.) (surveyor liable to person or class of persons who foreseeably might be expected to rely on survey); *Bell v. Manning*, 613 S.W.2d 335 (Tex. Civ. App.—Tyler 1981, writ ref'd n.r.e.) (attorney owes no duty to third-party nonclients and therefore is not liable to them for damages resulting from his performance of legal services).

Source of question and instruction.   The question and instruction are patterned after the supreme court's opinion in *Federal Land Bank Ass'n of Tyler v. Sloane*, 825 S.W.2d 439, 442 (Tex. 1991).

Damages—pecuniary loss.   Damages are limited to pecuniary loss. *Sloane*, 825 S.W.2d at 442–43. See PJC 110.21.

Justifiable reliance.   Although justifiable reliance is not required in a fraud case, the supreme court included it as an element of the cause of action for negligent misrepresentation in *Sloane*. Moreover, the court of appeals opinion held that contributory negligence is a defense to a negligent misrepresentation claim. *Federal Land Bank Ass'n of Tyler v. Sloane*, 793 S.W.2d 692, 696 n.4 (Tex. App.—Tyler 1990), *aff'd in part and rev'd in part*, 825 S.W.2d 439 (Tex. 1991).

Preference for broad form.   This broad-form question conforms to Tex. R. Civ. P. 277.

PJC 106.1   Question and Instruction—Intentional Interference with Existing Contract

QUESTION _____

Did *Don Davis* intentionally interfere with [*identify contract*]?

Interference is intentional if committed with the desire to interfere with the contract or with the belief that interference is substantially certain to result.

Answer: _____

COMMENT

When to use.   An existing contract is a necessary element of a claim of intentional interference with contract. PJC 106.1 should be used in cases involving claims for intentional interference with a contract if the existence of the contract is not in dispute. If the existence of the contract is in dispute, additional jury questions or instructions may be required. See chapter 101.

Source of question and instruction.   The four elements of intentional interference with a contract are (1) a contract subject to interference, (2) an act of interference that was willful and intentional, (3) the act being a proximate cause of the plaintiff's damage, and (4) actual damage or loss. *ACS Investors, Inc. v. McLaughlin*, 943 S.W.2d 426, 430 (Tex. 1997); *Holloway v. Skinner*, 898 S.W.2d 793, 795–96 (Tex. 1995); *Victoria Bank & Trust Co. v. Brady*, 811 S.W.2d 931, 939 (Tex. 1991); *see also Southwestern Bell Telephone Co. v. John Carlo Texas, Inc.*, 843 S.W.2d 470 (Tex. 1992); *Exxon Corp. v. Allsup*, 808 S.W.2d 648, 654 (Tex. App.—Corpus Christi 1991, writ denied). The third and fourth elements are submitted together with the question and instructions on damages in PJC 110.22.

Interference.   Interference can include conduct that prevents performance of a contract or makes performance of a contract impossible, more burdensome, or more difficult or of less or no value to the one entitled to performance. *See International Union UAW v. Johnson Controls, Inc.*, 813 S.W.2d 558, 568 (Tex. App.—Dallas 1991, writ denied); *Tippett v. Hart*, 497 S.W.2d 606, 610 (Tex. Civ. App.—Amarillo), *writ ref'd n.r.e. per curiam*, 501 S.W.2d 874 (Tex. 1973).

Damages.   Damages questions are set forth in chapter 110. PJC 110.22 submits actual damages in cases involving existing contracts and in cases involving prospective contractual relations.

Exemplary damages.

Pre-September 1995 cases.   To support a recovery of exemplary damages for intentional interference with an existing contract (where the cause of action accrued before September 1, 1995), the plaintiff must secure a finding of actual malice. *Clements v. Withers*, 437 S.W.2d 818, 822 (Tex. 1969). For submission of actual malice, see PJC 110.23.

Post-September 1995 cases.   Causes of action accruing on or after September 1, 1995, are governed by Tex. Civ. Prac. & Rem. Code Ann. ch. 41 (Vernon 1997 & Supp. 1998), as amended in 1995. See PJCs 110.33 and .34.

**PJC 106.2   Question and Instruction—Wrongful Interference
with Prospective Contractual Relations**

QUESTION _____

Did *Don Davis* wrongfully interfere with [*describe Paul Payne's prospective
contractual relations*]?

Wrongful interference occurred if—

a.   there was a reasonable probability that *Paul Payne* would have
      entered into the contractual relations and

b.   *Don Davis* intentionally prevented the contractual relations from
      occurring with the purpose of harming *Paul Payne.*

Answer: _____

COMMENT

When to use.   In *Morgan Stanley & Co., Inc. v. Texas Oil Co.*, 958 S.W.2d 178 (Tex.
1997), *Calvillo v. Gonzalez*, 922 S.W.2d 928 (Tex. 1996), *Juliette Fowler Homes, Inc. v.
Welch Associates*, 793 S.W.2d 660 (Tex. 1990), and *Sterner v. Marathon Oil Co.*, 767
S.W.2d 686 (Tex. 1989), the Supreme Court of Texas recognized the existence of a cause of
action for interference with a prospective contractual relationship.

Source of instruction on wrongful interference.   The instruction on wrongful interference is derived from *Exxon Corp. v. Allsup*, 808 S.W.2d 648, 659 (Tex. App.—Corpus
Christi 1991, writ denied). *See also Leonard Duckworth, Inc. v. Michael L. Field & Co.*,
516 F.2d 952, 956 (5th Cir. 1975). Based on *Calvillo*, the element of lack of justification is
omitted. For the submission of the affirmative defense of justification, see PJC 106.3. The
elements of proximate cause and actual damages are submitted in PJC 110.22.

Exemplary damages.

Pre-September 1995 cases.   For causes of action accruing before September 1, 1995,
an affirmative answer to PJC 106.2 includes a finding that the defendant intended to harm
the plaintiff and therefore satisfies the element of "purposing the injury of another"
included in "actual malice" as defined in *Clements v. Withers*, 437 S.W.2d 818, 822 (Tex.
1969). Thus, no separate finding of actual malice as a predicate for exemplary damages is
required, and PJC 110.33 may be submitted conditioned on an affirmative answer to PJC
106.2.

Post-September 1995 cases.   Causes of action accruing on or after September 1, 1995,
are governed by Tex. Civ. Prac. & Rem. Code Ann. ch. 41 (Vernon 1997 & Supp. 1998), as
amended in 1995. See PJCs 110.33 and .34.

PJC 106.3   Question—Defense of Legal Justification

If your answer to Question _____ [*106.1 or .2*] is "Yes," then answer the following question. Otherwise, do not answer the following question.

QUESTION _____

Did *Don Davis* interfere because he had a good-faith belief that he had a right to do so?

Answer: _____

COMMENT

When to use.   PJC 106.3 submits the affirmative defense of justification. *See Calvillo v. Gonzalez*, 922 S.W.2d 928, 929 (Tex. 1996) (justification is an affirmative defense to interference with prospective business relations); *Texas Beef Cattle Co. v. Green*, 921 S.W.2d 203 (Tex. 1996) (justification is affirmative defense to intentional interference with existing contract). The defendant has the burden of proof. *Texas Beef Cattle Co.*, 921 S.W.2d at 211.

Source of question and instruction.   PJC 106.3 is derived from *Texas Beef Cattle Co.*, 921 S.W.2d at 211, and *Southwestern Bell Telephone Co. v. John Carlo Texas, Inc.*, 843 S.W.2d 470, 472 (Tex. 1992). *See also Victoria Bank & Trust Co. v. Brady*, 811 S.W.2d 931, 939 (Tex. 1991); *Sterner v. Marathon Oil Co.*, 767 S.W.2d 686, 689–91 (Tex. 1989).

Questions of law or fact.   Whether the defendant has established a legal right to interfere is a question of law for the court. If no legal right exists as a matter of law, the court must then make a threshold determination if a mistaken but colorable legal right was asserted. If a colorable legal right was asserted, then the jury is to determine whether the defendant exercised that colorable legal right in good faith. *Texas Beef Cattle Co.*, 921 S.W.2d at 211.

Scope of instruction.   Interference may be justified under circumstances other than those addressed in PJC 106.3. *See, e.g., Eloise Bauer & Associates v. Electronic Realty Associates*, 621 S.W.2d 200, 203 (Tex. Civ. App.—Texarkana 1981, writ ref'd n.r.e.) (employee acting in good faith to further interests of employer); *see also Russell v. Edgewood Independent School District*, 406 S.W.2d 249, 252 (Tex. Civ. App.—San Antonio 1966, writ ref'd n.r.e.); *Restatement (Second) of Torts* §§ 769–772 (1977). Although *Texas Beef Cattle Co.* omitted reference to "interests that a party possesses in the subject matter equal or superior to that of the other party," the Committee believes that such interests are subsumed in the term "colorable legal right." *See Texas Beef Cattle Co.*, 921 S.W.2d at 211 (citing *Sakowitz, Inc. v. Steck*, 669 S.W.2d 105, 107 (Tex. 1984), *overruled on other grounds by Sterner*, 767 S.W.2d at 690); *John Carlo Texas, Inc.*, 843 S.W.2d at 472.

PJC 107.1   Breach of Employment Agreement (Comment)

Subject to general contract rules.   PJC chapter 101 governs the submission of breach of employment agreement cases. An express agreement limiting the employer's right to discharge an employee at will is subject to general rules governing contracts. *See, e.g., Mansell v. Texas & Pacific Railway Co.*, 137 S.W.2d 997, 999–1000 (Tex. 1940) (agreement that employment could not be terminated without a fair investigation); *Morgan v. Jack Brown Cleaners, Inc.*, 764 S.W.2d 825, 827 (Tex. App.—Austin 1989, writ denied) (oral agreement that plaintiff would be transferred to another position and not terminated if her department were shut down); *Ramos v. Henry C. Beck Co.*, 711 S.W.2d 331, 336 (Tex. App.—Dallas 1986, no writ) (agreement that plaintiff would not be discharged absent good cause). The Supreme Court of Texas has expressly reserved the question of whether an oral agreement is sufficient to modify an employment-at-will relationship. *Goodyear Tire & Rubber Co. v. Portilla*, 879 S.W.2d 47, 51–52 n.8 (Tex. 1994).

If an express agreement exists between an employer and an employee limiting the employer's right to discharge an employee and breach of that agreement is alleged, PJC 101.2 should be submitted. If there is a dispute about the existence of an agreement or its terms, PJC 101.1 should be submitted, with PJC 101.2 predicated on an affirmative answer to PJC 101.1. Any defense to breach of the employment agreement should be submitted under PJC 101.21.

If there is no specific contract term or express agreement to the contrary, the rule that either party may terminate the employment relationship at will with or without cause will control. *Federal Express Corp. v. Dutschmann*, 846 S.W.2d 282, 283 (Tex. 1993); *East Line & R.R. Co. v. Scott*, 10 S.W. 99, 102 (Tex. 1888).

Property interest.   A "for cause" or "good cause" limitation on dismissal of a public employee creates a property right in continued employment that is protected under the constitution's Due Process Clause. *Bexar County Sheriff's Civil Service Commission v. Davis*, 802 S.W.2d 659, 661 & n.2 (Tex. 1990), *cert. denied*, 112 S. Ct. 57 (1991); *Brandy v. City of Cedar Hill*, 884 S.W.2d 913, 915 (Tex. App.—Texarkana 1994, no writ). If a property interest in not being discharged only for good cause exists, the Committee suggests the following jury question with a modified definition of PJC 107.2's "good cause":

Did *Don Davis* terminate *Paul Payne* without good cause?

Accompanying instructions.   Depending on the nature of the specific contract terms or any defenses, additional instructions may be necessary for use with PJCs 101.2 and .21. See PJC 107.2 (instruction on good cause as defense to early discharge) and chapter 101 (general instructions on contracts).

PJC 107.2   Instruction on Good Cause as Defense to Early Discharge

Failure to comply by *Don Davis* is excused if there was good cause for discharging *Paul Payne* before the agreed term of employment expired. "Good cause" means that the employee failed to perform those duties in the scope of his employment as a person of ordinary prudence would have done under the same or similar circumstances, or that the employee committed acts in the scope of his employment which a person of ordinary prudence would not have done under the same or similar circumstances.

COMMENT

When to use.   PJC 107.2 submits the defense of "good cause" to breach of an agreement to employ for a definite term. *See, e.g., Lee-Wright, Inc. v. Hall*, 840 S.W.2d 572, 578 (Tex. App.—Houston [1st Dist.] 1992, no writ); *Watts v. St. Mary's Hall, Inc.*, 662 S.W.2d 55, 58–59 (Tex. App.—San Antonio 1983, writ ref'd n.r.e.); *Lone Star Steel Co. v. Wahl*, 636 S.W.2d 217, 220 (Tex. App.—Texarkana 1982, no writ). This instruction should be used with PJC 101.21, the basic contract defense question.

Source of instruction.   PJC 107.2 is derived from *Winograd v. Willis*, 789 S.W.2d 307, 311 (Tex. App.—Houston [14th Dist.] 1990, writ denied); *see also Dixie Glass Co. v. Pollak*, 341 S.W.2d 530, 541–42 (Tex. Civ. App.—Houston 1960) (defining "good cause"), *writ ref'd n.r.e. per curiam*, 347 S.W.2d 596 (Tex. 1961).

"Good cause" defined in agreement.   If "good cause" or a similar term, such as "just cause" or "proper cause," is explicitly defined in the agreement or if specific grounds for termination are recited in the agreement, PJC 107.2 should not be submitted.

PJC 107.3   **Question on Wrongful Discharge for Refusing to Perform an Illegal Act**

QUESTION _____

Was *Paul Payne* discharged for the sole reason that *he* refused to perform an illegal act?

As used in this question, an "illegal act" means any of the following:

[*Insert appropriate instructions.*]

Answer: _____

COMMENT

When to use.   PJC 107.3 should be used for a claim that the employee was discharged for the sole reason that he or she refused to perform an illegal act.

Source of question.   PJC 107.3 is derived from *Sabine Pilot Service, Inc. v. Hauck*, 687 S.W.2d 733, 735 (Tex. 1985), and *Paul v. P.B.-K.B.B., Inc.*, 801 S.W.2d 229, 230 (Tex. App.—Houston [14th Dist.] 1990, writ denied). *Burt v. City of Burkburnett*, 800 S.W.2d 625, 627 (Tex. App.—Fort Worth 1990, writ denied), interpreted *Sabine Pilot*'s use of the word *refused* to include a requirement that the employer, in some manner, must order, require, or request the employee to commit an illegal act.

Illegal act.   The trial court should make a threshold determination as a matter of law whether the act the employee refused to commit was illegal. In *Hancock v. Express One International, Inc.*, 800 S.W.2d 634, 636–37 (Tex. App.—Dallas 1990, writ denied), the court refused to extend the *Sabine Pilot* exception to illegal acts that carry only civil penalties.

After-acquired evidence of employee misconduct.   If the employer has pleaded the discovery of evidence of employee misconduct acquired only after the employee's employment was terminated, see PJC 107.7 for the applicable question.

PJC 107.4   **Question and Instruction on Retaliation under Texas Whistleblower Act**

QUESTION _____

Was *Paul Payne*'s report [*insert matter reported*] made in good faith and a cause of *Don Davis's* [*terminating, suspending, or (describe other discriminatory action)*] *Paul Payne* when *he* did?

> "Good faith" means that (1) *Paul Payne* believed that the conduct reported was a violation of law and (2) *his* belief was reasonable in light of *his* training and experience.

Answer: _____

COMMENT

When to use.   PJC 107.4 should be used if a violation of Tex. Gov't Code Ann. § 554.002 (Vernon Supp. 1998) is alleged. If the existence of an adverse personnel action is in dispute, a finding in addition to PJC 107.4 is necessary.

Source of question and instruction.   PJC 107.4 is derived from Tex. Gov't Code § 554.002, *Texas Department of Human Services v. Hinds*, 904 S.W.2d 629 (Tex. 1995), and *Texas Department of Human Services v. Green*, 855 S.W.2d 136, 150-51 (Tex. App.—Austin 1993, writ denied). The instruction was adopted by the supreme court in *Wichita County, Texas v. Hart*, 917 S.W.2d 779, 784-85 (Tex. 1996).

Provisions of Whistleblower Act.   The Texas Whistleblower Act is found at Tex. Gov't Code §§ 554.001-.010 (1994 & Supp. 1998). A state or local governmental body may not terminate, suspend, or otherwise discriminate against a public employee who in good faith reports a violation of law to an appropriate law enforcement authority. Tex. Gov't Code § 554.002 (Supp. 1998) (formerly Tex. Rev. Civ. Stat. Ann. art. 6252-16(a)); *see also Winters v. Houston Chronicle Publishing Co.*, 795 S.W.2d 723 (Tex. 1990) (declining to extend Whistleblower Act to private sector employees).

Questions of law.   Whether the report concerned a violation of "law" as defined by the statute is a question of law. *See* Tex. Gov't Code § 554.001 (defining "law"). The Committee believes that the question of whether the person or entity to which the employee made the report is "an appropriate law enforcement authority" is a question of law. *See City of Beaumont v. Bouillion*, 896 S.W.2d 143, 145-46 (Tex. 1995); *Travis County v. Colunga*, 753 S.W.2d 716, 719-20 (Tex. App.—Austin 1988, writ denied); *City of Dallas v. Moreau*, 697 S.W.2d 472, 474 (Tex. App.—Dallas 1985, no writ); *but see Castaneda v. Texas Department of Agriculture*, 831 S.W.2d 501, 504 (Tex. App.—Corpus Christi 1992, writ denied) (in reviewing summary judgment, court stated "appropriate law enforcement authority" is question of fact).

Other retaliation statutes. The Committee has not provided pattern jury charges for every statutory prohibition against retaliatory discharge. Other such statutes include—

- Tex. Civ. Prac. & Rem. Code Ann. § 122.001 (Vernon 1997) (jury duty; criminal statute);

- Tex. Elec. Code Ann. § 276.001 (Vernon 1986 & Supp. 1998) (voting for certain candidate or proposition or refusing to reveal how one voted);

- Tex. Fam. Code Ann. § 158.209 (Vernon 1996 & Supp. 1998) (child support or child custody order or writ relating to an employee);

- Tex. Gov't Code § 431.006 (1998) (active duty in state military forces);

- Tex. Health & Safety Code Ann. § 161.134 (Vernon Supp. 1996) (employees of hospital, mental health facility, or treatment facility reporting violation of law or rule);

- Tex. Health & Safety Code § 242.133 (1992) (employees of nursing home reporting patient abuse);

- Tex. Lab. Code Ann. § 52.041 (Vernon 1996) (employee refusing to make purchases from a specific person or place or refusing to engage in dealings with any person or business; criminal statute);

- Tex. Lab. Code § 52.051 (compliance with subpoena);

- Tex. Lab. Code § 101.052 (union membership or nonmembership);

- Tex. Lab. Code § 411.083 (using telephone service to report violation of occupational health or safety law);

- 29 U.S.C.A. § 158(a)(1), (3), (4) (West 1973) (engaging in union activities);

- 29 U.S.C.A. § 215(a)(3) (1965) (exercising rights to a minimum wage and overtime compensation);

- 29 U.S.C.A. § 1140 (1985) (exercising rights under employee benefit plan);

- 42 U.S.C.A. § 5851 (1995) (federal whistleblower provision).

Caveat: causes of action accruing on or after June 15, 1995. If the adverse personnel action occurred on or after June 15, 1995, it is an affirmative defense to a Whistleblower Act suit that the state or local governmental entity would have taken the action against the employee "based solely on information, observation, or evidence that is not related to the fact that the employee made a report" of a violation of law. Tex. Gov't Code § 554.004(b) (Supp. 1998). In *Hinds*, 904 S.W.2d at 637, the supreme court noted that it expressed no opinion on whether the amended statute shifted the burden of proof.

After-acquired evidence of employee misconduct. If the employer has pleaded the discovery of evidence of employee misconduct acquired only after the employee's employment was terminated, see PJC 107.7 for the applicable question.

**PJC 107.5   Question and Instruction on Retaliation for Seeking
Workers' Compensation Benefits**

QUESTION _____

Did *Don Davis* [*discharge or (describe other discriminatory action)*] *Paul
Payne* because *he* [*filed a worker's compensation claim in good faith, hired a lawyer to represent him in a worker's compensation claim, instituted or caused to be
instituted a worker's compensation claim in good faith, testified or is about to testify
in a worker's compensation proceeding*]?

> There may be more than one cause for an employment decision. An
> employer does not [*discharge or discriminate against*] an employee for
> [*filing a worker's compensation claim in good faith, hiring a lawyer to
> represent him in a worker's compensation claim, instituting or causing to
> be instituted a worker's compensation claim in good faith, testifying or
> intending to testify in a worker's compensation proceeding*] if the em-
> ployer would have [*insert employment decision—e.g., discharged*] the
> employee when he did even if the employee had not [*filed a worker's
> compensation claim in good faith, hired a lawyer to represent him in a
> worker's compensation claim, instituted or caused to be instituted a
> worker's compensation claim in good faith, testified or is about to testify
> in a worker's compensation proceeding*].

Answer: _____

COMMENT

When to use.   PJC 107.5 should be used for a claim that the employer has committed
an unlawful practice under Tex. Lab. Code Ann. § 451.001 (Vernon 1996) (formerly Tex.
Rev. Civ. Stat. Ann. art. 8307c).

Source of question and instruction.   PJC 107.5 is derived from Tex. Lab. Code
§ 451.001 (formerly Tex. Rev. Civ. Stat. Ann. art. 8307e) and *Azar Nut Co. v. Caille*, 720
S.W.2d 685, 687 (Tex. App.—El Paso 1986), *aff'd*, 734 S.W.2d 667 (Tex. 1987). The instruction is derived from *Texas Department of Human Services v. Hinds*, 904 S.W.2d 629,
637 (Tex. 1995).

Institution of proceeding.   If an employee has been discharged after injury, but before
claim paperwork has been filed, the following instruction may be given:

> "Instituting or causing to be instituted a worker's compensation pro-
> ceeding" includes reporting an injury to *Don Davis*, being furnished with
> medical benefits, or receiving weekly compensation benefits.

See Worsham Steel Co. v. Arias, 831 S.W.2d 81, 84 (Tex. App.—El Paso 1992, no writ), *Mid-South Bottling Co. v. Cigainero*, 799 S.W.2d 385, 389 (Tex. App.—Texarkana 1990, writ denied); *Texas Steel Co. v. Douglas*, 533 S.W.2d 111, 116 (Tex. Civ. App.—Fort Worth 1976, writ ref'd n.r.e.).

After-acquired evidence of employee misconduct.   If the employer has pleaded the discovery of evidence of employee misconduct acquired only after the employee's employment was terminated, see PJC 107.7 for the applicable question.

PJC 107.6 **Question and Instruction on Unlawful Employment Practices**

QUESTION _____

Was [*race, color, disability, religion, sex, national origin, or age*] a motivating factor in *Don Davis*'s decision to [*fail or refuse to hire, discharge, or (describe other discriminatory action)*] *Paul Payne*?

> A "motivating factor" in an employment decision is a reason for making the decision at the time it was made. There may be more than one motivating factor for an employment decision.

Answer: _____

COMMENT

When to use. PJC 107.6 should be used for a claim that the employer has committed an unlawful employment practice as set out in the Texas Commission on Human Rights Act, Tex. Lab. Code Ann. §§ 21.001–.306 (Vernon 1996 & Supp. 1998) (TCHRA). PJC 107.6 applies to employment practices prohibited by Tex. Lab. Code § 21.051(1) and will need to be modified according to the facts of the case. If there is a fact issue concerning the existence of an adverse employment action, an additional finding is necessary.

PJC 107.6 and the questions and instructions that follow are drafted for TCHRA cases, but may also be used in federal law claims, because TCHRA conforms substantially to Title VII of the 1964 Civil Rights Act, 42 U.S.C.A. §§ 2000e to e-17 (West 1994 & Supp. 1998), the Age Discrimination in Employment Act (ADEA), 29 U.S.C.A. §§ 621–634 (Pamph. 1998), and the Americans with Disabilities Act (ADA), 42 U.S.C.A. §§ 12101-12213 (1995 & Supp. 1998). TCHRA is not, however, always identical to federal law. Therefore, before using these submissions in cases based on federal law, the practitioner should compare the language of TCHRA with the language of the applicable federal statute and the cases construing those statutes.

Use of federal case law. TCHRA is expressly intended to implement policies of title VII of the Civil Rights Act of 1964. Tex. Lab. Code § 21.001(1); *Schroeder v. Texas Iron Works*, 813 S.W.2d 483, 485 (Tex. 1991). Because one of the purposes behind TCHRA is the "correlation of state law with federal law in the area of discrimination in employment," federal case law interpreting title VII serves as a guide for interpretation of cases brought under chapter 21 of the Labor Code. *Specialty Retailers, Inc. v. DeMoranville*, 933 S.W.2d 490, 492 (Tex. 1996) (per curiam); *Schroeder*, 813 S.W.2d at 485; *Farrington v. Sysco Food Services, Inc.*, 865 S.W.2d 247, 251 (Tex. App.—Houston [1st Dist.] 1993, writ denied).

Source of question and definition. PJC 107.6 is derived from Tex. Lab. Code § 21.051(1), which parallels 42 U.S.C.A. § 2000e-2(a)(1) and prohibits intentional discriminatory practices. *See also Texas Department of Community Affairs v. Burdine*, 101 S. Ct. 1089 (1981); *International Brotherhood of Teamsters v. United States,* 97 S. Ct. 1843 (1977); *McDonnell Douglas Corp. v. Green*, 93 S. Ct. 1817 (1973). The Committee believes that PJC 107.6 and the definition of "motivating factor" correctly state the ultimate fact-finding necessary to determine liability under the TCHRA; additional instructions may, however, be necessary in a particular case. *See Adams v. Valley Federal Credit Union*, 848 S.W.2d 182 (Tex. App.—Corpus Christi 1992, writ denied); *Lakeway Land Co. v. Kizer*, 796 S.W.2d 820, 825-26 (Tex. App.—Austin 1990, writ denied); *but see Olitsky v. Spencer Gifts, Inc.*, 964 F.2d 1471 (5th Cir. 1992), *cert. denied*, 113 S. Ct. 1253 (1993).

The definition of "motivating factor" is derived from the following: (1) Tex. Lab. Code § 21.125(a), which provides that "an unlawful employment practice is established when the complaint demonstrates that race, color, sex, national origin, religion, age, or disability was a motivating factor for an employment practice, even if other factors motivated the practice"; and (2) section 709 of the Civil Rights Act of 1991, 42 U.S.C.A. § 2000e, codifying a portion of the Supreme Court's definition of causation under title VII in *Price Waterhouse v. Hopkins*, 109 S. Ct. 1775 (1989).

Circumstantial evidence. A circumstantial evidence instruction may be appropriate. See PJC 100.8.

National origin. For a definition of "national origin," see Tex. Lab. Code § 21.110 and *EEOC Guidelines on Discrimination Because of National Origin*, 29 C.F.R. § 1606.1 (1995).

Disparate treatment versus disparate impact. There is a difference between disparate treatment (Tex. Lab. Code § 21.051(1)) and disparate impact (Tex. Lab. Code §§ 21.051(2), 21.122) cases. PJC 107.6 submits disparate treatment. In a disparate impact case, an employer may be held liable for unintentional discrimination where an employment practice or criterion, neutral on its face, has a disproportionate effect or impact on a protected group. *Griggs v. Duke Power Co.*, 91 S. Ct. 849 (1971). TCHRA defines "disparate impact" as a practice where the employer "limits, segregates or classifies an employee or applicant for employment in a manner that would deprive or tend to deprive an individual of any employment opportunity or adversely affect in any other manner the status of an employee." Tex. Lab. Code § 21.051(2). For example, height and weight requirements may unlawfully discriminate against women and some ethnic or racial minorities. *Dothard v. Rawlinson*, 97 S. Ct. 2720 (1977). Education requirements may impact impermissibly on historically disadvantaged minority groups. *See Griggs*, 91 S. Ct. at 853-54. Disparate impact is not restricted to objective criteria or written tests with a discriminatory effect. *Watson v. Fort Worth Bank & Trust*, 108 S. Ct. 2777, 2790 (1988).

"Business necessity" is an affirmative defense to a disparate impact claim if an employer can show that the job requirement is job-related and justified by a valid business necessity. *See* Tex. Lab. Code § 21.115. "Business necessity" is never a justification, however, for intentional discrimination (disparate treatment). *See* Tex. Lab. Code § 21.123.

Submission of disparate impact cases.   Tex. Lab. Code § 21.122 sets forth the elements and burden of proof necessary in a disparate impact case and is the basis of the Committee's following suggested questions and instructions:

QUESTION _____

Did *Don Davis*'s requirement that [*particular employment practice*] have a disparate impact on [*name of protected group, e.g., women, racial minorities, etc.*]?

"Disparate impact" is established if an employer uses a particular employment practice, even if apparently neutral, that has a significant adverse effect on the basis of [*race, color, sex, national origin, etc.*].

Answer: _____

If you have answered "Yes" to Question _____ [*disparate impact question*], then answer the following question. Otherwise, do not answer the following question.

QUESTION _____

Was the employment practice inquired about in Question _____ [*disparate impact question*] job-related to the position in question and consistent with business necessity?

An employment practice is job-related if the practice clearly relates to skills, knowledge, or ability required for successful performance on the job. For an employment practice to be consistent with business necessity, it must be necessary to safe and efficient job performance.

Answer: _____

If you have answered "Yes" to Question _____ [*employment practice question*], then answer the following question. Otherwise, do not answer the following question.

QUESTION _____

Has *Don Davis* refused to adopt an "alternative employment practice" to the job requirement inquired about in Question _____ [*disparate impact question*]?

An "alternative employment practice" is an employment practice that serves the employer's legitimate interest in an equally effective manner, but which does not have a disparate impact on [*name of protected group, e.g., women, racial minorities, etc.*].

Answer: _____

"Disparate impact" was defined by the Supreme Court in *Albemarle Paper Co. v. Moody*, 95 S. Ct. 2362, 2375 (1975). The requirements of business necessity are set forth in Tex. Lab. Code §§ 21.115, 21.122(a)(1). Tex. Lab. Code § 21.122(a)(2) states the burden of proof with respect to showing an alternative employment practice to be that "in accordance with federal law as that law existed on June 4, 1989"—a reference to the 1991 amendments to Title VII that changed those burdens following the June 5, 1989, Supreme Court decision in *Wards Cove Packing Co. v. Atonio*, 109 S. Ct. 2115 (1989). Therefore, the burden of proof, on a showing of disparate impact, is on the employer to demonstrate that the practice is "job-related" and consistent with business necessity. *Dothard*, 97 S. Ct. at 2727. The instruction on "job-relatedness" is derived from *Albemarle Paper Co.*, 95 S. Ct. at 2375; *Contreras v. City of Los Angeles*, 656 F.2d 1267 (9th Cir. 1981), *cert. denied*, 102 S. Ct. 1719 (1982); and 29 C.F.R. § 1607 (1997). *See also* Tex. Lab. Code § 21.115; *Davis v. Richmond, Fredericksburg & Potomac Railroad Co.*, 803 F.2d 1322, 1327–28 (4th Cir. 1986); *EEOC v. Rath Packing Co. Creditors' Trust*, 787 F.2d 318, 328 (8th Cir. 1986), *cert. denied*, 107 S. Ct. 307 (1986). The "alternative employment practice" definition is derived from *Watson*, 108 S. Ct. at 2790.

Damages.   See PJC 110.30 for the question submitting actual damages and PJC 110.31 regarding exemplary damages.

After-acquired evidence of employee misconduct.   If the employer has pleaded the discovery of evidence of employee misconduct acquired only after the employee's employment was terminated, see PJC 107.7 for the applicable question.

PJC 107.7   **Question on After-Acquired Evidence of Employee
                      Misconduct**

QUESTION _____

Did *Paul Payne* engage in misconduct for which *Don Davis* would have legiti-
mately discharged him solely on that basis?

Answer "Yes" or "No."

Answer: _____

COMMENT

When to use.   PJC 107.7 should be used if the employer pleads that evidence of the
employee's misconduct, acquired after the employee's discharge, should limit the employee's recovery, because the employer would either not have hired or would have terminated the employee on legitimate and lawful grounds had the evidence been discovered before discharge. The Committee believes that PJC 107.7 is appropriate to submit if
after-acquired evidence is pleaded by the defendant in any wrongful discharge claim. *See
McKennon v. Nashville Banner Publishing Co.*, 115 S. Ct. 879 (1995) (age discrimination);
Trico Technologies Corp. v. Mandel, 929 S.W.2d 308 (Tex. 1997) (worker's compensation
retaliation).

PJC 107.8   **Instruction on Damages Reduction for After-Acquired Evidence of Employee Misconduct**

If you have answered "Yes" to Question _____ [*107.7*], do not include any damages suffered past the date *Don Davis* discovered that *Paul Payne* engaged in the conduct you have found in answer to Question _____ [*107.3, .4, .5, or .6*].

COMMENT

When to use. PJC 107.8 should be predicated on a "Yes" answer to PJC 107.7. It should be used as the last sentence of the preliminary instruction in PJC 110.26, .27, .28, or .30.

Source of instruction. PJC 107.8 is derived from *McKennon v. Nashville Banner Publishing Co.*, 115 S. Ct. 879 (1995); *Trico Technologies Corp. v. Mandel*, 929 S.W.2d 308 (Tex. 1997).

PJC 107.9   Question on Retaliation

QUESTION _____

Was *Paul Payne*'s [*opposition to a discriminatory practice, making or filing a charge of discrimination, filing a complaint, or testifying, assisting, or participating in any manner in a discrimination investigation, proceeding, or hearing under the Texas Commission on Human Rights Act*] a motivating factor in *Don Davis*'s decision to [*fail or refuse to hire, discharge, or (describe other discriminatory or retaliatory action)*] *Paul Payne*?

[*Insert motivating factor instruction from PJC 107.6.*]

Answer: _____

COMMENT

When to use.   PJC 107.9 should be used for a claim that an employer retaliated or discriminated against an employee for engaging in conduct protected by Tex. Lab. Code Ann. § 21.055 (Vernon 1996).

Source of question.   PJC 107.9 is derived from Tex. Lab. Code § 21.055.

Caveat: causation standard.   Tex. Lab. Code § 21.055 contains no express standard of causation in retaliation cases. The Committee has incorporated the "motivating factor" causation standard applicable to an unlawful employment practice as set forth in Tex. Lab. Code § 21.125(a). *But see Jack v. Texaco Research Center*, 743 F.2d 1129, 1131 (5th Cir. 1984).

PJC 107.10   Instruction on Constructive Discharge

An employee is considered to have been discharged when an employer makes conditions so intolerable that a reasonable person in the employee's position would have felt compelled to resign.

COMMENT

When to use.   PJC 107.10 should be used with PJC 107.6 if an employee alleges that the conditions of his employment amounted to a constructive discharge. *See Jett v. Dallas Independent School District*, 798 F.2d 748, 755 (5th Cir. 1986), *modified on other grounds*, 109 S. Ct. 2702 (1989); *Kelleher v. Flawn*, 761 F.2d 1079, 1086 (5th Cir. 1985).

Source of instruction.   PJC 107.10 is derived from *Jett*, 798 F.2d at 755. *See also Hammond v. Katy Independent School District*, 821 S.W.2d 174 (Tex. App.—Houston [14th Dist.] 1991, no writ) (discussing doctrine of constructive discharge in context of reviewing summary judgment on breach of employment agreement).

PJC 107.11   Instruction on Disability

"Disability" means:

    a. a mental or physical impairment, or a record of mental or physical impairment that substantially limits at least one major life activity;

    b. a record of such an impairment; or

    c. being regarded as having such an impairment.

The term "mental or physical impairment" means any physiological disorder, condition, cosmetic disfigurement, or anatomical loss affecting one or more of the following body systems: neurological; musculoskeletal; special sense organs; respiratory (including speech organs); cardiovascular; reproductive; digestive; genitourinary; hemic; lymphatic; skin; and endocrine; or any mental or psychological disorder, such as mental retardation, organic brain syndrome, emotional or mental illness, and specific learning disabilities.

"Major life activities" means functions such as caring for oneself, performing manual tasks, walking, seeing, hearing, speaking, breathing, learning, or working.

"Substantially limits" (as applied to "major life activities" other than "working") means that an individual is unable to perform a major life activity that the average person in the general population can perform or that individual is significantly restricted as to the condition, manner, or duration under which an individual can perform a particular major life activity as compared to the condition, manner, or duration under which the average person in the general population can perform that same major life activity.

"Substantially limits" (as applied to the "major life activity" of "working") means that an individual is restricted in the ability to perform either a class of jobs or a broad range of jobs in various classes as compared to the average person having comparable training, skills, and abilities. The inability to perform a single, particular job does not constitute a substantial limitation in the major life activity of working.

"Record of such an impairment" means that an individual has a history of or has been misclassified as having a mental or physical impairment that substantially limits one or more major life activities.

"Being regarded as having such an impairment" means an individual: (a) has a physical or mental impairment that does not substantially limit a major life activity but is treated by the employer as having such a limitation; (b) has a physical or mental impairment that substantially limits a major life activity only as a result of the attitudes of others towards the impairment; or (c) does not have an impairment at all, but is regarded by the employer as having such a substantially limiting impairment.

Disability is not a motivating factor in an employment decision if an individual's disability impairs the individual's ability to reasonably perform the job in question.

COMMENT

When to use.   PJC 107.11 is to be used with PJC 107.6 if disability is alleged to be the basis of an employer's commission of an unlawful employment practice.

Source of instruction.   PJC 107.11 is derived from the Americans with Disabilities Act (ADA), 42 U.S.C.A. §§ 12101–12213 (West 1995 & Supp. 1998), and from Tex. Lab. Code Ann. §§ 21.002(6), 21.105 (Vernon 1996 & Supp. 1998). The definitions pertaining to disability are contained in the EEOC regulations implementing the equal employment provisions of the Americans with Disabilities Act, 29 C.F.R. § 1630.2(g)–(*l*) (1997). These definitions, first promulgated as part of the Rehabilitation Act of 1973 (29 U.S.C.A. § 31*et seq.*), were interpreted by the United States Supreme Court in *School Board of Nassau County, Florida v. Arline*, 107 S. Ct. 1123 (1987), and *Southeastern Community College v. Davis*, 99 S. Ct. 2361 (1979).

Additional instruction: substance addiction or communicable disease status.   In the appropriate case, use the following instruction:

> "Disability" does not include [*a current condition of addiction to the use of alcohol, a drug, an illegal substance, or a federally controlled substance*] [*a currently communicable disease or infection, including acquired immune deficiency syndrome or infection with the human immunodeficiency virus, that constitutes a direct threat to the health or safety of other persons or that makes the affected person unable to perform the duties of the person's employment*].

See Tex. Lab. Code § 21.002(6).

PJC 107.12   Instruction on Failure to Make Reasonable Workplace Accommodation

Disability is a motivating factor when an employer refuses or fails to make a reasonable workplace accommodation to a known physical or mental limitation of an otherwise qualified individual with a disability.

The term "reasonable workplace accommodation" means:

a.   modifications or adjustments to a job application process that enables an applicant with a disability to be considered for the position that the applicant desires;

b.   modifications or adjustments to the work environment, or to the manner or circumstances in which the position held or desired is customarily performed, that enables an individual with a disability to perform the essential functions of that position; or

c.   modifications or adjustments that enable an employee with a disability to enjoy equal benefits and privileges of employment as are enjoyed by other similarly situated employees without disabilities.

There may be more than one reasonable workplace accommodation.

COMMENT

When to use. PJC 107.12 is to be used in conjunction with PJC 107.6 and the definition of "disability" in PJC 107.11 if the discrimination alleged is a claim that the employer refused or failed to make a reasonable workplace accommodation to a known disability.

Source of instruction. PJC 107.12 is derived from Tex. Lab. Code Ann. § 21.128 (Vernon 1996) and 29 C.F.R. § 1630.2(*o*) (1997) (EEOC regulations implementing the equal employment provisions of the Americans with Disabilities Act).

PJC 107.13   Question and Instruction on Undue Hardship Defense

If you have answered Question _____ [*107.6*] "Yes," then answer the following question. Otherwise, do not answer the following question.

QUESTION _____

Would a reasonable workplace accommodation to *Paul Payne*'s known disability have caused undue hardship to the operation of *Don Davis*'s business?

> "Reasonable workplace accommodation" is defined in Question _____ [*107.12*].

> "Undue hardship" means a significant difficulty or expense incurred by an employer in light of the reasonableness of the costs of any necessary workplace accommodation considered in light of the availability of all alternatives or other appropriate relief.

Answer: _____

COMMENT

When to use.   PJC 107.13 should be used if the employer presents evidence of undue hardship in defense to a claim of lack of reasonable workplace accommodation under Tex. Lab. Code Ann. § 21.128 (Vernon 1996).

Source of question and instructions.   PJC 107.13 is derived from Tex. Lab. Code § 21.128 and 29 C.F.R. § 1630.2(p) (1997) (EEOC regulations implementing the equal employment provisions of the Americans with Disabilities Act).

PJC 107.14   Question on Good-Faith Effort to Make Reasonable Workplace Accommodation

If you have answered Question _____ [*107.6*] "Yes," then answer the following question. Otherwise, do not answer the following question.

QUESTION _____

Did *Don Davis* consult with *Paul Payne* in good faith in an effort to identify and make a reasonable workplace accommodation to *Paul Payne*'s disability that would not cause an undue hardship to the operation of *Don Davis*'s business?

> "Reasonable workplace accommodation" and "undue hardship" are defined in Questions _____ [*107.12*] and _____ [*107.13*].

Answer: _____

COMMENT

When to use.   PJC 107.14 should be used if the employer presents evidence that it has made a good-faith effort to identify and accommodate a known disability in defense to a claim of lack of reasonable accommodation under Tex. Lab. Code Ann. § 21.128 (Vernon 1996). The inquiry in PJC 107.14 is for use by the judge in entry of a judgment. *See* Tex. Lab. Code §§ 21.258, 21.2585, 21.259.

Source of question.   PJC 107.14 is derived from Tex. Lab. Code § 21.128(c). The employer bears the burden of proof on the issue.

PJC 107.15   Instruction on Sex Discrimination

In determining whether sex was a motivating factor, "sex" includes discrimination because of or on the basis of pregnancy, childbirth, or a related medical condition.

COMMENT

When to use.   PJC 107.15 is to be used with PJC 107.6 if pregnancy, childbirth, or a related medical condition is alleged to be the basis of an employer's commission of an unlawful employment practice.

Source of instruction.   PJC 107.15 is derived from Tex. Lab. Code Ann. § 21.106 (Vernon 1996).

PJC 107.16   Instruction on Religious Observance or Practice

Religion is a motivating factor if the decision to [*fail or refuse to hire, discharge, or (describe other discriminatory action)*] *Paul Payne* was made because of or on the basis of any aspect of religious [*observance, practice, or belief*].

COMMENT

When to use.   PJC 107.16 is to be used with PJC 107.6 if some aspect of observance of a religion, such as inability to work on a Sabbath, is alleged to be the basis of an employer's commission of an unlawful employment practice. This instruction, however, should not be used if religious preference alone is at issue. See PJC 107.6.

Source of instruction.   PJC 107.16 is derived from Tex. Lab. Code Ann. § 21.108 (Vernon 1996).

**PJC 107.17   Question and Instruction on Defense of Undue Hardship
to Accommodate Religious Observances or Practices**

QUESTION _____

Was *Don Davis* unable to reasonably accommodate *Paul Payne*'s religious observance or practice without undue hardship to the conduct of *his* business?

A reasonable accommodation to an employee's religious observances or practices constitutes an undue hardship when it requires the employer to bear more than a minimal cost, such cost including both monetary costs and burdens in conducting business.

COMMENT

When to use.   PJC 107.17 should be used if the employer alleges that reasonable accommodation to religious observances or practices would cause undue hardship.

Source of question and instruction.   PJC 107.17 is derived from Tex. Lab. Code Ann. § 21.108 (Vernon 1996) and *Trans World Airlines, Inc. v. Hardison*, 97 S. Ct. 2264, 2277 & n.15 (1977).

PJC 107.18   Question Limiting Relief in Unlawful Employment Practices

If you have answered "Yes" to Question _____ [*107.6*], then answer the following question. Otherwise, do not answer the following question.

QUESTION _____

Would *Don Davis* have taken the same action inquired about in Question _____ [*107.6*] when *he* did, in the absence of the impermissible motivating factor?

Answer: _____

COMMENT

When to use.   PJC 107.18 should be used if an employer claims that its employment decision would have been made in the absence of an impermissible motive. Tex. Lab. Code Ann. § 21.125(b) (Vernon 1996); *see also Price Waterhouse v. Hopkins*, 109 S. Ct. 1775 (1989). In such a mixed-motive case, a plaintiff may be entitled to declaratory or injunctive relief, attorney's fees, and costs, although not entitled to back pay or reinstatement. Tex. Lab. Code § 21.125(b). PJC 107.18 should not be submitted to the jury based on after-acquired evidence. *See McKennon v. Nashville Banner Publishing Co.*, 115 S. Ct. 879 (1995).

Source of question.   PJC 107.18 is derived from Tex. Lab. Code § 21.125(b).

PJC 107.19   **Question and Instruction on Bona Fide Occupational Qualification Defense**

QUESTION _____

Was *Don Davis*'s [*failure or refusal to hire, discharge, or (describe other discriminatory action)*] *Paul Payne* based on a bona fide occupational qualification reasonably necessary to the normal operation of *Don Davis*'s business?

"Bona fide occupational qualification" means a qualification (1) reasonably related to the satisfactory performance of the duties of a job, and (2) for which a factual basis exists for the belief that no person of an excluded group would be able to satisfactorily perform the duties of the job with safety or efficiency.

Answer: _____

COMMENT

When to use.   PJC 107.19 is to be used if an employer asserts a bona fide occupational qualification as the basis for any discrimination based on disability, religion, sex, national origin, or age of an employee. Tex. Lab. Code Ann. § 21.119 (Vernon 1996).

Source of instruction.   PJC 107.19 is derived from Tex. Lab. Code §§ 21.002, 21.119.

PJC 107.20   Question on Sexual Harassment

QUESTION _____

Was *Paul Payne* subjected to sexual harassment by *Don Davis*?

[*Insert appropriate instruction.*]

Answer: _____

COMMENT

When to use.   PJC 107.20 should be used if there is an allegation of sexual harassment.

Source of question and instruction.   PJC 107.20 is derived from *Nagel Manufacturing & Supply Co. v. Ulloa*, 812 S.W.2d 78, 80–81 (Tex. App.—Austin 1991, writ denied). *See also Harris v. Forklift Systems, Inc.*, 114 S. Ct. 367 (1993); *Meritor Savings Bank v. Vinson*, 103 S. Ct. 2399 (1986); *Benavides v. Moore*, 848 S.W.2d 190 (Tex. App.—Corpus Christi 1992, writ denied).

Accompanying instructions.   Instructions to accompany PJC 107.20 are at PJCs 107.21–.23. If more than one instruction is used, each should be separated by the word *or*.

PJC 107.21   Instruction on *Quid Pro Quo* Sexual Harassment

"Sexual harassment" occurred if:

    1. *Paul Payne* was subjected to unwelcome sexual advance(s) or demand(s);

    2. submission to or refusal to submit to the unwelcome sexual advance(s) or demand(s) resulted in [*discharge, demotion, undesirable reassignment, or (describe other tangible employment action)*]; and

    3. the conduct was committed by an employee who had authority over hiring, advancement, dismissals, discipline, or other employment decisions affecting *Paul Payne*.

[or]

COMMENT

When to use.   PJC 107.21 should be used with PJC 107.20 if it is alleged that the employee was subjected to what has traditionally been referred to as *quid pro quo* sexual harassment.

Source of instruction.   PJC 107.21 is derived from *Ewald v. Wornick Family Foods Corp.*, 878 S.W.2d 653 (Tex. App.—Corpus Christi 1994, writ denied). *See also Jones v. Flagship International*, 793 F.2d 714, 721–22 (5th Cir. 1986), *cert. denied*, 107 S. Ct. 952 (1987); *Henson v. City of Dundee*, 682 F.2d 897, 909–10 (11th Cir. 1982).

Tangible employment action.   The United States Supreme Court in *Burlington Industries, Inc. v. Ellerth*, 118 S. Ct. 2257, 2268 (1998), defined "tangible employment action" as "a significant change in employment status, such as hiring, firing, failing to promote, reassignment with significantly different responsibilities, or a decision causing a significant change in benefits."

Vicarious liability.   If a supervisor's harassment culminates in tangible employment action, the employer is vicariously liable for the supervisor's conduct. *Faragher v. City of Boca Raton*, 118 S. Ct. 2275, 2293 (1998). In that instance, the affirmative defense in PJC 107.24 is not available.

Caveat.   PJC 107.21 is largely derived from federal summary judgment and bench trial cases, not jury charge cases. *But see Nagel Manufacturing & Supply Co. v. Ulloa*, 812 S.W.2d 78, 80–81 (Tex. App.—Austin 1991, writ denied).

PJC 107.22   Instruction on Hostile Environment Sexual Harassment by Nonsupervisory Employee

"Sexual harassment" occurred if:

1. *Paul Payne* was subjected to sexual advances, requests for sexual favors, and/or other conduct of a sexual nature that was unwelcome and undesirable or offensive to *Paul Payne*;

2. the harassment complained of altered a term, condition, or privilege of employment; and

3. *Don Davis* knew or should have known of the harassment and *Don Davis* failed to take prompt, remedial action to eliminate the harassment.

Harassment alters a term, condition, or privilege of employment when a reasonable person would find that the harassment created an abusive working environment. In determining whether an abusive working environment existed, consider the following: the frequency of the conduct; its severity; whether it was physically threatening or humiliating or a mere offensive utterance; and whether it unreasonably interferes with an employee's work performance.

[*or*]

COMMENT

When to use.   PJC 107.22 should be used with PJC 107.20 if it is alleged that the plaintiff was subjected to a hostile environment based on sex.

Source of instruction.   PJC 107.22 is derived from *Burlington Industries, Inc. v. Ellerth*, 118 S. Ct. 2257, 2265 (1998), *Faragher v. City of Boca Raton*, 118 S. Ct. 2275, 2283 (1998), *Harris v. Forklift Systems, Inc.*, 114 S. Ct. 367, 371 (1993), and *Meritor Savings Bank v. Vinson*, 103 S. Ct. 2399 (1986). *See also Nash v. Electrospace System, Inc.*, 9 F.3d 401, 404 (5th Cir. 1993); *Jones v. Flagship International*, 793 F.2d 714, 719-20 (5th Cir. 1986), *cert. denied*, 107 S. Ct. 952 (1987); *Ewald v. Wornick Family Foods Corp.*, 878 S.W.2d 653, 659 (Tex. App.—Corpus Christi 1994, writ denied).

PJC 107.23   Instruction on Hostile Environment Sexual Harassment by Supervisory Employee

"Sexual harassment" occurred if:

1. *Paul Payne* was subjected to sexual advances, requests for sexual favors, and/or other conduct of a sexual nature that was unwelcome and undesirable or offensive to *Paul Payne*;

2. the harassment complained of altered a term, condition, or privilege of employment; and

3. the conduct was committed by a supervisor who had authority over hiring, advancement, dismissals, discipline, or other employment decisions affecting *Paul Payne*.

Harassment alters a term, condition, or privilege of employment when a reasonable person would find that the harassment created an abusive working environment. In determining whether an abusive working environment existed, consider the following: the frequency of the conduct; its severity; whether it was physically threatening or humiliating or a mere offensive utterance; and whether it unreasonably interferes with an employee's work performance.

[*or*]

COMMENT

When to use.   PJC 107.23 should be used with PJC 107.20 if it is alleged that the plaintiff was subjected to sexual harassment by a supervisor.

Source of instruction.   PJC 107.22 is derived from *Burlington Industries, Inc. v. Ellerth*, 118 S. Ct. 2257, 2265 (1998), *Faragher v. City of Boca Raton*, 118 S. Ct. 2275, 2283 (1998), *Harris v. Forklift Systems, Inc.*, 114 S. Ct. 367, 371 (1993), and *Meritor Savings Bank v. Vinson*, 103 S. Ct. 2399 (1986). *See also Nash v. Electrospace System, Inc.*, 9 F.3d 401, 404 (5th Cir. 1993); *Jones v. Flagship International*, 793 F.2d 714, 719–20 (5th Cir. 1986), *cert. denied*, 107 S. Ct. 952 (1987); *Ewald v. Wornick Family Foods Corp.*, 878 S.W.2d 653, 659 (Tex. App.—Corpus Christi 1994, writ denied).

Affirmative defense.   An employer is entitled to submission of the affirmative defense of reasonable care under PJC 107.24 if the supervisor's harassment does not culminate in a tangible employment action. *Ellerth*, 118 S.Ct. at 2270; *Faragher*, 118 S. Ct. at 2293. If the existence of a tangible employment action is in dispute, a separate question may need to be submitted.

PJC 107.24   Question on Affirmative Defense to Sexual Harassment Where No Tangible Employment Action Occurred

If your answer to Question _____ [*107.20*] is "Yes," then answer the following question. Otherwise, do not answer the following question.

QUESTION _____

Is *Don Davis* legally excused from responsibility for the conduct of [*insert name of supervisor(s)*] found in Question _____ [*107.20*]?

> *Don Davis* is legally excused if—

1. *Don Davis* exercised reasonable care to prevent and correct promptly any sexual harassment behavior; and

2. *Paul Payne* unreasonably failed to take advantage of any preventive or corrective opportunities by *his* employer or to avoid harm otherwise.

Answer "Yes" or "No."

Answer: _____

COMMENT

When to use. PJC 107.24 should be used if the defendant employer alleges the affirmative defense of reasonable care and there has been no tangible employment action taken by the employer against the employee alleging sexual harassment.

Source of question. PJC 107.24 is derived from *Burlington Industries, Inc. v. Ellerth*, 118 S. Ct. 2257, 2270 (1998), and *Faragher v. City of Boca Raton*, 118 S. Ct. 2275, 2293 (1998).

CHAPTER 108   PIERCING THE CORPORATE VEIL

PJC 108.1 Basic Question

QUESTION _____

Is *Don Davis* responsible for the conduct of [*name of corporation*]?

Don Davis is "responsible" for the conduct of [*name of corporation*] if:

[*Insert appropriate instruction(s); see PJCs 108.2–.7.*]

Answer "Yes" or "No."

Answer: _____

COMMENT

When to use. PJC 108.1 is a basic question that is appropriate to submit in all cases in which the claimant seeks to disregard the corporate fiction and pierce the corporate veil.

Accompanying instructions. PJC 108.1 should be accompanied with appropriate instructions and definitions informing the jury of the applicable bases for disregarding the corporate fiction, "an equitable doctrine [that] takes a flexible, fact-specific approach focusing on equity." *See Castleberry v. Branscum*, 721 S.W.2d 270, 275–76 (Tex. 1986); *see also Stewart & Stevenson Services, Inc. v. Serv-Tech, Inc.*, 879 S.W.2d 89, 110 (Tex. App.—Houston [14th Dist.] 1994, writ denied). Instructions to accompany PJC 108.1, informing the jury what type of conduct should be considered under the question, are at PJCs 108.2–.7.

Use of "or." If more than one instruction is used, each must be separated by the word *or*, because a finding of any one of the theories for disregarding the corporate fiction defined in the instructions would support an affirmative answer to the question.

PJC 108.2   Instruction on Alter Ego

[*Name of corporation*] was organized and operated as a mere tool or business conduit of *Don Davis*; there was such unity between [*name of corporation*] and *Don Davis* that the separateness of [*name of corporation*] had ceased and holding only [*name of corporation*] responsible would result in injustice; and *Don Davis* caused [*name of corporation*] to be used for the purpose of perpetuating and did perpetuate an actual fraud on *Paul Payne* primarily for the direct personal benefit of *Don Davis*.

In deciding whether there was such unity between [*name of corporation*] and *Don Davis* that the separateness of [*name of corporation*] had ceased, you are to consider the total dealings of [*name of corporation*] and *Don Davis*, including:

1. the degree to which [*name of corporation's*] property had been kept separate from that of *Don Davis*;

2. the amount of financial interest, ownership, and control *Don Davis* maintained over [*name of corporation*]; and

3. whether [*name of corporation*] had been used for personal purposes of *Don Davis*.

[*or*]

COMMENT

When to use.   PJC 108.2 should be used as an instruction accompanying the question in PJC 108.1 if it is alleged that a corporation is the alter ego of another person or entity in a case relating to or arising from a contractual obligation. See comment below, "Noncontract case," for charge language to be used in other cases.

Use of "or."   If used with other instructions (see PJCs 108.3 –.7), PJC 108.2 must be followed by the word *or*, because a finding of any one of the theories for disregarding the corporate fiction defined in the instructions would support an affirmative answer to the question.

Source of instruction.   PJC 108.2 is based on the supreme court's discussion of alter ego in *Castleberry v. Branscum*, 721 S.W.2d 270, 272 (Tex. 1986). The language of *Castleberry* has been modified to reflect the enactment of Tex. Bus. Corp. Act Ann. art 2.21(A) (Vernon Supp. 1998), which eliminated constructive fraud and the failure to observe corporate formalities as considerations for piercing the corporate veil in contract-based claims. *See Farr v. Sun World Savings Ass'n*, 810 S.W.2d 294, 296 (Tex. App.—El Paso 1991, no writ).

"Injustice."   No Texas case has stated whether *injustice* must be defined in alter ego cases. For a case discussing the term *injustice* in an alter ego context, see *Mancorp, Inc. v. Culpepper*, 836 S.W.2d 844 (Tex. App.—Houston [1st Dist.] 1992), *on remand from* 802 S.W.2d 226 (Tex. 1990).

"Actual fraud."   The term *actual fraud* appearing in Tex. Bus. Corp. Act art. 2.21(A) is not defined in the statute. In *Castleberry*, the supreme court defined actual fraud in the context of piercing the corporate veil as "involv[ing] dishonesty of purpose or intent to deceive." 721 S.W.2d at 273 (quoting *Archer v. Griffith*, 390 S.W.2d 735, 740 (Tex. 1964)).

Actions against persons other than owners and subscribers.   Tex. Bus. Corp. Act art. 2.21 and PJC 108.2 apply in actions based on a contractual obligation brought against holders of shares, owners of beneficial interests in shares, subscribers whose subscriptions have been accepted, their affiliates, and the affiliates of the corporation. For such actions brought against persons or entities other than holders, owners, subscribers, or affiliates, use the instruction shown below in the comment "Noncontract case."

Noncontract case.   For those cases not relating to or arising from a corporate obligation, use the following instruction:

> [*Name of corporation*] was organized and operated as a mere tool or business conduit of *Don Davis* and there was such unity between [*name of corporation*] and *Don Davis* that the separateness of [*name of corporation*] had ceased and holding only [*name of corporation*] responsible would result in injustice.
>
> In deciding whether there was such unity between [*name of corporation*] and *Don Davis* that the separateness of [*name of corporation*] had ceased, you are to consider the total dealings of [*name of corporation*] and *Don Davis*, including—
>
> 1. the degree to which [*name of corporation's*] property had been kept separate from that of *Don Davis*;
>
> 2. the amount of financial interest, ownership, and control *Don Davis* maintained over [*name of corporation*]; and
>
> 3. whether [*name of corporation*] had been used for personal purposes of *Don Davis*.

This instruction is derived from *Castleberry*, 721 S.W.2d at 271–73. By its terms, the restrictions of Tex. Bus. Corp. Act art. 2.21(A)(2) do not apply in a noncontract case. *See Farr*, 810 S.W.2d at 296. *See also Stewart & Stevenson Services, Inc. v. Serv-Tech, Inc.*, 879 S.W.2d 89, 110 (Tex. App.—Houston [14th Dist.] 1994, writ denied) (recommending that trial courts follow an alter ego instruction that came "verbatim" from *Castleberry*).

If the corporation whose veil is sought to be pierced is a close corporation organized under Tex. Bus. Corp. Act arts. 12.01–.54, one or more of the indicia of unity may not apply.

Actions brought before September 1, 1997. Tex. Bus. Corp. Act art. 2.21 was amended in 1997 as follows:

1. The list of persons or entities protected from liability (except for actual fraud) was expanded to include "affiliates"; Tex. Bus. Corp. Act art. 2.21;

2. Not only contractual obligations of the corporation but "matters relating to or arising from contractual obligations" were excluded as grounds for disregarding the corporate fiction unless actual fraud was proved; Tex. Bus. Corp. Act art. 2.21(A)(2); and

3. Failure of the corporation to observe a corporate formality is no longer a ground for piercing the corporate veil in any case, not just contract cases. Tex. Bus. Corp. Act art. 2.21(A)(3).

These amendments affect all corporations, regardless of the date of formation or incorporation, but do *not* affect actions or proceedings commenced before September 1, 1997. Act of May 13, 1997, 75th Leg., R.S., ch. 375, § 125, 1997 Tex. Gen. Laws 1516, 1610. For an action or proceeding governed by the prior law, amend the charge language accordingly. See also State Bar of Texas, *Texas Pattern Jury Charges—Business, Consumer & Employment* (1997).

PJC 108.3   Instruction on Sham to Perpetrate a Fraud

Don Davis used [*name of corporation*] for the purpose of perpetrating and did perpetrate an actual fraud on *Paul Payne* primarily for the direct personal benefit of *Don Davis*.

[*or*]

COMMENT

When to use.   PJC 108.3 should be used as an instruction accompanying the question in PJC 108.1 if it is alleged that a corporation has been used by another person or entity as a sham to perpetrate a fraud in a case relating to or arising from a contractual obligation. See comment below, "Noncontract case," for charge language to be used in other cases.

Use of "or."   If used with other instructions (see PJCs 108.2 and .4–.7), PJC 108.3 must be followed by the word *or*, because a finding of any one of the theories for disregarding the corporate fiction defined in the instructions would support an affirmative answer to the question.

Source of instruction.   PJC 108.3 is based on the supreme court's discussion of the theories for disregarding the corporate fiction in *Castleberry v. Branscum*, 721 S.W.2d 270, 271–73 (Tex. 1986). The language of *Castleberry* has been modified to reflect the enactment of Tex. Bus. Corp. Act Ann. art. 2.21(A) (Vernon Supp. 1998), which eliminated constructive fraud and the failure to observe corporate formalities as considerations for piercing the corporate veil in contract-based claims. *See Farr v. Sun World Savings Ass'n*, 810 S.W.2d 294, 296 (Tex. App.—El Paso 1991, no writ).

"Actual fraud."   The term *actual fraud* appearing in Tex. Bus. Corp. Act art. 2.21(A) is not defined in the statute. In *Castleberry*, the supreme court defined actual fraud in the context of piercing the corporate veil as "involv[ing] dishonesty of purpose or intent to deceive." 721 S.W.2d at 273 (quoting *Archer v. Griffith*, 390 S.W.2d 735, 740 (Tex. 1964)).

Actions against persons other than owners and subscribers.   Tex. Bus. Corp. Act art. 2.21 and PJC 108.3 apply in actions based on a contractual obligation brought against holders of shares, owners of beneficial interests in shares, subscribers whose subscriptions have been accepted, their affiliates, and the affiliates of the corporation. For such actions brought against persons or entities other than holders, owners, subscribers, or affiliates, use the instruction shown below in the comment "Noncontract case."

Noncontract case.   For those cases not relating to or arising from a corporate obligation, use the following instruction:

Don Davis used [*name of corporation*] as a means of perpetrating a fraud, and holding only [*name of corporation*] responsible would result in injustice.

"Fraud" is the breach of some legal or equitable duty which, irrespective of moral guilt, the law declares fraudulent because of its tendency to deceive others, to violate confidence, or to injure public interests.

This instruction is derived from *Castleberry*, 721 S.W.2d at 271–73. By its terms, the restrictions of Tex. Bus. Corp. Act art. 2.21(A)(2) do not apply in a noncontract case. *See Farr*, 810 S.W.2d at 296.

"[C]onstructive fraud, not intentional fraud, is the standard for disregarding the corporate fiction on the basis of a sham to perpetrate a fraud." *Castleberry*, 721 S.W.2d at 273. The definition of "fraud" in the instruction is of constructive fraud and is taken from *Castleberry*, 721 S.W.2d at 273 (quoting *Archer*, 390 S.W.2d at 740). *See also Seaside Industries, Inc. v. Cooper*, 766 S.W.2d 566, 568 (Tex. App.—Dallas 1989, no writ).

"Injustice."   No Texas case has stated whether *injustice* must be defined in cases of the type covered by this instruction. For a case discussing the term *injustice* in the context of piercing the corporate veil, see *Mancorp, Inc. v. Culpepper*, 836 S.W.2d 844 (Tex. App.—Houston [1st Dist.] 1992), *on remand from* 802 S.W.2d 226 (Tex. 1990).

Actions brought before September 1, 1997.   Tex. Bus. Corp. Act art. 2.21 was amended in 1997 as follows:

1. The list of persons or entities protected from liability (except for actual fraud) was expanded to include "affiliates"; Tex. Bus. Corp. Act art. 2.21;

2. Not only contractual obligations of the corporation but "matters relating to or arising from contractual obligations" were excluded as grounds for disregarding the corporate fiction unless actual fraud was proved; Tex. Bus. Corp. Act art. 2.21(A)(2); and

3. Failure of the corporation to observe a corporate formality is no longer a ground for piercing the corporate veil in any case, not just contract cases. Tex. Bus. Corp. Act art. 2.21(A)(3).

These amendments affect all corporations, regardless of the date of formation or incorporation, but do *not* affect actions or proceedings commenced before September 1, 1997. Act of May 13, 1997, 75th Leg., R.S., ch. 375, § 125, 1997 Tex. Gen. Laws 1516, 1610. For an action or proceeding governed by the prior law, amend the charge language accordingly. See also State Bar of Texas, *Texas Pattern Jury Charges—Business, Consumer & Employment* (1997).

PJC 108.4   Instruction on Evasion of Existing Legal Obligation

Don Davis used [*name of corporation*] as a means of evading an existing legal obligation for the purpose of perpetrating and did perpetrate an actual fraud on *Paul Payne* primarily for the direct personal benefit of *Don Davis*.

[*or*]

COMMENT

When to use.   PJC 108.4 should be used as an instruction accompanying the question in PJC 108.1 if it is alleged that a corporation has been used by another person or entity to evade an existing legal obligation in a case relating to or arising from a contractual obligation. See comment below, "Noncontract case," for charge language to be used in other cases.

Use of "or."   If used with other instructions (see PJCs 108 2–,3 and .5–.7), PJC 108.4 must be followed by the word *or*, because a finding of any one of the theories for disregarding the corporate fiction defined in the instructions would support an affirmative answer to the question.

Source of instruction.   PJC 108.4 is based on the supreme court's discussion of the theories for disregarding the corporate fiction in *Castleberry v. Branscum*, 721 S.W.2d 270, 271–73 (Tex. 1986). The language of *Castleberry* has been modified to reflect the enactment of Tex. Bus. Corp. Act Ann. art. 2.21(A) (Vernon Supp. 1998), which eliminated constructive fraud and the failure to observe corporate formalities as considerations for piercing the corporate veil in contract-based claims. *See Farr v. Sun World Savings Ass'n*, 810 S.W.2d 294, 296 (Tex. App.—El Paso 1991, no writ).

"Actual fraud."   The term *actual fraud* appearing in Tex. Bus. Corp. Act art. 2.21(A) is not defined in the statute. In *Castleberry*, the supreme court defined actual fraud in the context of piercing the corporate veil as "involv[ing] dishonesty of purpose or intent to deceive." 721 S.W.2d at 273 (quoting *Archer v. Griffith*, 390 S.W.2d 735, 740 (Tex. 1964)).

Actions against persons other than owners and subscribers.   Tex. Bus. Corp. Act art. 2.21 and PJC 108.4 apply in actions based on a contractual obligation brought against holders of shares, owners of beneficial interests in shares, subscribers whose subscriptions have been accepted, their affiliates, and the affiliates of the corporation. For such actions brought against persons or entities other than holders, owners, subscribers, or affiliates, use the instruction shown below in the comment "Noncontract case."

Noncontract case.   For those cases not relating to or arising from a corporate obligation, use the following instruction:

> *Don Davis* used [*name of corporation*] as a means of evading an existing legal obligation and holding only [*name of corporation*] responsible would result in injustice.

This instruction is derived from *Castleberry*, 721 S.W.2d at 271–73. By its terms, the restrictions of Tex. Bus. Corp. Act art. 2.21(A)(2) do not apply in a noncontract case. *See Farr*, 810 S.W.2d at 296.

"Injustice." No Texas case has stated whether *injustice* must be defined in cases of the type covered by this instruction. For a case discussing the term *injustice* in the context of piercing the corporate veil, see *Mancorp, Inc. v. Culpepper*, 836 S.W.2d 844 (Tex. App.— Houston [1st Dist.] 1992), *on remand from* 802 S.W.2d 226 (Tex. 1990).

Actions brought before September 1, 1997. Tex. Bus. Corp. Act art. 2.21 was amended in 1997 as follows:

1. The list of persons or entities protected from liability (except for actual fraud) was expanded to include "affiliates"; Tex. Bus. Corp. Act art. 2.21;

2. Not only contractual obligations of the corporation but "matters relating to or arising from contractual obligations" were excluded as grounds for disregarding the corporate fiction unless actual fraud was proved; Tex. Bus. Corp. Act art. 2.21(A)(2); and

3. Failure of the corporation to observe a corporate formality is no longer a ground for piercing the corporate veil in any case, not just contract cases. Tex. Bus. Corp. Act art. 2.21(A)(3).

These amendments affect all corporations, regardless of the date of formation or incorporation, but do *not* affect actions or proceedings commenced before September 1, 1997. Act of May 13, 1997, 75th Leg., R.S., ch. 375, § 125, 1997 Tex. Gen. Laws 1516, 1610. For an action or proceeding governed by the prior law, amend the charge language accordingly. See also State Bar of Texas, *Texas Pattern Jury Charges—Business, Consumer & Employment* (1997).

PJC 108.5   Instruction on Circumvention of a Statute

Don Davis used [*name of corporation*] to circumvent a statute for the purpose of perpetrating and did perpetrate an actual fraud on *Paul Payne* primarily for the direct personal benefit of *Don Davis*.

[*or*]

COMMENT

When to use.   PJC 108.5 should be used as an instruction accompanying the question in PJC 108.1 if it is alleged that a corporation has been used by another person or entity to circumvent a statute in a case relating to or arising from a contractual obligation. See comment below, "Noncontract case," for charge language to be used in other cases.

Use of "or."   If used with other instructions (see PJCs 108.2–.4 and .6–.7), PJC 108.5 must be followed by the word *or*, because a finding of any one of the theories for disregarding the corporate fiction defined in the instructions would support an affirmative answer to the question.

Source of instruction.   PJC 108.5 is based on the supreme court's discussion of the theories for disregarding the corporate fiction in *Castleberry v. Branscum*, 721 S.W.2d 270, 271–73 (Tex. 1986). The language of *Castleberry* has been modified to reflect the enactment of Tex. Bus. Corp. Act Ann. art. 2.21(A) (Vernon Supp. 1998), which eliminated constructive fraud and the failure to observe corporate formalities as considerations for piercing the corporate veil in contract-based claims. *See Farr v. Sun World Savings Ass'n*, 810 S.W.2d 294, 296 (Tex. App.—El Paso 1991, no writ).

"Actual fraud."   The term *actual fraud* appearing in Tex. Bus. Corp. Act art. 2.21(A) is not defined in the statute. In *Castleberry*, the supreme court defined actual fraud in the context of piercing the corporate veil as "involv[ing] dishonesty of purpose or intent to deceive." 721 S.W.2d at 273 (quoting *Archer v. Griffith*, 390 S.W.2d 735, 740 (Tex. 1964)).

Actions against persons other than owners and subscribers.   Tex. Bus. Corp. Act art. 2.21 and PJC 108.5 apply in actions based on a contractual obligation brought against holders of shares, owners of beneficial interests in shares, subscribers whose subscriptions have been accepted, their affiliates, and the affiliates of the corporation. For such actions brought against persons or entities other than holders, owners, subscribers, or affiliates, use the instruction shown below in the comment "Noncontract case."

Noncontract case.   For those cases not relating to or arising from a corporate obligation, use the following instruction:

> *Don Davis* used [*name of corporation*] as a means of circumventing a statute, and holding only [*name of corporation*] responsible would result in injustice.

This instruction is derived from *Castleberry*, 721 S.W.2d at 271–73. By its terms, the restrictions of Tex. Bus. Corp. Act art. 2.21(A)(2) do not apply in a noncontract case. *See Farr*, 810 S.W.2d at 296.

"Injustice." No Texas case has stated whether *injustice* must be defined in cases of the type covered by this instruction. For a case discussing the term *injustice* in the context of piercing the corporate veil, see *Mancorp, Inc. v. Culpepper*, 836 S.W.2d 844 (Tex. App.—Houston [1st Dist.] 1992), *on remand from* 802 S.W.2d 226 (Tex. 1990).

Actions brought before September 1, 1997. Tex. Bus. Corp. Act art. 2.21 was amended in 1997 as follows:

1. The list of persons or entities protected from liability (except for actual fraud) was expanded to include "affiliates"; Tex. Bus. Corp. Act art. 2.21;

2. Not only contractual obligations of the corporation but "matters relating to or arising from contractual obligations" were excluded as grounds for disregarding the corporate fiction unless actual fraud was proved; Tex. Bus. Corp. Act art. 2.21(A)(2); and

3. Failure of the corporation to observe a corporate formality is no longer a ground for piercing the corporate veil in any case, not just contract cases. Tex. Bus. Corp. Act art. 2.21(A)(3).

These amendments affect all corporations, regardless of the date of formation or incorporation, but do *not* affect actions or proceedings commenced before September 1, 1997. Act of May 13, 1997, 75th Leg., R.S., ch. 375, § 125, 1997 Tex. Gen. Laws 1516, 1610. For an action or proceeding governed by the prior law, amend the charge language accordingly. See also State Bar of Texas, *Texas Pattern Jury Charges—Business, Consumer & Employment* (1997).

PJC 108.6   Instruction on Protection of Crime or Justification of Wrong

Don Davis used [*name of corporation*] to protect a crime or to justify a wrong for the purpose of perpetrating and did perpetrate an actual fraud on *Paul Payne* primarily for the direct personal benefit of *Don Davis*.

[*or*]

COMMENT

When to use.   PJC 108.6 should be used as an instruction accompanying the question in PJC 108.1 if it is alleged that a corporation has been used by another person or entity to protect a crime or to justify a wrong in a case relating to or arising from a contractual obligation. See comment below, "Noncontract case," for charge language to be used in other cases.

Use of "or."   If used with other instructions (see PJCs 108.2–.5 and .7), PJC 108.6 must be followed by the word *or*, because a finding of any one of the theories for disregarding the corporate fiction defined in the instructions would support an affirmative answer to the question.

Source of instruction.   PJC 108.6 is based on the supreme court's discussion of the theories for disregarding the corporate fiction in *Castleberry v. Branscum*, 721 S.W.2d 270, 271–73 (Tex. 1986). The language of *Castleberry* has been modified to reflect the enactment of Tex. Bus. Corp. Act Ann. art. 2.21(A) (Vernon Supp. 1998), which eliminated constructive fraud and the failure to observe corporate formalities as considerations for piercing the corporate veil in contract-based claims. *See Farr v. Sun World Savings Ass'n*, 810 S.W.2d 294, 296 (Tex. App.—El Paso 1991, no writ).

"Actual fraud."   The term *actual fraud* appearing in Tex. Bus. Corp. Act art. 2.21(A) is not defined in the statute. In *Castleberry*, the supreme court defined actual fraud in the context of piercing the corporate veil as "involv[ing] dishonesty of purpose or intent to deceive." 721 S.W.2d at 273 (quoting *Archer v. Griffith*, 390 S.W.2d 735, 740 (Tex. 1964)).

"Protection of crime."   "Protection of crime" is one of the grounds given by the supreme court in *Castleberry* for disregarding the corporate fiction. This phrase appears to include but not be limited to "perpetration of crime." Its scope includes, therefore, not only those situations where the party commits a crime, but also situations where a crime has been abetted or the criminal has otherwise received assistance. The practitioner should amend this question as appropriate to reflect the facts of the case.

Actions against persons other than owners and subscribers.   Tex. Bus. Corp. Act art. 2.21 and PJC 108.6 apply in actions based on a contractual obligation brought against holders of shares, owners of beneficial interests in shares, subscribers whose subscriptions have been accepted, their affiliates, and the affilates of the corporation. For such actions brought against persons or entities other than holders, owners, subscribers, or affiliates, use the instruction shown below in the comment "Noncontract case."

Noncontract case. For those cases not relating to or arising from a corporate obligation, use the following instruction:

> *Don Davis* used [*name of corporation*] to protect a crime or to justify a wrong and holding only [*name of corporation*] responsible would result in injustice.

This instruction is derived from *Castleberry*, 721 S.W.2d at 271–73. By its terms, the restrictions of Tex. Bus. Corp. Act art. 2.21(A)(2) do not apply in a noncontract case. *See Farr*, 810 S.W.2d at 296.

"Injustice." No Texas case has stated whether *injustice* must be defined in cases of the type covered by this instruction. For a case discussing the term *injustice* in the context of piercing the corporate veil, see *Mancorp, Inc. v. Culpepper*, 836 S.W.2d 844 (Tex. App.— Houston [1st Dist.] 1992), *on remand from* 802 S.W.2d 226 (Tex. 1990).

Actions brought before September 1, 1997. Tex. Bus. Corp. Act art. 2.21 was amended in 1997 as follows:

1. The list of persons or entities protected from liability (except for actual fraud) was expanded to include "affiliates"; Tex. Bus. Corp. Act art. 2.21;

2. Not only contractual obligations of the corporation but "matters relating to or arising from contractual obligations" were excluded as grounds for disregarding the corporate fiction unless actual fraud was proved; Tex. Bus. Corp. Act art. 2.21(A)(2); and

3. Failure of the corporation to observe a corporate formality is no longer a ground for piercing the corporate veil in any case, not just contract cases. Tex. Bus. Corp. Act art. 2.21(A)(3).

These amendments affect all corporations, regardless of the date of formation or incorporation, but do *not* affect actions or proceedings commenced before September 1, 1997. Act of May 13, 1997, 75th Leg., R.S., ch. 375, § 125, 1997 Tex. Gen. Laws 1516, 1610. For an action or proceeding governed by the prior law, amend the charge language accordingly. See also State Bar of Texas, *Texas Pattern Jury Charges—Business, Consumer & Employment* (1997).

PJC 108.7   Instruction on Monopoly

Don Davis used [*name of corporation*] to achieve a monopoly for the purpose of perpetrating and did perpetrate an actual fraud on *Paul Payne* primarily for the direct personal benefit of *Don Davis*.

[*or*]

COMMENT

When to use.   PJC 108.7 should be used as an instruction accompanying the question in PJC 108.1 if it is alleged that a corporation has been used by another person or entity to achieve or perpetrate a monopoly in a case relating to or arising from a contractual obligation. See comment below, "Noncontract case," for charge language to be used in other cases.

Use of "or."   If used with other instructions (see PJCs 108.2–.6), PJC 108.7 must be followed by the word *or*, because a finding of any one of the theories for disregarding the corporate fiction defined in the instructions would support an affirmative answer to the question.

Source of instruction.   PJC 108.7 is based on the supreme court's discussion of the theories for disregarding the corporate fiction in *Castleberry v. Branscum*, 721 S.W.2d 270, 271–73 (Tex. 1986). The language of *Castleberry* has been modified to reflect the enactment of Tex. Bus. Corp. Act Ann. art. 2.21(A) (Vernon Supp. 1998), which eliminated constructive fraud and the failure to observe corporate formalities as considerations for piercing the corporate veil in contract-based claims. *See Farr v. Sun World Savings Ass'n*, 810 S.W.2d 294, 296 (Tex. App.—El Paso 1991, no writ).

"Actual fraud."   The term *actual fraud* appearing in Tex. Bus. Corp. Act art. 2.21(A) is not defined in the statute. In *Castleberry*, the supreme court defined actual fraud in the context of piercing the corporate veil as "involv[ing] dishonesty of purpose or intent to deceive." 721 S.W.2d at 273 (quoting *Archer v. Griffith*, 390 S.W.2d 735, 740 (Tex. 1964)).

Actions against persons other than owners and subscribers.   Tex. Bus. Corp. Act art. 2.21 and PJC 108.7 apply in actions based on a contractual obligation brought against holders of shares, owners of beneficial interests in shares, subscribers whose subscriptions have been accepted, their affiliates, and the affiliates of the corporation. For such actions brought against persons or entities other than holders, owners, subscribers, or affiliates, use the instruction shown below in the comment "Noncontract case."

Noncontract case.   For those cases not relating to or arising from a corporate obligation, use the following instruction:

Don Davis used [*name of corporation*] to achieve or perpetrate a monopoly and holding only [*name of corporation*] liable would result in injustice.

This instruction is derived from *Castleberry*, 721 S.W.2d at 271–73. By its terms, the restrictions of Tex. Bus. Corp. Act art. 2.21(A)(2) do not apply in a noncontract case. *See Farr*, 810 S.W.2d at 296.

"Injustice."   No Texas case has stated whether *injustice* must be defined in cases of the type covered by this instruction. For a case discussing the term *injustice* in the context of piercing the corporate veil, see *Mancorp, Inc. v. Culpepper*, 836 S.W.2d 844 (Tex. App.— Houston [1st Dist.] 1992), *on remand from* 802 S.W.2d 226 (Tex. 1990).

Actions brought before September 1, 1997.   Tex. Bus. Corp. Act art. 2.21 was amended in 1997 as follows:

1. The list of persons or entities protected from liability (except for actual fraud) was expanded to include "affiliates"; Tex. Bus. Corp. Act art. 2.21;

2. Not only contractual obligations of the corporation but "matters relating to or arising from contractual obligations" were excluded as grounds for disregarding the corporate fiction unless actual fraud was proved; Tex. Bus. Corp. Act art. 2.21(A)(2); and

3. Failure of the corporation to observe a corporate formality is no longer a ground for piercing the corporate veil in any case, not just contract cases. Tex. Bus. Corp. Act art. 2.21(A)(3).

These amendments affect all corporations, regardless of the date of formation or incorporation, but do *not* affect actions or proceedings commenced before September 1, 1997. Act of May 13, 1997, 75th Leg., R.S., ch. 375, § 125, 1997 Tex. Gen. Laws 1516, 1610. For an action or proceeding governed by the prior law, amend the charge language accordingly. See also State Bar of Texas, *Texas Pattern Jury Charges—Business, Consumer & Employment* (1997).

CHAPTER 109   CIVIL CONSPIRACY

PJC 109.1   Question and Instruction on Conspiracy

QUESTION _____

> *[Conditioned on findings of a tort or statutory violation that*
> *proximately caused damages.]*

Was *Connie Conspirator* part of a conspiracy that damaged *Paul Payne*?

   To be part of a conspiracy, *Connie Conspirator* and another person or persons must have had knowledge of, agreed to, and intended a common objective or course of action that resulted in the damages to *Paul Payne*. One or more persons involved in the conspiracy must have performed some act or acts to further the conspiracy.

Answer: _____

COMMENT

   When to use.   PJC 109.1 submits the question of conspiracy to accomplish the unlawful objective of harming another by committing a tort or statutory violation. See comment below, "Conspiracy to accomplish lawful objective by unlawful means," for the situation involving a conspiracy to employ an unlawful means to accomplish a lawful objective. Civil conspiracy to unlawfully harm another is a derivative tort. Liability is dependent on participation in some underlying tort or statutory violation. It is a means for imposing joint and several liability on persons in addition to the actual perpetrator(s) of the underlying tort.

   Source of question and instruction.   A civil conspiracy is a combination by two or more persons to accomplish an unlawful purpose or to accomplish a lawful purpose by unlawful means. The elements of civil conspiracy have been stated as (1) two or more persons; (2) an object to be accomplished; (3) a meeting of the minds on the object or course of action; (4) one or more unlawful, overt acts; and (5) damages as the proximate result. *Massey v. Armco Steel Co.*, 652 S.W.2d 932, 934 (Tex. 1983); *see also Schlumberger Well Surveying Corp. v. Nortex Oil & Gas Corp.*, 435 S.W.2d 854, 856 (Tex. 1968); *Triplex Communications, Inc. v. Riley*, 900 S.W.2d 716, 719–20 (Tex. 1995).

   Knowledge, intent, and agreement.   To be liable for conspiracy, a party must be shown to have intended to do more than engage in the conduct that resulted in the injury. It must be shown that from the inception of the combination or agreement the party intended to cause the injury or was aware of the harm likely to result from the wrongful conduct. *Triplex Communications, Inc.*, 900 S.W.2d at 720; *Great National Life Insurance Co. v. Chapa*, 377 S.W.2d 632, 635 (Tex. 1964). Thus, a party must be shown to have known the object and purpose of the conspiracy and to have had a meeting of the minds with the other conspirators to accomplish that object and purpose, intending to bring about the resulting injury. *Nortex Oil & Gas Corp.*, 435 S.W.2d at 857.

Unlawful act. A defendant's liability for conspiracy is based on participation in the underlying tort that would have been actionable against at least one of the conspirators individually. *Tilton v. Marshall*, 925 S.W.2d 672, 681 (Tex. 1996); *International Bankers Life Insurance Co. v. Holloway*, 368 S.W.2d 567, 581 (Tex. 1963). An act or declaration by a conspirator not in pursuance of the common objective is not actionable against coconspirators. *Chapa*, 377 S.W.2d at 635. Likewise, an improper motive in performing a lawful action will not support liability for conspiracy. *Kingsbery v. Phillips Petroleum Co.*, 315 S.W.2d 561, 576 (Tex. Civ. App.—Austin 1958, writ ref'd n.r.e.). The injury must have been caused by the tort or statutory violation that the conspirator agreed with the perpetrator to bring about while intending the resulting harm. *Triplex Communications, Inc.*, 900 S.W.2d at 720; *Nortex Oil & Gas Corp.*, 435 S.W.2d at 857. Once a civil conspiracy is found, each coconspirator is responsible for the actions of any coconspirator in furtherance of the conspiracy. Thus, each element of the underlying tort or violation is imputed to each participant. *Akin v. Dahl*, 661 S.W.2d 917, 921 (Tex. 1983).

Conspiracy to accomplish lawful objective by unlawful means. PJC 109.1 submits the proper question if a court or jury has established the existence of an unlawful objective, that is, a tort or statutory violation. The supreme court's opinions regarding conspiracy also define a conspiracy cause of action arising when the conspirators pursue a lawful objective by unlawful means. *Triplex Communications, Inc.*, 900 S.W.2d at 719–20; *Massey*, 652 S.W.2d at 934; *Chapa*, 377 S.W.2d at 635; *Berry v. Golden Light Coffee Co.*, 327 S.W.2d 436, 438 (Tex. 1959); *State v. Standard Oil Co.*, 107 S.W.2d 550, 559 (Tex. 1937). The Committee believes PJC 109.1 can be used to submit either theory, but may need modification in some instances depending on the facts of the case.

Damages. The damages recoverable in an action for civil conspiracy are those damages resulting from the commission of the wrong, not the conspiratorial agreement. *Triplex Communications, Inc.*, 900 S.W.2d at 720; *Carroll v. Timmers Chevrolet, Inc.*, 592 S.W.2d 922, 925 (Tex. 1979). Therefore, the Committee recommends that PJC 109.1 be submitted after, and conditioned on, an affirmative finding of damages caused by the underlying tort or statutory violation.

Exemplary damages. An affirmative finding of an underlying cause of action that includes a finding sufficient to impose exemplary damages may be imputed to all participants in the conspiracy on an affirmative conspiracy finding. *Akin*, 661 S.W.2d at 921. Exemplary damages questions may then be submitted conditioned on an affirmative finding to PJC 109.1. See PJCs 110.33 and .34.

PJC 110.1   Predicate—Instruction Conditioning Damages Question on Liability

If your answer to Question _____ [*insert number of appropriate liability question*] is "Yes," then answer the following question. Otherwise, do not answer the following question.

COMMENT

When to use.   PJC 110.1 is used to condition answers to damages questions. The damages questions in this chapter assume liability in the question, so this predicate should always precede those questions. The comments following damages questions in this chapter refer to the corresponding liability questions in other chapters.

PJC 110.2   **Question on Contract Damages**

[Insert predicate, PJC 110.1.]

QUESTION _____

What sum of money, if any, if paid now in cash, would fairly and reasonably compensate *Paul Payne* for *his* damages, if any, that resulted from such failure to comply?

Consider the following elements of damages, if any, and none other.

[Insert appropriate instructions. See samples in PJC 110.3
and instructions in PJC 110.4.]

Do not add any amount for interest on damages, if any.

Answer in dollars and cents for damages, if any, that—

were sustained in the past;   Answer: _____

in reasonable probability will
be sustained in the future.   Answer: _____

COMMENT

When to use.   PJC 110.2 should be predicated on a "Yes" answer to PJC 101.2 and may be adapted for use in most breach-of-contract cases by the addition of appropriate instructions setting out legally available measures of damages. See PJCs 110.3-.4. If only one measure of damages is supported by the pleadings and proof, the measure may be incorporated into the question.

Instruction required.   PJC 110.2 *may not* be submitted without an instruction on the appropriate measure of damages. *Jackson v. Fontaine's Clinics, Inc.*, 499 S.W.2d 87, 90 (Tex. 1973). See PJCs 110.3-.4 for sample instructions.

Causation.   The phrase *resulted from* is derived from *McKnight v. Hill & Hill Exterminators*, 689 S.W.2d 206, 209 (Tex. 1985).

Alternative submissions.   If separate answers for each measure of damages are desired, the following instruction should be given in lieu of the one above, and an answer blank will then follow each damages instruction.

Answer separately in dollars and cents, if any, for each of the following elements of damages.

Parallel theories.   If the breach-of-contract cause of action is only one of several theories of recovery submitted in the charge and any theory has a different legal measure of damages to be applied to a factually similar claim for damages, a separate damages question for each theory may be submitted and the following additional instruction may be included earlier in the charge:

> If you answer questions about damages, answer each question separately. Do not increase or reduce the amount in one answer because of the instructions in or your answers to any other questions about damages. Do not speculate about what any party's ultimate recovery may or may not be. Any recovery will be determined by the court when it applies the law to your answers at the time of judgment.

Prejudgment interest.   Instructing the jury not to add interest is suggested because prejudgment interest, if recoverable, will be calculated by the court at the time of judgment. If interest paid on an obligation is claimed as an element of damages, it may be necessary to modify the instruction on interest.

PJC 110.3 Sample Instructions on Direct and Incidental Damages— Contracts

Explanatory note: Damages instructions in contract actions are often necessarily fact-specific. Unlike most other form instructions in this volume, therefore, the following sample instructions are illustrative only, using a hypothetical situation to give a few examples of how instructions may be worded to submit various legal measures of damages for use in connection with the contract damages question, PJC 110.2.

Sample A—Loss of the benefit of the bargain

> The difference, if any, between the value of the paint job agreed to by the parties and the value of the paint job performed by *Don Davis*. The difference in value, if any, shall be determined at the time and place the paint job was performed.

Sample B—Remedial damages

> The reasonable and necessary cost to repaint *Paul Payne*'s truck.

Sample C—Loss of contractual profit

> The difference between the agreed price and the cost *Paul Payne* would have incurred in painting the truck.

Sample D—Loss of contractual profit plus expenses incurred before breach

> The amount *Don Davis* agreed to pay *Paul Payne* less the expenses *Paul Payne* saved by not completing the paint job.

Sample E—Damages after mitigation

> The difference between the amount paid by *Paul Payne* to *John Jones* for painting the truck and the amount *Paul Payne* had agreed to pay *Don Davis* for that work.

Sample F—Mitigation expenses

> Reasonable and necessary expenses incurred in attempting to have the truck repainted.

Sample G—Incidental damages

> Reasonable and necessary costs to store *Paul Payne*'s tools while the truck was being repainted.

COMMENT

When to use.   See explanatory note above. Because damages instructions in contract suits are necessarily fact-specific, no true "pattern" instructions are given—only samples of some measures of general damages available in contract actions. This list is not exhaustive. The samples are illustrative only, adapted to a hypothetical fact situation, and must be rewritten to fit the particular damages raised by the pleadings and proof and recoverable under a legally accepted theory. The instructions should be drafted in an attempt to make the plaintiff factually whole but not to put the plaintiff in a better position than he would have been in had the defendant fully performed the contract. *See Osoba v. Bassichis*, 679 S.W.2d 119, 122 (Tex. App.—Houston [14th Dist.] 1984, writ ref'd n.r.e.). For a comprehensive discussion of the theories of contract damages, see *Restatement (Second) of Contracts* §§ 346–356 (1981).

Measures generally alternative.   The measures outlined here are generally alternatives, although some, particularly incidental damages, may be available in addition to one of the other measures, as may consequential damages (see PJC 110.4).

Direct damages.   Since *Hadley v. Baxendale*, 9 Exch. 341, 156 Eng. Rep. 145 (1854), contract damages have been divided into two categories: direct and consequential. *See Mead v. Johnson Group, Inc.*, 615 S.W.2d 685 (Tex. 1981). Direct damages

> are those which naturally and necessarily flow from a wrongful act, are so usual an accompaniment of the kind of breach alleged that the mere allegation of the breach gives sufficient notice, and are conclusively presumed to have been foreseen or contemplated by the party as a consequence of his breach of contract.

Hess Die Mold, Inc. v. American Plasti-Plate Corp., 653 S.W.2d 927, 929 (Tex. App.—Tyler 1983, no writ). The general or direct nature of a type of damages is a determination of law to be made by the court. No question should be submitted concerning the foreseeability of direct damages; even if the evidence shows that was not factually foreseeable to the parties, recovery is permitted if the damages are properly characterized by the court as direct rather than consequential. *American Bank v. Thompson*, 660 S.W.2d 831, 834 (Tex. App.—Waco 1983, writ ref'd n.r.e.).

Even damages usually not considered recoverable may be deemed direct damages if they stem as a matter of law from the breach of the contract in question. *Cactus Utility Co. v. Larson*, 709 S.W.2d 709, 716 (Tex. App.—Corpus Christi 1986), *rev'd in part on other grounds*, 730 S.W.2d 640 (Tex. 1987) (expert witness fee, for accountant, recoverable as direct damages for breach of agreement to provide accounting services).

Benefit of the bargain and remedial damages.   Whether difference in value or cost of repair is the proper measure of damages depends on the particular facts and circumstances in each case. *Fidelity & Deposit Co. of Maryland v. Stool*, 607 S.W.2d 17, 21 (Tex. Civ. App.—Tyler 1980, no writ); *Smith v. Kinslow*, 598 S.W.2d 910 (Tex. Civ. App.—Dallas 1980, no writ); *P.G. Lake, Inc. v. Sheffield*, 438 S.W.2d 952 (Tex. Civ. App.—Tyler 1969, writ ref'd n.r.e.).

Loss of contractual profit.   Lost profits from collateral contracts are generally classi-
fied as consequential damages. Profits lost from the actual contract in question, however,
are direct damages for the seller. *Community Development Service, Inc. v. Replacement
Parts Manufacturing, Inc.*, 679 S.W.2d 721, 725 (Tex. App.—Houston [1st Dist.] 1984, no
writ).

Lost profit plus capital expenditures.   If the plaintiff has incurred expenses in preparation or performance and reasonably expected to recoup that investment as well as make a
profit, this lost profit plus capital expenditures may be an appropriate measure of damages.
Houston Chronicle Publishing Co. v. McNair Trucklease, Inc., 519 S.W.2d 924, 929-31
(Tex. Civ. App.—Houston [1st Dist.] 1975, writ ref'd n.r.e.).

Reliance damages.   The plaintiff may elect to recover expenditures made in preparation or performance instead of claiming lost benefit of the bargain or profit damages. If the
plaintiff makes this election because he would have lost money had the contract been completed and the defendant proves the amount of loss avoided as a result of the breach, the jury
should also be instructed to deduct those prospective losses from the reliance damages.
Mistletoe Express Service v. Locke, 762 S.W.2d 637 (Tex. App.—Texarkana 1988, no writ).

Mitigation damages.   Although normally raised defensively, the reasonable expenses
of mitigating an economic loss are recoverable as actual damages for breach of contract.
Hycel, Inc. v. Wittstruck, 690 S.W.2d 914, 924 (Tex. App.—Waco 1985, writ dism'd).

Incidental damages.   A variety of expenditures and other incidental damages may be
recoverable as direct damages, depending on the particular facts and circumstances of each
case. *Cactus Utility Co.*, 709 S.W.2d at 716; *LaChance v. Hollenbeck*, 695 S.W.2d 618
(Tex. App.—Austin 1985, writ ref'd n.r.e.); *Anderson Development Corp. v. Coastal States
Crude Gathering Co.*, 543 S.W.2d 402 (Tex. Civ. App.—Houston [14th Dist.] 1976, writ
ref'd n.r.e.). Whether any particular incidental damages are characterized as direct or consequential is, as discussed above, a question for the court. If a claimed expense is deemed
consequential, it should be submitted as such, using the form in PJC 110.4.

UCC cases.   If the contract is for the sale of goods, the damages instructions should be
drafted to incorporate the appropriate damages provisions in Tex. Bus. & Com. Code Ann.
§§ 2.701-.724 (Tex. UCC) (Vernon 1994). The following examples are illustrative only,
using only a few damages provisions in the Uniform Commercial Code.

Sample A—(§ 2.708) Seller's damages for nonacceptance

> The difference between the market price of the goods at the
> time and place *Paul Payne* was to tender them to *Don Davis*
> and the unpaid contract price.

Sample B—(§ 2.710) Seller's incidental damages

> Commercially reasonable charges, expenses, or commis-
> sions *Paul Payne* incurred in stopping delivery of goods.

Commercially reasonable charges *Paul Payne* incurred for transportation, care, and custody of goods in connection with their return or resale.

Sample C—(§ 2.713) Buyer's damages for nondelivery

The difference between the market price at the time *Paul Payne* learned of *Don Davis*'s failure to comply and the contract price.

PJC 110.4   Instructions on Consequential Damages—Contracts

Lost profits that were a natural, probable, and foreseeable consequence of *Don Davis*'s failure to comply.

Damage to credit reputation that was a natural, probable, and foreseeable consequence of *Don Davis*'s failure to comply.

COMMENT

When to use.   PJC 110.4, with its added element of foreseeability, should be used for recoverable elements of consequential damages that do not, as a matter of law, directly flow from the defendant's breach. See PJC 110.3 Comment.

Foreseeability.   Consequential damages may be recovered only if proved to be the "natural, probable, and foreseeable consequence" of the defendant's breach. *Mead v. Johnson Group, Inc.*, 615 S.W.2d 685, 687 (Tex. 1981). The instruction does not state to whom the damage must be foreseeable. In *Mead*, 615 S.W.2d at 687, the court indirectly gave conflicting answers to this question, recognizing both the rule in *Hadley v. Baxendale*, 9 Exch. 341, 156 Eng. Rep. 145 (1854) (both parties), and the rule in *Restatement (Second) of Contracts* § 365 (1981) (party in breach).

Caveat.   Damages usually characterized as consequential may be deemed direct if they are so directly related to the contract that they stem as a matter of law from the breach. Conversely, not all factually foreseeable damages are legally recoverable. *Myrtle Springs Reverted Independent School District v. Hogan*, 705 S.W.2d 707, 710 (Tex. App.—Texarkana 1985, writ ref'd n.r.e.), *cert. denied*, 107 S. Ct. 1350 (1987) (loss of earning capacity and mental anguish not recoverable for breach of teaching contract).

Lost profits.   If evidence of lost profits is merely speculative, no recovery is allowed as a matter of law, and this instruction should not be included in the damages question. If, however, there is some legally sufficient evidence, a fact question is raised. *Southwest Battery Corp. v. Owen*, 115 S.W.2d 1097, 1099 (Tex. 1938). The Committee has not found any cases holding that, once this "no evidence" threshold is passed, any additional instructions should be given concerning the quality or amount of evidence necessary to support the jury's findings.

UCC cases.   For transactions covered by article 2 of the Uniform Commercial Code, see Tex. Bus. & Com. Code Ann. § 2.715(b)(1) (Tex. UCC) (Vernon 1994) (buyer's consequential damages).

PJC 110.5   Question on Promissory Estoppel—Reliance Damages

[*Insert predicate, PJC 110.1.*]

QUESTION _____

What sum of money, if any, if paid now in cash, would fairly and reasonably compensate *Paul Payne* for *his* damages, if any, that resulted from *his* reliance on *Don Davis*'s promise?

Consider the following elements of damages, if any, and none other.

[*Insert appropriate instructions.*]

Answer in dollars and cents, if any.

Answer: _____

COMMENT

When to use.   PJC 110.5 and appropriate instructions tailored to the specific reliance damages alleged by the plaintiff should be submitted following the liability question for promissory estoppel. See PJC 101.41.

Reliance damages only.   In a claim based on promissory estoppel, the plaintiff is not entitled to recover expectancy damages or to receive the full benefit of the bargain. Only reliance damages are allowed. *Fretz Construction Co. v. Southern National Bank,* 626 S.W.2d 478, 483 (Tex. 1981); *Wheeler v. White,* 398 S.W.2d 93, 96–97 (Tex. 1965).

PJC 110.6   Question on Quantum Meruit Recovery

[*Insert predicate, PJC 110.1.*]

QUESTION _____

What is the reasonable value of such compensable work at the time and place it was performed?

Answer in dollars and cents, if any.

Answer: _____

COMMENT

When to use.   PJC 110.6 submits the measure of recovery for quantum meruit. *Colbert v. Dallas Joint Stock Land Bank,* 150 S.W.2d 771, 776 (Tex. 1941) (ultimate question is reasonable value of work performed); *see, e.g., Texas Delta Upsilon Foundation v. Fehr,* 307 S.W.2d 124, 127 (Tex. Civ. App.—Austin 1957, writ ref'd n.r.e.); *Blalack v. Johnson,* 293 S.W.2d 811, 813 (Tex. Civ. App.—Texarkana 1956, no writ) (jury questions in these cases quoted with approval). The question must be predicated on an affirmative finding that the work is compensable under this theory. See PJC 101.42.

PJC 110.7   Defensive Instruction on Mitigation—Contract Damages

Do not include in your answer any amount that you find *Paul Payne* could have avoided by the exercise of reasonable care.

COMMENT

When to use.   If the evidence raises a question about the plaintiff's failure to mitigate damages after the defendant's actionable conduct, an instruction on mitigation should be included with the damages question. *Alexander & Alexander, Inc. v. Bacchus Industries, Inc.*, 754 S.W.2d 252, 253 (Tex. App.—El Paso 1988, writ denied); *Cook Consultants, Inc. v. Larson*, 700 S.W.2d 231, 238 (Tex. App.—Dallas 1985, writ ref'd n.r.e.).

Defendant's burden of proof.   The defendant must offer evidence showing not just the plaintiff's lack of care but also the amount by which the damages were increased by such failure to mitigate. *Cocke v. White*, 697 S.W.2d 739, 744 (Tex. App.—Corpus Christi 1985, writ ref'd n.r.e.); *R.A. Corbett Transport v. Oden*, 678 S.W.2d 172, 176 (Tex. App.—Tyler 1984, no writ); *Copenhaver v. Berryman*, 602 S.W.2d 540, 544 (Tex. Civ. App.—Corpus Christi 1980, writ ref'd n.r.e.).

DTPA and Insurance Code.   Several appellate opinions have cited the duty to mitigate as grounds for allowing DTPA consumers to recover mitigation expenses as actual damages. *Hycel, Inc. v. Wittstruck*, 690 S.W.2d 914, 924 (Tex. App.—Waco 1985, writ dism'd); *Orkin Exterminating Co. v. Lesassier*, 688 S.W.2d 651, 653 (Tex. App.—Beaumont 1985, no writ). At least three courts have allowed the duty to mitigate to be used defensively in DTPA and Insurance Code suits. *Pinson v. Red Arrow Freight Lines*, 801 S.W.2d 14 (Tex. App.—Austin 1990, no writ) (DTPA); *Alexander & Alexander, Inc.*, 754 S.W.2d at 253 (Insurance Code article 21.21); *Town East Ford Sales, Inc. v. Gray*, 730 S.W.2d 796 (Tex. App.—Dallas 1987, no writ) (DTPA).

Mitigation damages.   Mitigation may also be the basis for an affirmative recovery of damages for the plaintiff. See PJC 110.3.

UCC cases.   A buyer's recovery of consequential damages is limited to those "which could not reasonably be prevented by cover or otherwise." Tex. Bus. & Com. Code Ann. § 2.715(b)(1) (Tex. UCC) (Vernon 1994).

PJC 110.8   **Question and Instruction on Deceptive Trade Practice Damages**

[Insert predicate, PJC 110.1.]

QUESTION _____

What sum of money, if any, if paid now in cash, would fairly and reasonably compensate *Paul Payne* for *his* damages, if any, that resulted from such conduct?

Consider the following elements of damages, if any, and none other.

Answer separately in dollars and cents, if any, for each of the following:

[Insert appropriate instructions. See examples in PJCs 110.3 and .9.]

In answering questions about damages, answer each question separately. Do not increase or reduce the amount in one answer because of your answer to any other question about damages. Do not speculate about what any party's ultimate recovery may or may not be. Any recovery will be determined by the court when it applies the law to your answers at the time of judgment. Do not add any amount for interest on damages, if any.

COMMENT

When to use.   PJC 110.8 should be predicated on a "Yes" answer to PJC 102.1, .7, or .8, finding a violation of section 17.46(b) of the Texas Deceptive Trade Practices-Consumer Protection Act (Tex. Bus. & Com. Code Ann. §§ 17.41–.63 (Vernon 1987 & Supp. 1998)) (DTPA), a breach of warranty, or an unconscionable action. It may be adapted for use in most DTPA cases by the addition of appropriate instructions setting out legally available measures of damages. See PJCs 110.3, .9, and .10.

Instruction required.   Failure to instruct the jury on appropriate measures of damages is error. *Jackson v. Fontaine's Clinics, Inc.*, 499 S.W.2d 87 (Tex. 1973).

1995 amendments.   The 1995 amendments to the DTPA altered the grounds of recovery available to plaintiffs as well as the availability of exemplary and discretionary damages. See the Comments to PJCs 110.9–.11. The amendments apply to causes of action accruing on or after September 1, 1995, and all suits filed on or after September 1, 1996.

Alternative measures.   The DTPA permits the injured consumer to recover the greatest amount of actual damages caused by the wrongful conduct. Thus, the consumer may submit to the jury alternative measures of damages for the same loss and then elect after the verdict the recovery desired by waiving the surplus findings on damages. *Kish v. Van Note*,

692 S.W.2d 463, 466–67 (Tex. 1985). Similarly, if the DTPA claim is only one of several theories of recovery, each cause of action will have its own damages question inquiring about similar claims of damages.

Separating measures of damages.   PJC 110.8 should, typically, submit damages measures that separate both economic from noneconomic damages, and past from future damages. This separation is needed—

1. to allow the court to apply the proper standards for recovery of economic and mental anguish damages under DTPA § 17.50(b) (Supp. 1998);

2. to allow the court to apply the limits on recovery of exemplary damages based on economic and noneconomic damages as required by Tex. Civ. Prac. & Rem. Code Ann. § 41.008(b) (Vernon 1997); and

3. to allow calculation of prejudgment interest on damages in cases governed by *Cavnar v. Quality Control Parking, Inc.*, 696 S.W.2d 549 (Tex. 1985).

See PJC 110.9 for sample damages instructions.

Prejudgment interest.   Instructing the jury not to add interest is suggested because prejudgment interest, if recoverable, will be calculated by the court at the time of judgment. If interest paid on an obligation is claimed as an element of damages, it may be necessary to modify the instruction on interest. In cases involving wrongful death, personal injury, or property damage, prejudgment interest is governed by statute, which does not require separation of past and future damages. Tex. Fin. Code Ann. §§ 304.101–.108 (Vernon 1998). Cases not governed by the statute require separation. *Cavnar*, 696 S.W.2d 549.

PJC 110.9   Sample Instructions—Deceptive Trade Practice Damages

Explanatory note: Damages instructions in DTPA actions are necessarily fact-specific. Unlike most other form instructions in this volume, therefore, the following sample instructions are illustrative only, using a hypothetical situation to give a few examples of how instructions may be worded to submit various legal measures of damages for use in connection with the DTPA damages question, PJC 110.8.

Sample A—Loss of the benefit of the bargain

> The difference, if any, in the value of the paint job as it was received and the value it would have had if it had been as [*represented*] [*warranted*]. The difference in value, if any, shall be determined at the time and place the paint job was done.

Sample B—Out of pocket

> The difference, if any, in the value of the paint job as it was received and the price *Paul Payne* paid for it. The difference, if any, shall be determined at the time and place the paint job was done.

Sample C—Expenses

> The reasonable and necessary cost to repaint the truck.

> The reasonable and necessary interest expense that *Paul Payne* incurred on the loan *he* received to pay for the paint job.

Sample D—Loss of use

> [The reasonable and necessary expense incurred in renting a car.] [The reasonable rental value of a replacement vehicle.]

Sample E—Lost profits

> *Paul Payne*'s lost profits sustained in the past.

> *Paul Payne*'s lost profits that, in reasonable probability, *he* will sustain in the future.

Sample F—Lost time

> The reasonable value of the time spent by *Paul Payne* correcting or attempting to correct the problems with the paint job.

Sample G—Damage to credit

> Damage to *Paul Payne*'s credit reputation sustained in the past.

Damage to *Paul Payne*'s credit reputation that, in reasonable probability, *he* will sustain in the future.

Sample H—Medical care

Medical care in the past.

Medical care that, in reasonable probability, *Paul Payne* will sustain in the future.

Sample I—Loss of earning capacity

Loss of earning capacity sustained in the past.

Loss of earning capacity that, in reasonable probability, *Paul Payne* will sustain in the future.

Sample J—Mental anguish

Paul Payne's mental anguish sustained in the past.

Paul Payne's mental anguish that, in reasonable probability, *he* will sustain in the future.

COMMENT

When to use.   See explanatory note above. Because damages instructions in DTPA suits are necessarily fact-specific, no true "pattern" instructions are given—only samples of damages available in DTPA actions. This list is not exhaustive. The samples are illustrative only, adapted to a hypothetical fact situation, and must be rewritten to fit the particular damages raised by the pleadings and proof. Instructions on one or more measures of damages must be submitted with the DTPA damages question, PJC 110.8. In addition to the measures outlined above, any of the common-law measures of damages for breach of contract may be available to the plaintiff in a DTPA action. See PJC 110.3.

Instruction required.   Failure to instruct the jury on an appropriate measure of damages is error. *Jackson v. Fontaine's Clinics, Inc.*, 499 S.W.2d 87, 90 (Tex. 1973).

Separation of measures of damages.   Actual damages questions (as opposed to exemplary damages questions) should, typically, submit questions that separate both economic from noneconomic damages, and past from future damages. This separation is needed—

1. to allow the court to apply the proper standards for recovery of economic and mental anguish damages under Tex. Bus. & Com. Code Ann. § 17.50(b) (Vernon Supp. 1998) (DTPA);

2. to allow the court to apply the limits on recovery of exemplary damages based on economic and noneconomic damages as required by Tex. Civ. Prac. & Rem. Code Ann. § 41.008(b) (Vernon 1997); and

3. to allow calculation of prejudgment interest on damages in cases governed by *Cavnar v. Quality Control Parking, Inc.*, 696 S.W.2d 549 (Tex. 1985).

Available measures. Damages available to DTPA plaintiffs are those recoverable at common law. *Brown v. American Transfer & Storage Co.*, 601 S.W.2d 931, 939 (Tex. 1980). Traditional measures of damages for misrepresentation are the out-of-pocket and benefit-of-the-bargain measures, the first two samples listed above. *W.O. Bankston Nissan, Inc. v. Walters*, 754 S.W.2d 127 (Tex. 1988); *Leyendecker & Associates v. Wechter*, 683 S.W.2d 369, 373 (Tex. 1984). Cost of repair is another recognized measure. *Nobility Homes of Texas, Inc. v. Shivers*, 557 S.W.2d 77, 78 (Tex. 1977). Cost of repair and permanent reduction in market value after repair are cumulative, and both may be recovered in a proper case. *See Ludt v. McCollum*, 762 S.W.2d 575 (Tex. 1988). A wide variety of incidental and consequential damages are recoverable. *Henry S. Miller Co. v. Bynum*, 836 S.W.2d 160 (Tex. 1992); *Kish v. Van Note*, 692 S.W.2d 463, 466–67 (Tex. 1985).

Alternative measures. The DTPA permits the injured consumer to recover the greatest amount of actual damages caused by the wrongful conduct. Thus, the consumer may submit to the jury alternative measures of damages for the same loss and then elect after the verdict the recovery desired by waiving the surplus findings on damages. *Kish*, 692 S.W.2d at 466–67.

Loss of use. The consumer does not need to actually incur out-of-pocket expenses to recover for loss of use of an item. Evidence of the reasonable rental value of the substitute is sufficient. *Luna v. North Star Dodge Sales*, 667 S.W.2d 115, 118–19 (Tex. 1984).

Expenses. Recoverable damages include reasonably necessary expenses shown to be factually caused by the defendant's conduct. *Kish*, 692 S.W.2d at 466. In *Jacobs v. Danny Darby Real Estate, Inc.*, 750 S.W.2d 174 (Tex. 1988), the supreme court raised, but, because it was not asserted by point of error, left unanswered, the question of whether those expenses must be proved reasonable and necessary.

Lost time. *See Village Mobile Homes, Inc. v. Porter*, 716 S.W.2d 543, 549 (Tex. App.—Austin 1986, writ ref'd n.r.e.); *Ybarra v. Saldana*, 624 S.W.2d 948 (Tex. App.—San Antonio 1981, no writ).

Consideration paid. Another accepted measure of damages is the consumer's net economic loss, determined by subtracting the amount of any benefits received from the consideration the consumer has paid. For example, in *Woo v. Great Southwestern Acceptance Corp.*, 565 S.W.2d 290 (Tex. Civ. App.—Waco 1978, writ ref'd n.r.e.), the consumer recovered as damages the amount paid for a distributorship, less the value of certain materials she had received, and in *Henry S. Miller Co. v. Bynum*, 797 S.W.2d 51 (Tex. App.—Houston [1st Dist.] 1990), *aff'd*, 836 S.W.2d 160 (Tex. 1992), the consumer recovered the amounts spent to open a business, less the amount he recouped when the business was sold. If the consumer receives nothing or if what is received is worthless, then the recovery under this measure of damages would be simply the consideration paid. *Vogelsang v. Reece Im-*

port Autos, Inc., 745 S.W.2d 47, 48 (Tex. App.—Dallas 1987, no writ). In addition to being a measure of damages, restoration of money paid is available under a theory of rescission and restitution in DTPA § 17.50(b)(3). *Carrow v. Bayliner Marine Corp.*, 781 S.W.2d 691, 696 (Tex. App.—Austin 1989, no writ); *Green Tree Acceptance, Inc. v. Pierce*, 768 S.W.2d 416, 419 (Tex. App.—Tyler 1989, no writ); *Smith v. Kinslow*, 598 S.W.2d 910, 915 (Tex. Civ. App.—Dallas 1980, no writ).

Medical care.   If there is a question whether medical expenses are reasonable or medical care is necessary, the phrase *Reasonable expenses for necessary medical care* should be substituted for the phrase *Medical care* in sample *H*.

No foreseeability required.   Proof of foreseeability is not required to recover consequential damages, such as lost profits, under the DTPA. *Hycel, Inc. v. Wittstruck*, 690 S.W.2d 914, 922-23 (Tex. App.—Waco 1985, writ dism'd); *cf. Investors, Inc. v. Hadley*, 738 S.W.2d 737 (Tex. App.—Austin 1987, writ denied).

Mental anguish, pre-1995 cases.   The supreme court has stated that mental anguish damages may not be recovered in a DTPA or Insurance Code article 21.21 action unless a willful or grossly negligent violation is shown. *State Farm Life Insurance Co. v. Beaston*, 907 S.W.2d 430, 435-36 (Tex. 1995); *Boyles v. Kerr*, 855 S.W.2d 593 (Tex. 1993).

Mental anguish and additional damages, post-1995 cases.   The 1995 amendments to the DTPA limit damages recovery by plaintiffs to "economic damages" unless the conduct was committed knowingly; in that case, the plaintiff may recover damages for mental anguish as well. DTPA § 17.50(b). A finding that the conduct was committed knowingly is also required for the plaintiff to recover discretionary, additional damages; the amendments abolish the mandatory trebling of the first $1,000 of actual damages. See PJC 110.11 Comment, "Treble damages."

PJC 110.10   Personal Injury Damages—Deceptive Trade Practices
(Comment)

Availability of personal injury damages, pre-1995 cases.   Before its amendment in 1995, the DTPA allowed recovery of the actual damages found by the trier of fact. "Actual damages" included personal injury damages. *See Keller Industries, Inc. v. Reeves*, 656 S.W.2d 221, 224-25 (Tex. App.—Austin 1983, writ ref'd n.r.e.). Personal injury damages typically include physical pain, disfigurement, and physical impairment. See State Bar of Texas, *Texas Pattern Jury Charges—General Negligence & Intentional Personal Torts* PJC 8.2 (1998), for general comments.

Availability of personal injury damages, post-1995 cases.   Damages for personal injury or death are exempted from DTPA coverage. Tex. Bus. & Com. Code Ann. § 17.49(e) (Vernon Supp. 1998) (DTPA). This exemption applies to causes of action accruing on or after September 1, 1995, and all suits filed on or after September 1, 1996.

Prejudgment interest.   In personal injury cases filed after September 1, 1987, there is no need for separate answers for past and future damages. Prejudgment interest on the entire damages award will be calculated by the court. Tex. Fin. Code Ann. §§ 304.101-.108 (Vernon 1998).

**PJC 110.11   Question on Additional Damages—Deceptive Trade
                 Practices**

[*Insert predicate, PJC 110.1.*]

QUESTION _____

What sum of money, if any, in addition to actual damages, should be awarded to
Paul Payne against *Don Davis* because *Don Davis*'s conduct was committed knowingly [*intentionally*]?

Answer in dollars and cents, if any.

Answer: _____

COMMENT

When to use.   PJC 110.11 should be predicated on a jury finding that the defendant's
deceptive trade practice, breach of warranty, or unconscionable act was committed knowingly or intentionally. See PJC 102.21.

Factors to consider.   In light of the constitutional concerns raised in *Transportation
Insurance Co. v. Moriel*, 879 S.W.2d 10, 29–30 (Tex. 1994), an instruction on the exemplary damages factors set out at PJC 110.33 should be submitted with the question at PJC
110.11. *See also TXO Production Corp. v. Alliance Resources Corp.*, 113 S. Ct. 2711
(1993); *Pacific Mutual Life Insurance Co. v. Haslip*, 111 S. Ct. 1032 (1991). Some trial
courts have, without objection, given instructions similar to the definition of exemplary
damages in connection with submission of these DTPA enhancement damages. *Ortiz v.
Flintkote Co.*, 761 S.W.2d 531, 537 (Tex. App.—Corpus Christi 1988, writ denied); *Ren-
don v. Sanchez*, 737 S.W.2d 122, 126 (Tex. App.—San Antonio 1987, no writ).

Treble damages.

A. *Pre-1995 DTPA suits.*   Except for cases covered by the 1995 DTPA amendments
(see below), the first $1,000 in actual damages is automatically trebled, and no instruction
is needed to inform the jury of this recovery. See *Blue Island, Inc. v. Taylor*, 706 S.W.2d 668
(Tex. App.—Corpus Christi 1985, writ ref'd n.r.e.).

B. *1995 DTPA amendments.*   For DTPA causes of action accruing on or after September 1, 1995, and all cases filed after September 1, 1996, the first $1,000 is not automati-
cally trebled. A finding of knowing or intentional conduct is required for any award of discretionary damages. Tex. Bus. & Com. Code Ann. § 17.50(b)(1) (Vernon Supp. 1998)
(DTPA). See PJC 102.21.

C. *Insurance Code article 21.21.*   Recovery of treble damages under article 21.21 varies depending on which version of the statute applies. Treble damages are mandatory and automatic in causes of action arising in whole or in part before April 4, 1985. *State Farm Fire & Casualty Co. v. Gros*, 818 S.W.2d 908, 917 (Tex. App.—Austin 1991, no writ); *Rainey-Mapes v. Queen Charters, Inc.*, 729 S.W.2d 907, 915 (Tex. App.—San Antonio 1987, writ granted, dism'd as moot). In these cases, a finding of liability alone was enough to support recovery of treble damages.

After the 1985 amendments, but before the 1995 amendments, treble damages were mandatory, but only if the jury found the defendant acted "knowingly." Act of March 19, 1985, 69th Leg., R.S., ch. 22, § 3, 1985 Tex. Gen. Laws 395, *amended by* Act of May 19, 1995, 74th Leg., R.S., ch. 414, § 13, 1995 Tex. Gen. Laws 2988, 3000. See PJC 102.21 for a question on knowing conduct.

The 1995 amendments to article 21.21 make additional damages discretionary with the trier of fact, if the defendant acted knowingly. The amendments apply to all causes of action that accrue on or after September 1, 1995, and to all suits filed on or after September 1, 1996. In suits subject to the 1995 amendments, the plaintiff should submit the question of knowing conduct as in PJC 102.21 and then should ask the jury to determine the amount of additional damages as in PJC 110.11. *See* Tex. Ins. Code Ann. art. 21.21, § 16(b) (Vernon Supp. 1998).

Under each of these versions, recovery of treble damages is the same whether the claim is brought directly under article 21.21 or is brought through DTPA § 17.50(a)(4). In *Vail v. Texas Farm Bureau Mutual Insurance Co.*, 754 S.W.2d 129, 137 (Tex. 1988), the supreme court held that this DTPA section "incorporates article 21.21 . . . in its entirety," including the treble damages provision in article 21.21, section 16.

Cap on treble damages.   The maximum recovery under DTPA § 17.50(b)(1) is treble damages. *Jim Walter Homes, Inc. v. Valencia*, 690 S.W.2d 239, 241 (Tex. 1985). Rather than submit to the jury the rather convoluted formula in section 17.50(b)(1), it is preferable to have the jury supply whatever amount it wishes as "additional damages" and have the court impose the statutory ceiling on the recovery actually awarded at judgment.

PJC 110.12   Contribution—Deceptive Trade Practices Act and Insurance Code Article 21.21 (Comment)

DTPA and article 21.21 incorporate existing principles.   DTPA section 17.555 provides that a DTPA defendant "may seek contribution or indemnity from one who, under the statute law or at common law, may have liability for the damaging event of which the consumer complains." Tex. Bus. & Com. Code Ann. § 17.555 (Vernon 1987) (DTPA). No new contribution scheme was created; rather, the section incorporates "existing principles of contribution and indemnity law into DTPA cases." *Plas-Tex, Inc. v. U.S. Steel Corp.*, 772 S.W.2d 442, 446 (Tex. 1989). Though Insurance Code article 21.21 does have a section like DTPA § 17.555 incorporating existing contribution principles, the supreme court applied the original statutory pro rata scheme in chapter 32 of the Civil Practice and Remedies Code to an article 21.21 case in *Stewart Title Guaranty Co. v. Sterling*, 822 S.W.2d 1, 6 n.7 (Tex. 1991).

1989-1995 DTPA claims.   In claims commenced between August 31, 1989, and September 1, 1996 (unless the cause of action accrued on or after September 1, 1995), if the DTPA damages sought are for death, personal injury, or damage to property other than the property involved in the consumer transaction, the prior version of Tex. Civ. Prac. & Rem. Code Ann. ch. 33 (Vernon 1997) applies. Act of May 29, 1989, 71st Leg., R.S., ch. 380, § 2, 1989 Tex. Gen. Laws 1490, 1491, *amended by* Act of May 19, 1995, 74th Leg., R.S., ch. 414, § 5, 1995 Tex. Gen. Laws 2988, 2992. The contribution responsibility of the parties, therefore, including that of the consumer, may be submitted as in other personal injury cases. *See, e.g.*, State Bar of Texas, *Texas Pattern Jury Charges—Malpractice, Premises & Products* PJCs 51.7, 71.3, 71.12, and 71.13 (1998).

DTPA claims not covered by 1989 amendments and claims under article 21.21.   For DTPA claims not covered by the 1989 amendments and for claims under article 21.21, contribution is governed by the original contribution statute, Tex. Civ. Prac. & Rem. Code ch. 32. *Stewart Title Guaranty Co.*, 822 S.W.2d 1, 6 n.7.

1995 DTPA amendments.   In DTPA causes of action accruing on or after September 1, 1995, and for all such suits filed on or after September 1, 1996, contribution is governed by chapter 33 of the Texas Civil Practice & Remedies Code. *See* Tex. Civ. Prac. & Rem. Code Ann. § 33.002(h). For a discussion and a sample submission, see PJC 110.32 Comment, "Contribution defendants."

PJC 110.13   **Question and Instruction on Actual Damages under Insurance Code Article 21.21**

[Insert predicate, PJC 110.1.]

QUESTION _____

What sum of money, if any, if paid now in cash, would fairly and reasonably compensate *Paul Payne* for *his* damages, if any, that resulted from such unfair or deceptive act or practice?

Consider the following elements of damages, if any, and none other.

Answer separately in dollars and cents, if any, for each of the following:

[Insert appropriate instructions. See examples in PJC 110.9.]

In answering questions about damages, answer each question separately. Do not increase or reduce the amount in one answer because of your answer to any other question about damages. Do not speculate about what any party's ultimate recovery may or may not be. Any recovery will be determined by the court when it applies the law to your answers at the time of judgment. Do not add any amount for interest on damages, if any.

COMMENT

When to use.   PJC 110.13 should be used if the insured is claiming damages for a violation of Tex. Ins. Code Ann. art. 21.21 (Vernon 1981 & Supp. 1998). PJC 110.13 should be predicated on a "Yes" answer to PJC 102.14.

Instruction required.   PJC 110.13 *may not* be submitted without an instruction on the appropriate measure of damages. *Jackson v. Fontaine's Clinics, Inc.*, 499 S.W.2d 87, 90 (Tex. 1973). See PJC 110.9 for sample instructions.

Causation.   The phrase *resulted from* is derived from *Aetna Casualty & Surety Co. v. Marshall*, 724 S.W.2d 770, 772 (Tex. 1987), and former Tex. Ins. Code art. 21.21, § 16. Act of March 19, 1985, 69th Leg., R.S., ch. 22, § 3, 1985 Tex. Gen. Laws 395, *amended by* Act of May 19, 1995, 74th Leg., R.S., ch. 414, § 13, 1995 Tex. Gen. Laws 2988, 3000. For causes of action accruing on or after September 1, 1995, and all suits filed on or after September 1, 1996, the phrase *resulted from* should be replaced with the phrase *were caused by*. Tex. Ins. Code art. 21.21, § 16(a) (Supp. 1998). See PJC 102.14 Comment, "Causation."

Policy benefits.   The supreme court held in *Vail v. Texas Farm Bureau Mutual Insurance Co.*, 754 S.W.2d 129, 136 (Tex. 1988), that policy benefits were recoverable as a matter of law. Subsequent cases have limited *Vail* and held that a causation finding may nonetheless be required. *See Twin City Fire Insurance Co. v. Davis*, 904 S.W.2d 663 (Tex. 1995); *Seneca Resources Corp. v. Marsh & McLennan, Inc.*, 911 S.W.2d 144 (Tex. App.—Houston [1st Dist.] 1995, no writ); *Beaston v. State Farm Life Insurance Co.*, 861 S.W.2d 268 (Tex. App.—Austin 1993), *rev'd on other grounds*, 907 S.W.2d 430 (Tex. 1995). Unless both the amount and causation of policy benefits as damages are conclusively established, the Committee believes it prudent to submit this element of damages to the jury.

Mental anguish.   Mental anguish damages may not be recovered under the DTPA or Insurance Code article 21.21 unless a knowing violation is shown. *State Farm Life Insurance Co. v. Beaston*, 907 S.W.2d 430, 435–36 (Tex. 1995) (article 21.21). See PJC 110.9 concerning when mental anguish damages may be trebled.

PJC 110.14 Question and Instruction on Actual Damages for Breach of Duty of Good Faith and Fair Dealing

[Insert predicate, PJC 110.1.]

QUESTION _____

What sum of money, if any, if paid now in cash, would fairly and reasonably compensate *Paul Payne* for *his* damages, if any, that were proximately caused by such conduct?

[Insert definition of proximate cause, PJC 100.9.]

Consider the following elements of damages, if any, and none other.

Answer separately in dollars and cents, if any, for each of the following:

[Insert appropriate instructions. See sample instructions in PJC 110.9 for format.]

In answering questions about damages, answer each question separately. Do not increase or reduce the amount in one answer because of your answer to any other question about damages. Do not speculate about what any party's ultimate recovery may or may not be. Any recovery will be determined by the court when it applies the law to your answers at the time of judgment. Do not add any amount for interest on damages, if any.

COMMENT

When to use. PJC 110.14 should be used if the insured is claiming damages other than policy benefits. PJC 110.14 should be predicated on a "Yes" answer to PJC 103.1.

Instruction required. PJC 110.14 *may not* be submitted without an instruction on the appropriate measure of damages. *Jackson v. Fontaine's Clinics, Inc.*, 499 S.W.2d 87, 90 (Tex. 1973). See PJC 110.9 for sample instructions.

Proximate cause. For a definition of proximate cause, see PJC 100.9.

Policy benefits. Unpaid benefits due under the policy may or may not be recoverable as damages, depending on the circumstances of the case. *See Twin City Fire Insurance Co. v. Davis*, 904 S.W.2d 663 (Tex. 1995); *Seneca Resources Corp. v. Marsh & McLennan, Inc.*, 911 S.W.2d 144 (Tex. App.—Houston [1st Dist.] 1995, no writ). If policy benefits are wrongfully withheld, they are properly submitted as damages. *See Vail v. Texas Farm Bu-*

reau Mutual Insurance Co., 754 S.W.2d 129 (Tex. 1988) (policy benefits wrongfully withheld recoverable as a matter of law in DTPA or article 21.21 case).

Damages other than policy benefits.   If there is delay or denial of payment of an insurance claim, there may be personal injury damages, damage to credit, lost profits, and other damages. For sample instructions that may apply, see PJC 110.9.

Prejudgment interest.   Instructing the jury not to add interest is suggested because prejudgment interest will be calculated by the court at the time of judgment. If interest paid on an obligation is claimed as an element of damages, it may be necessary to modify the instruction on interest. In cases involving wrongful death, personal injury, or property damage, prejudgment interest is governed by statute, which does not require separation of past and future damages. Tex. Fin. Code Ann. §§ 304.101–.108 (Vernon 1998). Cases not governed by the statute require separation. *Cavnar v. Quality Control Parking, Inc.*, 696 S.W.2d 549 (Tex. 1985).

**PJC 110.15   Equitable Remedies and Damages for Breach
of Fiduciary Duty (Comment)**

Equitable relief generally.   Where a fiduciary has profited or benefited from a transaction with the beneficiary, as described in PJC 104.2, the plaintiff is entitled to equitable relief (such as rescission, constructive trust, profit disgorgement, or fee forfeiture) as a matter of law, without having to show that the breach caused damages. *Kinzbach Tool Co. v. Corbett-Wallace Corp.*, 160 S.W.2d 509, 514 (Tex. 1942); *Watson v. Limited Partners of WCKT, Ltd.*, 570 S.W.2d 179, 182 (Tex. Civ. App.—Austin 1978, writ ref'd n.r.e.); *Russell v. Truitt*, 554 S.W.2d 948, 952 (Tex. Civ. App.—Fort Worth 1977, writ ref'd n.r.e.); *see also Restatement (Second) of Agency* § 399 (1958) (listing remedies).

Rescission.   The court may grant rescission of a transaction accomplished by a breach of the defendant's fiduciary duty. *See Allison v. Harrison*, 156 S.W.2d 137, 141 (Tex. 1941) (purchase of land done without full disclosure by the fiduciary was voidable and could be set aside at plaintiff's option, even without proof that the price obtained was unreasonable); *see also Schiller v. Elick*, 240 S.W.2d 997, 1000 (Tex. 1951) (setting aside deed obtained through fiduciary's breach).

Constructive trust.   The court may impose a constructive trust to restore property or profits lost through the fiduciary's breach. *Consolidated Gas & Equipment Co. v. Thompson*, 405 S.W.2d 333, 336 (Tex. 1966); *International Bankers Life Insurance v. Holloway*, 368 S.W.2d 567, 577 (Tex. 1963); *Slay v. Burnett Trust*, 187 S.W.2d 377, 388 (Tex. 1945).

Injunction.   The court may grant injunctive relief. *Hyde Corp. v. Huffines*, 314 S.W.2d 763, 773 (Tex. 1958) (injunction allowed to prevent damage through abuse of confidence in wrongfully appropriating trade secrets); *Elcor Chemical Corp. v. Agri-Sul, Inc.*, 494 S.W.2d 204, 212 (Tex. Civ. App.—Dallas 1973, writ ref'd n.r.e.) (enjoining unfair use of trade secret by party breaching confidential relationship).

Profit disgorgement, fee forfeiture.   See PJCs 110.16 and .17.

Jury questions.   Because the plaintiff is entitled to equitable relief as a matter of law once breach is found, there is no jury question on this remedy. However, jury questions may be needed if the amount of profits or fees is disputed. See PJCs 110.16 (profit disgorgement) and 110.17 (fee forfeiture).

Actual and exemplary damages.   In a proper case, in addition to equitable relief, the plaintiff may also recover actual and exemplary damages caused by the fiduciary's breach. *Manges v. Guerra*, 673 S.W.2d 180, 184 (Tex. 1984); *see also Cantu v. Butron*, 921 S.W.2d 344, 351–53 (Tex. App.—Corpus Christi 1996, writ denied). See PJCs 110.18 (actual damages for breach of fiduciary duty) and 110.33–.34 (exemplary damages).

PJC 110.16   Question on Profit Disgorgement—Amount of Profit

QUESTION _____

What was the amount of *Don Davis*'s profit in [*describe the transaction in question, e.g., Don Davis's leasing of mineral rights to himself*]?

Answer in dollars and cents, if any.

Answer: _____

COMMENT

When to use. Profit disgorgement does not present a jury question. If the amount of profit is disputed, however, PJC 110.16 may be used. See PJC 110.15.

Amount of profit. A fiduciary cannot use his position to gain any benefit for himself at the expense of his principal. *Schiller v. Elick*, 240 S.W.2d 997, 999 (Tex. 1951); *Fitz-Gerald v. Hull*, 237 S.W.2d 256, 264–65 (Tex. 1951); *Slay v. Burnett Trust*, 187 S.W.2d 377, 388 (Tex. 1945); *McDonald v. Follett*, 180 S.W.2d 334, 338 (Tex. 1944). A fiduciary must account for, and yield to the beneficiary, any profit that he makes as a result of a breach of his fiduciary duty. *International Bankers Life Insurance Co. v. Holloway*, 368 S.W.2d 567, 576–77 (Tex. 1963); *Restatement (Second) of Agency* §§ 388, 404A (1958).

PJC 110.17   Question on Fee Forfeiture—Amount of Fee

QUESTION _____

What was the amount of *Don Davis*'s fees in [*describe the transaction in question, e.g., Don Davis's brokerage of the real estate transaction*]?

Answer in dollars and cents, if any.

Answer: _____

COMMENT

When to use.   The right to fee forfeiture does not present a jury question. If the amount earned is disputed, however, PJC 110.17 may be used. See PJC 110.15.

Amount of fees forfeited.   The traditional rule is that a fiduciary who breaches his fiduciary duties forfeits all fees in the transaction and the right to compensation. *Kinzbach Tool Co. v. Corbett-Wallace Corp.*, 160 S.W.2d 509, 514 (Tex. 1942); *Armstrong v. O'Brien*, 19 S.W. 268, 274 (Tex. Civ. App.—Amarillo 1892, writ ref'd); *Murphy v. Canion*, 797 S.W.2d 944, 947 (Tex. App.—Houston [14th Dist.] 1990, no writ); *Russell v. Truitt*, 554 S.W.2d 948, 951 (Tex. Civ. App.—Fort Worth 1977, writ ref'd n.r.e.); *Anderson v. Griffith*, 501 S.W.2d 695, 702 (Tex. Civ. App.—Fort Worth 1973, writ ref'd n.r.e.). However, the supreme court has suggested that a breaching fiduciary may receive partial compensation. *Archer v. Griffith*, 390 S.W.2d 735, 741 (Tex. 1964) (canceling a contingent fee agreement as exorbitant, but suggesting that quantum meruit recovery might be proper); *see also Arce v. Burrow*, 958 S.W.2d 239, 250 (Tex. App.—Houston [14th Dist.] 1997, writ granted); *Cantu v. Butron*, 921 S.W.2d 344, 354 (Tex. App.—Corpus Christi 1996, writ denied). Neither the *Arce* nor *Cantu* courts treated the amount of partial recovery as a question for the jury; in *Arce*, the court of appeals held that the amount to be forfeited was an equitable determination for the trial court. 958 S.W.2d at 250–51.

Causation not required.   It is not necessary to prove that the fiduciary's breach caused damages to have the fiduciary forfeit compensation. *Kinzbach*, 160 S.W.2d at 514; *Armstrong*, 19 S.W. at 274.

PJC 110.18   Question on Actual Damages for Breach of Fiduciary Duty

[*Insert predicate, PJC 110.1.*]

QUESTION _____

What sum of money, if any, if paid now in cash, would fairly and reasonably compensate *Paul Payne* for *his* damages, if any, that were proximately caused by such conduct?

[*Insert appropriate instructions. See examples in PJCs 110.3 and .9.*]

Answer in dollars and cents, if any.

Answer: _____

COMMENT

When to use. Breach of fiduciary duty is an independent tort that will support an award of actual damages. *Manges v. Guerra*, 673 S.W.2d 180, 184 (Tex. 1984). A fiduciary is liable for any loss or damages suffered by the plaintiff. *Slay v. Burnett Trust*, 187 S.W.2d 377, 391 (Tex. 1945); *NRC v. Huddleston*, 886 S.W.2d 526, 530 (Tex. App.—Austin 1994, no writ); *Restatement of Trusts* § 205(a) (1962); *Restatement (Second) of Agency* § 401 (1958). PJC 110.18 may be used when the plaintiff seeks actual damages in addition to equitable relief or as an alternate remedy. *Cantu v. Butron*, 921 S.W.2d 344 (Tex. App.—Corpus Christi 1996, writ denied); see also PJCs 110.4 and .20.

PJC 110.19   Question and Instruction on Direct Damages Resulting from Fraud

[Insert predicate, PJC 110.1.]

QUESTION _____

What sum of money, if any, if paid now in cash, would fairly and reasonably compensate *Paul Payne* for *his* damages, if any, that resulted from such fraud?

Consider the following elements of damages, if any, and none other.

Answer separately in dollars and cents, if any, for each of the following:

[Insert appropriate instructions. See sample instructions in PJCs 110.3 and .9 for format.]

In answering questions about damages, answer each question separately. Do not increase or reduce the amount in one answer because of your answer to any other question about damages. Do not speculate about what any party's ultimate recovery may or may not be. Any recovery will be determined by the court when it applies the law to your answers at the time of judgment. Do not add any amount for interest on damages, if any.

COMMENT

When to use.   PJC 110.19 should be predicated on a "Yes" answer to PJC 105.1 and may be adapted for use in most fraud cases by the addition of appropriate instructions setting out legally available measures of direct damages. See PJCs 110.3 and .9. If only one measure of damages is supported by the pleadings and proof, the measure may be incorporated into the question.

Instruction required.   PJC 110.19 *may not* be submitted without an instruction on the appropriate measure of damages. *Jackson v. Fontaine's Clinics, Inc.*, 499 S.W.2d 87, 90 (Tex. 1973). See PJCs 110.3 and .9 for sample instructions.

Direct damages.   PJC 110.19 should be used only for the submission of direct damages in fraud cases. For a discussion of direct damages, see PJC 110.3 Comment. In fraud cases, direct damages are sometimes referred to as general damages—that is, damages that are the necessary and usual result of the wrong complained of. *Airborne Freight Corp. v. C.R. Lee Enterprises*, 847 S.W.2d 289, 295 (Tex. App.—El Paso 1992, writ denied). The measure of direct damages in fraud cases has been held to be either "out of pocket" or "benefit of the bargain." *Streller v. Hecht*, 859 S.W.2d 114, 116 (Tex. App.—Houston [14th

Dist.] 1993, writ denied); *LSR Joint Venture No. 2 v. Callewart*, 837 S.W.2d 693, 701–02 (Tex. App.—Dallas 1992, writ denied); *Matthews v. AmWest Savings Ass'n*, 825 S.W.2d 552, 554 (Tex. App.—Beaumont 1992, writ denied).

PJC 110.20 may be used to submit consequential damages, and PJC 110.34 may be used to submit exemplary damages.

Prejudgment interest.   Instructing the jury not to add interest is suggested because prejudgment interest, if recoverable, will be calculated by the court at the time of judgment. If interest paid on an obligation is claimed as an element of damages, it may be necessary to modify the instruction on interest. In cases involving wrongful death, personal injury, or property damage, prejudgment interest is governed by statute, which does not require separation of past and future damages. Tex. Fin. Code Ann. §§ 304.101–.108 (Vernon 1998). Cases not governed by the statute require separation. *Cavnar v. Quality Control Parking, Inc.*, 696 S.W.2d 549 (Tex. 1985).

PJC 110.20   Question and Instruction on Consequential Damages Caused by Fraud

[*Insert predicate, PJC 110.1.*]

QUESTION _____

What sum of money, if any, if paid now in cash, would fairly and reasonably compensate *Paul Payne* for *his* damages, if any, that were proximately caused by such fraud?

[*Insert definition of proximate cause, PJC 100.9.*]

Consider the following elements of damages, if any, and none other.

Answer separately in dollars and cents, if any, for each of the following:

[*Insert appropriate instructions. See sample instructions in PJCs 110.3 and .9 for format, and see PJC 110.4.*]

In answering questions about damages, answer each question separately. Do not increase or reduce the amount in one answer because of your answer to any other question about damages. Do not speculate about what any party's ultimate recovery may or may not be. Any recovery will be determined by the court when it applies the law to your answers at the time of judgment. Do not add any amount for interest on damages, if any.

COMMENT

When to use.   PJC 110.20 should be predicated on a "Yes" answer to PJC 105.1 and may be adapted for use in most fraud cases by the addition of appropriate instructions setting out legally available measures of damages. See PJCs 110.3, .4, and .9. If only one measure of damages is supported by the pleadings and proof, the measure may be incorporated into the question.

Instruction required.   PJC 110.20 *may not* be submitted without an instruction on the appropriate measure of damages. *Jackson v. Fontaine's Clinics, Inc.*, 499 S.W.2d 87, 90 (Tex. 1973). See PJCs 110.3, .4, and .9 for sample instructions.

Proximate cause—consequential damages.   PJC 110.20 should be used only for the submission of consequential or special damages in fraud cases. To be recoverable, such damages must be the "proximate result" of fraud. *Airborne Freight Corp. v. C.R. Lee Enterprises*, 847 S.W.2d 289, 295 (Tex. App.—El Paso 1992, writ denied); *El Paso Development*

Co. v. Ravel, 339 S.W.2d 360, 363 (Tex. Civ. App.—El Paso 1960, writ ref'd n.r.e.), *cited and relied on in Trenholm v. Ratcliff*, 646 S.W.2d 927, 933 (Tex. 1983); *see also Morriss-Buick Co. v. Pondrom*, 113 S.W.2d 889, 890 (Tex. 1938) (loss resulting directly and proximately from fraud). For a description of general and special damages, see *Sherrod v. Bailey*, 580 S.W.2d 24, 28 (Tex. Civ. App.—Houston [1st Dist.] 1979, writ ref'd n.r.e.).

PJC 110.19 should be used to submit direct damages, and PJC 110.34 may be used to submit exemplary damages.

Prejudgment interest.   Instructing the jury not to add interest is suggested because prejudgment interest, if recoverable, will be calculated by the court at the time of judgment. If interest paid on an obligation is claimed as an element of damages, it may be necessary to modify the instruction on interest. In cases involving wrongful death, personal injury, or property damage, prejudgment interest is governed by statute, which does not require separation of past and future damages. Tex. Fin. Code Ann. §§ 304.101–.108 (Vernon 1998). Cases not governed by the statute require separation. *Cavnar v. Quality Control Parking, Inc.*, 696 S.W.2d 549 (Tex. 1985).

PJC 110.21 **Question and Instruction on Monetary Loss Caused by Negligent Misrepresentation**

[Insert predicate, PJC 110.1.]

QUESTION _____

What sum of money, if any, if paid now in cash, would fairly and reasonably compensate *Paul Payne* for *his* damages, if any, that were proximately caused by such negligent misrepresentation?

[Insert definition of proximate cause, PJC 100.9.]

Consider the following elements of damages, if any, and none other.

The difference, if any, between the value of what *Paul Payne* has received in the transaction and the purchase price or value given.

The pecuniary loss, if any, otherwise suffered as a consequence of *Paul Payne*'s reliance on the misrepresentation.

Do not add any amount for interest on past damages, if any.

Answer in dollars and cents for damages, if any, that—

were sustained in the past;   Answer: _____

in reasonable probability will
be sustained in the future.   Answer: _____

COMMENT

When to use. PJC 110.21 should be predicated on a "Yes" answer to PJC 105.16. If only one measure of damages is supported by the pleadings and proof, the measure may be incorporated into the question.

Instruction required. PJC 110.21 *may not* be submitted without an instruction on the appropriate measure of damages. *Jackson v. Fontaine's Clinics, Inc.*, 499 S.W.2d 87, 90 (Tex. 1973).

Source of instructions. The measures of damages set forth in the instructions are prescribed by the *Restatement (Second) of Torts* § 552B (1977) and have been adopted by the Supreme Court of Texas. *Federal Land Bank Ass'n of Tyler v. Sloane*, 825 S.W.2d 439 (Tex. 1991).

Alternative submissions.   If separate answers for each measure of damages are desired, the following instruction should be given in lieu of the one above, and an answer blank will then follow each instruction on damages:

> Answer separately in dollars and cents, if any, for each of the following elements of damages.

Parallel theories.   If the negligent misrepresentation cause of action is only one of several theories of recovery submitted in the charge and any theory has a different legal measure of damages to be applied to a factually similar claim for damages, a separate damages question for each theory may be submitted and the following additional instruction may be included earlier in the charge:

> If you answer questions about damages, answer each question separately. Do not increase or reduce the amount in one answer because of the instructions in or your answers to any other questions about damages. Do not speculate about what any party's ultimate recovery may or may not be. Any recovery will be determined by the court when it applies the law to your answers at the time of judgment.

Prejudgment interest.   Instructing the jury not to add interest is suggested because prejudgment interest, if recoverable, will be calculated by the court at the time of judgment. If interest paid on an obligation is claimed as an element of damages, it may be necessary to modify the instruction on interest. In cases involving wrongful death, personal injury, or property damage, prejudgment interest is governed by statute, which does not require separation of past and future damages. Tex. Fin. Code Ann. §§ 304.101–.108 (Vernon 1998). Cases not governed by the statute require separation. *Cavnar v. Quality Control Parking, Inc.*, 696 S.W.2d 549 (Tex. 1985).

PJC 110.22   **Question on Damages for Intentional Interference with Existing Contract or for Wrongful Interference with Prospective Contractual Relations**

[Insert predicate, PJC 110.1.]

QUESTION _____

What sum of money, if any, if paid now in cash, would fairly and reasonably compensate *Paul Payne* for *his* damages, if any, proximately caused by such interference?

[Insert definition of proximate cause, PJC 100.9.]

Consider the following elements of damages, if any, and none other.

[Insert appropriate instructions. See examples in PJC 110.3 and instructions in PJC 110.4.]

Do not add any amount for interest on damages, if any.

Answer in dollars and cents for damages, if any, that—

were sustained in the past;	Answer: _____
in reasonable probability will be sustained in the future.	Answer: _____

COMMENT

When to use.   PJC 110.22 should be predicated on a "Yes" answer to PJC 106.1 or .2 finding interference with an existing contract or with prospective contractual relations. PJC 110.22 is used to establish the proximate cause and actual damages elements of intentional interference with an existing contract as set forth in the comments to PJC 106.1 and of wrongful interference with prospective contractual relations as stated in the comments to PJC 106.2.

Instruction required.   PJC 110.22 *may not* be submitted without an instruction on the appropriate measure of damages. *Jackson v. Fontaine's Clinics, Inc.*, 499 S.W.2d 87, 90 (Tex. 1973). See PJCs 110.3–.4 for sample instructions.

Damages. PJC 110.22 submits actual damages in interference cases. Exemplary damages are submitted at PJC 110.34. In some cases, submission of PJC 110.34 must be predicated on a specific finding of actual malice in response to PJC 110.23. See comments to PJC 106.1.

The basic measure of damages is the same as for breach of contract. In some instances, however, basic contract damages are not sufficient and the entire range of tort damages may be recovered. Damages for interference with existing contract or prospective contractual relations include the pecuniary loss of the contract's benefit, consequential losses, and emotional distress. *Exxon Corp. v. Allsup*, 808 S.W.2d 648, 660 (Tex. App.—Corpus Christi 1991, writ denied); *Restatement (Second) of Torts* § 774A (1977). The loss incurred does not have to be one contemplated by the parties when the contract was made. *Allsup*, 808 S.W.2d at 660.

Alternative submissions. If separate answers for each measure of damages are desired, the following instruction should be given in lieu of the one above, and an answer blank will then follow each instruction on damages:

> Answer separately in dollars and cents, if any, for each of the following elements of damages.

Parallel theories. If theories of recovery other than those addressed in PJC 110.22 are submitted in the charge and any theory has a different legal measure of damages to be applied to a factually similar claim for damages, a separate damages question for each theory may be submitted and the following additional instruction may be included earlier in the charge:

> If you answer questions about damages, answer each question separately. Do not increase or reduce the amount in one answer because of the instructions in or your answers to any other questions about damages. Do not speculate about what any party's ultimate recovery may or may not be. Any recovery will be determined by the court when it applies the law to your answers at the time of judgment.

Prejudgment interest. Instructing the jury not to add interest is suggested because prejudgment interest, if recoverable, will be calculated by the court at the time of judgment. If interest paid on an obligation is claimed as an element of damages, it may be necessary to modify the instruction on interest. In cases involving wrongful death, personal injury, or property damage, prejudgment interest is governed by statute, which does not require separation of past and future damages. Tex. Fin. Code Ann. §§ 304.101–.108 (Vernon 1998). Cases not governed by the statute require separation. *Cavnar v. Quality Control Parking, Inc.*, 696 S.W.2d 549 (Tex. 1985).

PJC 110.23   **Question and Instruction on Exemplary Damages for Interference with Existing Contract (Pre-September 1995 Cases)**

[Insert predicate, PJC 110.1.]

QUESTION _____

Did *Don Davis* act with actual malice?

"Actual malice" means ill will, spite, evil motive, or purpose to injure another.

Answer "Yes" or "No."

Answer: _____

COMMENT

When to use.   PJC 110.23 should be predicated on a "Yes" answer to PJC 106.1. An affirmative answer to PJC 110.23 is required for recovery of exemplary damages in cases involving intentional interference with an existing contract, where the cause of action accrued before September 1, 1995. *See Clements v. Withers*, 437 S.W.2d 818, 822 (Tex. 1969); *Exxon Corp. v. Allsup*, 808 S.W.2d 648, 661 (Tex. App.—Corpus Christi 1991, writ denied); *Corporate Wings, Inc. v. King*, 767 S.W.2d 485, 487 (Tex. App.—Dallas 1989, no writ); *Armendariz v. Mora*, 553 S.W.2d 400, 407 (Tex. Civ. App.—El Paso 1977, writ ref'd n.r.e.).

Causes of action accruing on or after September 1, 1995, are governed by Tex. Civ. Prac. & Rem. Code Ann. ch. 41 (Vernon 1997 & Supp. 1998). Instead of PJC 110.23, PJC 110.33 should be submitted in such cases. PJC 110.34 submits exemplary damages in both pre-1995 and post-1995 cases. For the reasons set out in the comments to PJC 106.2, in cases involving prospective contractual relations, the submission of PJC 110.34 need not be predicated on a finding of actual malice.

Source of instruction.   In cases of intentional interference with contract, malice for purposes of exemplary damages is defined as "ill-will, spite, evil motive, or purposing the injury of another." *Clements*, 437 S.W.2d at 822; *see Allsup*, 808 S.W.2d at 661.

PJC 110.23 enables the jury to determine if the defendant's intent is to maliciously harm another. *Clements*, 437 S.W.2d at 822; *see Armendariz*, 553 S.W.2d at 407 (action motivated by spite and revenge was malicious); *Anthony Pools v. Charles & David, Inc.*, 797 S.W.2d 666, 677 (Tex. App.—Houston [14th Dist.] 1990, writ denied) (action motivated by business interest was willful but not malicious).

Caveat.   Do not confuse the actual malice standard of PJC 110.23 with the "actual malice" standard of defamation cases. *See, e.g., Milkovich v. Lorain Journal Co.,* 110 S. Ct. 2695 (1990); *New York Times Co. v. Sullivan,* 84 S. Ct. 710 (1964); *Doubleday & Co. v. Rogers,* 674 S.W.2d 751 (Tex. 1984); *Foster v. Upchurch,* 624 S.W.2d 564 (Tex. 1981); *Dun & Bradstreet, Inc. v. O'Neil,* 456 S.W.2d 896 (Tex. 1970).

**PJC 110.24   Sample Instructions on Direct and Incidental Damages—
Breach of Employment Agreement**

Explanatory note: Damages instructions in a breach of an employment agreement
case, like contract actions, are necessarily fact-specific and can vary with the circumstances of each case. The elements listed below are those commonly used in employment
contract cases, but do not represent an exhaustive list. These instructions are to be used in
conjunction with the contract damages question, PJC 110.2.

Sample A—Lost earnings

> "Lost earnings" equal the present cash value of the employment agree-
> ment to the employee had it not been breached, less amounts actually
> earned.

Sample B—Lost employee benefits other than earnings

> "Benefits" include [*sick-leave pay, vacation pay, cost of living in-
> creases, profit-sharing benefits, stock options, pension fund benefits,
> health insurance, life insurance, housing or transportation subsidies,
> bonuses*].

Sample C—Loss of insurance coverage

> Losses incurred as a result of the loss of health, life, dental, or similar
> insurance coverage.

Sample D—Mitigation expenses

> Reasonable and necessary expenses in obtaining other employment.

COMMENT

When to use.   See explanatory note above. Because damages instructions are necessarily fact-specific, no true "pattern" instructions are given—only samples of general damages available in employment contract actions. This list is not exhaustive. The samples are
illustrative only and must be rewritten to fit the particular damages raised by the pleadings
and proof and recoverable under a legally accepted theory.

Measure of damages.   The legal measure of damages for the breach of an employment
agreement is the present cash value of the agreement to the employee had it not been
breached, less any amounts the employee should in the exercise of reasonable diligence be
able to earn through other employment. *Gulf Consolidated International, Inc. v. Murphy,*

658 S.W.2d 565, 566 (Tex. 1983); *Greater Fort Worth & Tarrant County Community Action Agency v. Mims*, 627 S.W.2d 149, 151 (Tex. 1982); *see also Southwest Airlines Co. v. Jaeger*, 867 S.W.2d 824, 835 (Tex. App.—El Paso 1993, writ denied) (approving jury question and instructions on damages for breach of employment contract);*Lone Star Steel Co. v. Wahl*, 636 S.W.2d 217, 221 (Tex. App.—Texarkana 1982, no writ) (measure of damages is all wages past due and all future promised wages less what can be earned by reasonable effort in similar employment). There may be elements of actual damages that are recoverable other than those listed in PJC 110.24.

Consequential damages. If foreseeability is at issue, see PJC 110.4 and make appropriate modifications.

PJC 110.25 **Defensive Instruction on Mitigation—**
Breach of Employment Agreement Damages

Do not include in your answer any amount that you find *Paul Payne* could have earned by exercising reasonable diligence in seeking other employment.

COMMENT

When to use. PJC 110.25 should be included with the damages question (see PJC 110.2) if the evidence raises a question about the employee's failure to mitigate damages after the employer's actionable conduct. *Gulf Consolidated International, Inc. v. Murphy*, 658 S.W.2d 565, 566 (Tex. 1983); *Southwest Airlines Co. v. Jaeger*, 867 S.W.2d 824, 835 (Tex. App.—El Paso 1993, writ denied).

The general rules concerning mitigation found in the Comment to PJC 110.7 are also applicable to mitigation in employment contracts.

Source of instruction. PJC 110.25 is derived from *Gulf Consolidated International, Inc.*, 658 S.W.2d at 566, and *Lee-Wright, Inc. v. Hall*, 840 S.W.2d 572, 581 (Tex. App.—Houston [1st Dist.] 1992, no writ). See also PJC 110.7.

PJC 110.26   **Question and Instruction on Damages for Wrongful Discharge for Refusing to Perform an Illegal Act**

QUESTION _____

What sum of money, if any, if paid now in cash, would fairly and reasonably compensate *Paul Payne* for *his* damages, if any, that resulted from such conduct?

Consider the following elements of damages, if any, and none other.

    a.   Lost earnings.

    b.   Lost employee benefits other than earnings.

        "Benefits" include [*sick-leave pay, vacation pay, profit-sharing benefits, stock options, pension fund benefits, housing or transportation subsidies, bonuses, monetary losses incurred as a result of the loss of health, life, dental, or similar insurance coverage*].

Answer in dollars and cents for damages, if any, that—

were sustained in the past;	Answer: _____
in reasonable probability will be sustained in the future.	Answer: _____

COMMENT

When to use. PJC 110.26 should be predicated on a "Yes" answer to PJC 107.3, finding wrongful discharge for refusing to perform an illegal act.

Source of question and instruction. No Texas court has specifically addressed the measure of damages under *Sabine Pilot Service, Inc. v. Hauck*, 687 S.W.2d 733 (Tex. 1985); however, the concurring opinion in *Sabine Pilot* suggests that article 8307c (now codified at Tex. Lab. Code Ann. § 451.001 (Vernon 1996)), prohibiting firing an employee for filing a workers' compensation claim, should serve as a guide. *Sabine Pilot Service, Inc.*, 687 S.W.2d at 736; *see also Worsham Steel Co. v. Arias*, 831 S.W.2d 81, 84 (Tex. App.—El Paso 1992, no writ) (approving above as measures of damages in article 8307c case). There may be other elements of common-law damages, e.g., mental anguish, that are recoverable other than those listed in PJC 110.26. The Committee expresses no opinion concerning the recoverability of these common-law damages.

Mitigation. For a defensive instruction on mitigation, see PJCs 110.7 and .25.

Prejudgment interest. PJC 110.26 assumes that, for the purposes of computation of prejudgment interest, all elements of damages are governed by *Cavnar v. Quality Control*

Parking, Inc., 696 S.W.2d 549 (Tex. 1985). If Tex. Fin. Code Ann. §§ 304.101–.108 (Vernon 1998) apply to the mental anguish element, then it should be submitted separately so the appropriate statutory calculation can be made.

Exemplary damages. No Texas case has established whether exemplary damages are recoverable in a *Sabine Pilot* case or, if recoverable, what predicate state of mind or conduct is required. For causes of action accruing on or after September 1, 1995, the predicate state of mind or conduct for an award of exemplary damages is set out in Tex. Civ. Prac. & Rem. Code Ann. § 41.003(a) (Vernon 1997). See PJC 110.33. *Cf. Azar Nut Co. v. Caille*, 734 S.W.2d 667, 669 (Tex. 1987) (exemplary damages are within article 8307c "reasonable damages suffered by employee" terminated in a retaliatory manner). If exemplary damages are recoverable, see PJC 110.34.

After-acquired evidence of employee misconduct. If the employer has pleaded the discovery of evidence of employee misconduct acquired only after the employee's employment was terminated, see PJC 107.8 for the applicable instruction.

**PJC 110.27   Question and Instructions on Damages for Retaliation
                under Texas Whistleblower Act**

QUESTION _____

What sum of money, if any, if paid now in cash, would fairly and reasonably compensate *Paul Payne* for *his* damages, if any, that resulted from such conduct?

Consider the elements of damages listed below and none other. Consider each element separately. Do not include damages for one element in any other element. Do not include interest on any amount of damages you may find.

Answer separately, in dollars and cents, for damages, if any.

    a.   Lost wages during the period of suspension or termination.

Answer: _____

    b.   Lost employee benefits other than loss of earnings.

      "Benefits" include [*sick-leave pay, vacation pay, profit-sharing benefits, stock options, pension fund benefits, housing or transportation subsidies, bonuses, monetary losses incurred as a result of the loss of health, life, dental, or similar insurance coverage*].

Answer: _____

    c.   Compensatory damages.

      "Compensatory damages" include future pecuniary losses, emotional pain, suffering, inconvenience, mental anguish, loss of enjoyment of life, and other nonpecuniary damages. Do not include back pay or interest in calculating compensatory damages, if any.

Answer: _____

COMMENT

When to use.   PJC 110.27 should be predicated on a "Yes" answer to PJC 107.4, finding retaliation under the Texas Whistleblower Act, Tex. Gov't Code Ann. §§ 554.001–.010 (Vernon 1994 & Supp. 1998).

Source of question and instructions.   PJC 110.27 is derived from *City of Ingleside v. Kneuper*, 768 S.W.2d 451, 454 (Tex. App.—Austin 1989, writ denied). *See also Texas Department of Human Services v. Green*, 855 S.W.2d 136, 150-51 (Tex. App.—Austin 1993, writ denied).

Statutory relief.   Tex. Gov't Code § 554.003 (Supp. 1998) provides for recovery of actual damages and attorney's fees for a violation of the Whistleblower Act. The statute, however, does not define "actual damages." The elements given above are not meant to be exclusive, but rather are those most commonly allowed in employment cases.

The statute also provides for equitable relief in the nature of an injunction or reinstatement of employment and/or benefits, which is to be determined by the trial court. Tex. Gov't Code § 554.003; *see Caballero v. Central Power & Light Co.*, 858 S.W.2d 359 (Tex. 1993) (equitable relief under Texas Commission on Human Rights Act is to be determined by judge).

Mitigation.   For a defensive instruction on mitigation, see PJCs 110.7 and .25.

Attorney's fees.   For submission of attorney's fees, see PJC 110.43.

Exemplary damages, pre-June 15, 1995, cases.   The pre-1995 version of Tex. Gov't Code § 554.003 made no express requirement of a predicate mental state for the recovery of exemplary damages. Act of April 30, 1993, 73rd Leg., R.S., ch. 268, § 1, 1993 Tex. Gen. Laws 587, 613, *amended by* Act of May 25, 1995, 74th Leg., R.S., ch. 721, § 1, 1995 Tex. Gen. Laws 3812. In some cases, however, a predicate mental state was submitted. *Kneuper*, 768 S.W.2d at 455, held that the legislative history of the Whistleblower Act does not support omitting the traditional prerequisite findings of malice, willful and wanton conduct, fraud, or gross negligence to support an award of exemplary damages. Other cases have also submitted a predicate mental state. *See also Texas Department of Human Services v. Hinds*, 860 S.W.2d 893, 901 (Tex. App.—El Paso 1993), *rev'd on other grounds*, 904 S.W.2d 629 (Tex. 1995); *City of Beaumont v. Bouillion*, 873 S.W.2d 425, 444–45 (Tex. App.—Beaumont 1993), *rev'd on other grounds*, 896 S.W.2d 143 (Tex. 1995). For submission of exemplary damages, see PJC 110.34.

Exemplary damages unavailable, post-June 15, 1995, cases.   If the suspension or termination of the employee or other adverse personnel action was taken on or after June 15, 1995, exemplary damages are not available. Tex. Gov't Code § 554.003(a).

Prejudgment interest.   PJC 110.27 assumes that, for the purposes of computation of prejudgment interest, all elements of damages are governed by *Cavnar v. Quality Control Parking, Inc.*, 696 S.W.2d 549 (Tex. 1985). If Tex. Fin. Code Ann. §§ 304.101–.108 (Vernon 1998) apply to the mental anguish element, then it should be submitted separately so that the appropriate statutory calculation can be made.

After-acquired evidence of employee misconduct.   If the employer has pleaded the discovery of evidence of employee misconduct acquired only after the employee's employment was terminated, see PJC 107.8 for the applicable instruction.

PJC 110.28   Question and Instruction on Damages—Retaliation for Seeking Workers' Compensation Benefits

QUESTION _____

What sum of money, if any, if paid now in cash, would fairly and reasonably compensate *Paul Payne* for *his* damages, if any, that resulted from such conduct?

Consider the elements of damages listed below and none other. Consider each element separately. Do not include damages for one element in any other element. Do not include interest on any amount of damages you may find.

Reduce lost wages, if any, by wages earned, if any, in the past and wages, if any, which in reasonable probability will be earned in the future.

Answer separately, in dollars and cents for damages, if any.

   a.   Lost earnings and employee benefits in the past (between date of [*discharge or discriminatory event*] and today).

Answer: _____

   b.   Lost earnings and employee benefits that in reasonable probability will be lost in the future.

Answer: _____

   c.   Compensatory damages in the past, which may include [*emotional pain and suffering, inconvenience, mental anguish, loss of enjoyment of life, and other nonpecuniary losses*].

Answer: _____

   d.   Compensatory damages in the future, which may include [*emotional pain and suffering, inconvenience, mental anguish, loss of enjoyment of life, and other nonpecuniary losses*].

Answer: _____

COMMENT

When to use.   PJC 110.28 should be predicated on a "Yes" answer to PJC 107.5.

Source of question and instructions.   Tex. Lab. Code Ann. § 451.002 (Vernon 1996) provides for recovery of reasonable damages. The elements of damages given in PJC

110.28 are not meant to be exclusive, but rather are those most commonly allowed in employment cases. *See, e.g., Carnation Co. v. Borner,* 610 S.W.2d 450, 453–54 (Tex. 1980) (permitting recovery for future lost wages, retirement benefits, and other benefits ascertainable with reasonable certainty); *Pacesetter Corp. v. Barrickman,* 885 S.W.2d 256, 259 (Tex. App.—Tyler 1994, no writ) (award of past and future employee benefits); *Worsham Steel Co. v. Arias,* 831 S.W.2d 81, 85–86 (Tex. App.—El Paso 1992, no writ) (mental anguish as a compensable injury); *DeFord Lumber Co. v. Roys,* 615 S.W.2d 235, 237–38 (Tex. Civ. App.—Dallas 1981, no writ) (award of damages for lost wages in the past). In this instruction, damages for "lost earnings" subsumes the elements of lost earnings and loss of earning capacity. *See Texas Department of Human Services v. Hinds,* 860 S.W.2d 893, 900–901 (Tex. App.—El Paso 1993), *rev'd on other grounds,* 904 S.W.2d 629 (Tex. 1995) (discussing distinction between lost earning capacity and loss of actual earnings).

Equitable relief.   In addition to the reasonable damages allowed under Tex. Lab. Code § 451.002, the trial court may reinstate the employee (Tex. Lab. Code § 451.002) or restrain for cause a violation of section 451.001 (Tex. Lab. Code § 451.003).

Mitigation.   For a defensive instruction on mitigation, see PJCs 110.7 and .25.

Exemplary damages.   See PJC 110.29.

After-acquired evidence of employee misconduct.   If the employer has pleaded the discovery of evidence of employee misconduct acquired only after the employee's employment was terminated, see PJC 107.8 for the applicable instruction.

PJC 110.29   Predicate Question and Instruction on Exemplary Damages—Retaliation for Seeking Workers' Compensation Benefits

If you have answered "Yes" to Question _____ [*107.5*], then answer the following question. Otherwise, do not answer the following question.

QUESTION _____

Do you find that the harm to *Paul Payne* resulted from actual malice?

"Actual malice" means ill will, spite, evil motive, or purpose to injure another.

Answer "Yes" or "No."

Answer: _____

COMMENT

When to use.   PJC 110.29 should be used for a claim for exemplary damages if the plaintiff alleges retaliation for seeking workers' compensation benefits.

Bifurcation.   On timely motion, the trial court must bifurcate the determination of the amount of exemplary damages from the remaining issues. *Transportation Insurance Co. v. Moriel*, 879 S.W.2d 10, 30 (Tex. 1994).

Modification of "factors to consider" in PJC 110.34.   Use PJC 110.34 as the question asking the jury to fix the amount of exemplary damages, modifying the "factors to consider" in awarding exemplary damages to read as follows:

a.   The nature of the wrong.

b.   The frequency of the wrongs committed.

c.   The character of the conduct involved.

d.   The degree of culpability of *Don Davis*.

e.   The situation and sensibilities of the parties involved.

f.   The extent to which such conduct offends a public sense of justice and propriety.

g.   The size of the award needed to deter similar wrongs in the future.

Moriel, 879 S.W.2d at 27 n.1.

Source of question and instruction.   The question and instruction are derived from *Continental Coffee Supply Co. v. Cazarez*, 937 S.W.2d 444, 452 (Tex. 1996), and *Clements v. Withers*, 437 S.W.2d 818, 822 (Tex. 1969). Note that Tex. Civ. Prac. & Rem. Code Ann. ch. 41 (Vernon 1997) does not apply to any cause of action brought under title 5 of the Texas Labor Code (workers' compensation).

PJC 110.30 Question and Instruction on Unlawful Employment Practices Damages

QUESTION _____

What sum of money, if any, if paid now in cash, would fairly and reasonably compensate *Paul Payne* for *his* damages, if any, that resulted from such conduct?

Consider the elements of damages listed below and none other. Consider each element separately. Do not include damages for one element in any other element. Do not include interest on any damages you may find.

Answer in dollars and cents for damages, if any.

    a.   Back pay.

    "Back pay" is that amount of wages and employment benefits that *Paul Payne* would have earned if *he* had not been subjected to *his* employer's unlawful conduct less any wages, unemployment compensation benefits or workers' compensation benefits *he* received in the interim.

    "Employment benefits" include [*sick-leave pay, vacation pay, profit-sharing benefits, stock options, pension fund benefits, housing or transportation subsidies, bonuses, monetary losses incurred as a result of the loss of health, life, dental, or similar insurance coverage*].

Answer: _____

    b.   Compensatory damages.

    "Compensatory damages" include future pecuniary losses, emotional pain, suffering, inconvenience, mental anguish, loss of enjoyment of life, and other nonpecuniary damages. Do not include back pay or interest in calculating compensatory damages, if any.

Answer: _____

COMMENT

When to use.   PJC 110.30 should be predicated on a "Yes" answer to PJC 107.6.

Source of question and instruction.   PJC 110.30 is based on Tex. Lab. Code Ann. §§ 21.258, 21.2585 (Vernon 1996). *See also Speer v. Presbyterian Children's Home & Service Agency*, 847 S.W.2d 227, 228 (Tex. 1993) (Texas Commission on Human Rights Act specifically allows for compensatory relief).

Equitable relief. In addition to actual and exemplary damages allowed under Tex. Lab. Code § 21.2585 and attorney's fees under Tex. Lab. Code § 21.259, on a finding that an employer has engaged in unlawful employment practices, the trial court may order an injunction or additional equitable relief under Tex. Lab. Code § 21.2584. *See also Caballero v. Central Power & Light Co.*, 858 S.W.2d 359, 361 (Tex. 1993) (equitable relief under TCHRA is to be determined by judge).

Attorney's fees. See PJC 110.43.

Caveat. PJC 110.30 is based on the statutory delineation of back pay and compensatory damages as recoverable damages pursuant to Tex. Lab. Code §§ 21.258, 21.2585. The Committee expresses no opinion on whether front pay is a separate element of damages awardable by the jury.

After-acquired evidence of employee misconduct. If the employer has pleaded the discovery of evidence of employee misconduct acquired only after the employee's employment was terminated, see PJC 107.8 for the applicable instruction.

PJC 110.31   Predicate Question and Instruction on Punitive Damages for Unlawful Employment Practices

QUESTION _____

Do you find *by clear and convincing evidence* that *Don Davis* engaged in the discriminatory practice that you have found in answer to Question ____ [*107.6*] with malice or with reckless indifference to the right of *Paul Payne* to be free from such practices?

> "Clear and convincing evidence" means the measure or degree of proof that produces a firm belief or conviction of the truth of the allegations sought to be established.

> "Malice" means:

> (a)   a specific intent by *Don Davis* to cause substantial injury to *Paul Payne*; or

> (b)   an act or omission:

> > (i)   which, when viewed objectively from the standpoint of *Don Davis* at the time of its occurrence, involved an extreme degree of risk, considering the probability and magnitude of the potential harm to others; and

> > (ii)   of which *Don Davis* had actual, subjective awareness of the risk involved, but nevertheless proceeded with conscious indifference to the rights, safety, or welfare of others.

Answer "Yes" or "No."

Answer: _____

COMMENT

When to use.   PJC 110.31 should be used for a claim for punitive damages under the Texas Commission on Human Rights Act, Tex. Lab. Code Ann. §§ 21.001–.306 (Vernon 1996 & Supp. 1998) and:

1.   the evidence indicates that the discriminatory employment practice was motivated by malice or reckless indifference, Tex. Lab. Code § 21.2585 (1996); and

2.   the cause of action arose on or after September 1, 1995. See comment below, "1993–1995 causes of action," for a discussion of such causes of action.

1993–1995 causes of action. Cases where (1) the complaint was filed on or after September 1, 1993, and (2) the cause of action accrued before September 1, 1995, are governed by former Tex. Rev. Civ. Stat. Ann. art. 5221k, § 7.01. Act of May 14, 1993, 73rd Leg., R.S., ch. 276, § 7, 1993 Tex. Gen. Laws 1287, 1292. In those cases, the standard of proof is preponderance of the evidence, not clear and convincing evidence. Note also that the definition of malice given above is taken from the 1995 amendments to Tex. Civ. Prac. & Rem. Code Ann. § 41.001 (Vernon 1997). The definition of "malice" before the 1995 amendments read as follows: "'Malice' means: (A) conduct that is specifically intended by the defendant to cause substantial injury to the claimant; or (B) an act that is carried out by the defendant with a flagrant disregard for the rights of others and with actual awareness on the part of the defendant that the act will, in reasonable probability, result in human death, great bodily harm, or property damage." Act of June 3, 1987, 70th Leg., 1st C.S., ch. 2, § 2.12, 1987 Tex. Gen. Laws 71, 85–86, *amended by* Act of April 6, 1995, 74th Leg., R.S., ch. 19, § 1, 1995 Tex. Gen. Laws 108, 109.

Source of question and instruction. PJC 110.31 is derived from Tex. Lab. Code § 21.2585 and Tex. Civ. Prac. & Rem. Code § 41.001(2), (7).

PJC 110.32   Proportionate Responsibility

If you have answered Questions _____ and _____ [*the liability questions, e.g., 102.1, 103.1, or 105.1*] "Yes" as to more than one of the *persons* named below, then answer the following question. Otherwise, do not answer the following question.

You should only assign percentages to the *persons* you find caused the damages. The percentages you find must total 100 percent. The percentages must be expressed in whole numbers. The responsibility attributable to any one named below is not necessarily measured by the number of acts or omissions found.

QUESTION _____

For each *person* found by you to have caused the damages to *Paul Payne*, find the percentage caused by:

a.	*Don Davis*	_____	%
b.	*Paul Payne*	_____	%
c.	*Sam Settlor*	_____	%
d.	*Responsible Ray*	_____	%
	Total	_____100_____	%

COMMENT

When to use. Tex. R. Civ. P. 277 requires a percentage question "in any case in which the jury is required to apportion the loss among the parties." For causes of action based on tort accruing on or after September 1, 1995, and in all such suits filed on or after September 1, 1996, the trier of fact must determine the percentage of responsibility of each defendant, claimant, settling person, or responsible third party with respect to each person's causing or contributing to cause the harm for which damages are sought. Tex. Civ. Prac. & Rem. Code Ann. § 33.003 (Vernon 1997). The responsibility to be determined must arise from a negligent act or omission, a defective or unreasonably dangerous product, or other conduct or activity that violates an applicable legal standard. Tex. Civ. Prac. & Rem. Code Ann. § 33.003. The DTPA, chapter 21 of the Texas Insurance Code, and intentional tort causes of action accruing before September 1, 1995, were exempted from the provisions of Civil Practice and Remedies Code chapter 33. Those exemptions were removed by the 1995 legislature for causes of action accruing on or after September 1, 1995, and for all such suits filed on or after September 1, 1996. Act of June 16, 1987, 70th Leg., 1st C.S., ch. 2, § 2.05, 1987 Tex. Gen. Laws 71, 78, *amended by* Act of May 18, 1995, 74th Leg., R.S., ch. 136, § 1, 1995 Tex. Gen. Laws 971, 971–72. Note that the 1995 amendments to Civil Practice and Remedies Code chapter 33 expressly refer to the DTPA, but not to Insurance Code article 21.21. *See* Tex. Civ. Prac. & Rem. Code § 33.002(h).

Conditioned on responsibility of more than one person. PJC 110.32 is conditioned on findings that the acts or omissions of more than one person caused the damages or injury, because otherwise no comparison is possible.

Plaintiff's conduct. The plaintiff (*Paul Payne*) should be submitted in this question if the law governing the cause of action provides an "applicable legal standard" by which the plaintiff's conduct is measured and the jury is asked in a predicate question whether *Paul Payne* violated that standard. Tex. Civ. Prac. & Rem. Code § 33.003.

If there is more than one responsible person. If more than one responsible person has been found liable in a liability question, separate percentage answers should be sought for each person. For example:

a. *Don Davis* _____ %

b. *Davis Corporation* _____ %

c. *Paul Payne* _____ %

d. *Sam Settlor* _____ %

e. *Responsible Ray* _____ %

Settling persons. The proportionate responsibility statute requires the responsibility of a settling person (*Sam Settlor*) to be determined by the trier of fact. Tex. Civ. Prac. & Rem. Code §§ 33.003, 33.011. "Settling person" is defined as one—

> who at the time of submission has paid or promised to pay money or anything of monetary value to a claimant at any time in consideration of potential liability pursuant to the provisions of Section 33.001 with respect to the personal injury, property damage, death, or other harm for which recovery of damages is sought.

Tex. Civ. Prac. & Rem. Code § 33.011(5). To include a settling person, that person's name must be included in a basic liability question.

Responsible third parties. The liability of a "responsible third party" (*Responsible Ray*) should only be inquired into if that party is joined under Tex. Civ. Prac. & Rem. Code § 33.004. A "responsible third party" is defined in Tex. Civ. Prac. & Rem. Code § 33.011(6). If submitted in a basic liability question, a responsible third party should also be submitted in the proportionate responsibility question. Tex. Civ. Prac. & Rem. Code § 33.003.

Contribution defendants.

A. *Inclusion in liability question.* If there is a contribution defendant (*Connie Contributor*), that party's liability should be determined in a separate liability question. *See* Tex. Civ. Prac. & Rem. Code §§ 33.003, 33.011. "Contribution defendant" is defined as "any defendant, counterdefendant, or third-party defendant from whom any party seeks contribution with respect to any portion of damages for which that party may be liable, but from whom the claimant seeks no relief at the time of submission." Tex. Civ. Prac. & Rem. Code § 33.016.

B. *Separate comparative question necessary.*   The responsibility of the contribution defendant should *not* be included in the question comparing the responsibility of the plaintiff with that of the other defendants. A separate comparative question is necessary. An example of a question on comparative responsibility of a contribution defendant is as follows:

If you have answered Questions _____ and _____ *[102.1 or other applicable liability question]* "Yes" as to more than one of the persons named below, then answer the following question. Otherwise, do not answer the following question.

You should only assign percentages to the persons you find caused the damages. The percentages you find must total 100 percent. The percentages must be expressed in whole numbers. The responsibility attributable to a person named below is not necessarily measured by the number of acts or omissions found.

QUESTION _____

With respect to causing or contributing to cause in any way the injury to *Paul Payne*, find the percentage of responsibility, if any, attributable as between or among—

a.	*Don Davis*	_____	%
b.	*Connie Contributor*	_____	%
	Total	_____100_____	%

Exceptions to the limitations on joint and several liability.   The limitations on joint and several liability set forth in chapter 33 of the Civil Practice and Remedies Code are not applicable where a defendant (1) with the specific intent to do harm to others, acts in concert with another person to engage in conduct described in the sections of the Texas Penal Code referenced in section 33.002; (2) is found to have caused harm by depositing, discharging, or releasing into the environment a hazardous or harmful substance (section 33.013(c)(1)); or (3) causes harm resulting from a "toxic tort" (section 33.013(c)(2)).

To create an exception to the limitations on joint and several liability, in an appropriate case separate findings establishing such conduct may be necessary, e.g., whether the defendant acted in concert with another person to engage in the type of unlawful conduct referenced in section 33.002. However, though definitions or acts may be borrowed from the Penal Code to craft the jury question, the jury shall *not* be advised that the conduct in question is actually a violation of the Penal Code. Tex. Civ. Prac. & Rem. Code § 33.002(g). Similarly, under section 33.013, a fact finding may be required about whether the defendant deposited, discharged, or released into the environment a hazardous or harmful substance or caused harm resulting from a "toxic tort."

Several of the examples of criminal conduct constituting exceptions to the limitations on joint and several liability also constitute exceptions to the cap or limitation on exemplary damages, such as forgery, securing execution of a document by deception, fraudulent removal of a document, or theft. See PJCs 110.36–.42 for examples of those charges and for applicable comments. Note, however, that a jury question seeking to establish conduct sufficient to lift the limitation on joint and several liability must ask whether the defendant, with the specific intent to do harm to others, acted in concert with another person to engage in the conduct described in the applicable Penal Code section. Tex. Civ. Prac. & Rem. Code § 33.002(b). These elements are not contained in the charges found at PJCs 110.36–.42.

PJC 110.33   Predicate Question and Instruction on Award of Exemplary Damages (Post-September 1995 Cases)

If you have answered "Yes" to Question _____ [*103.1, 106.1, or other applicable liability question*], then answer the following question. Otherwise, do not answer the following question.

QUESTION _____

Do you find by clear and convincing evidence that the harm to *Paul Payne* resulted from [*malice* or *fraud*]?

"Clear and convincing evidence" means the measure or degree of proof that produces a firm belief or conviction of the truth of the allegations sought to be established.

"Malice" means:

(a)   a specific intent by *Don Davis* to cause substantial injury to *Paul Payne*; or

(b)   an act or omission by *Don Davis*,

(i)   which, when viewed objectively from the standpoint of *Don Davis* at the time of its occurrence, involved an extreme degree of risk, considering the probability and magnitude of the potential harm to others; and

(ii)   of which *Don Davis* had actual, subjective awareness of the risk involved, but nevertheless proceeded with conscious indifference to the rights, safety, or welfare of others.

[*and/or use appropriate definition for "fraud"; see comment below, "Fraud as a ground for exemplary damages"*]

Answer "Yes" or "No."

Answer: _____

COMMENT

When to use.   PJC 110.33 is used as a predicate question to PJC 110.34, the question for exemplary damages. It is based on an affirmative finding to a liability question such as the following: PJCs 103.1 (tort duty of good faith and fair dealing), 106.1 (interference with existing contract), or 106.2 (interference with prospective contractual relations). This question only applies to causes of action arising on or after September 1, 1995.

In a case where a defendant has requested a bifurcated trial pursuant to Tex. Civ. Prac. & Rem. Code Ann. § 41.009 (Vernon 1997), PJC 110.33 should be answered in the first phase of the trial.

See PJC 110.34 Comment, "Predicate finding, pre-September 1995 cases," for a discussion of the prerequisites for exemplary damages for causes of action arising before September 1, 1995.

Actual damages generally required. In general, exemplary damages may be awarded only if damages other than nominal damages are awarded. If, however, the jury finds that the harm suffered by the plaintiff was caused by a specific intent by the defendant to cause substantial injury to the plaintiff (the first definition of "malice" in the question above), then an award of nominal damages will support an award of exemplary damages. Tex. Civ. Prac. & Rem. Code § 41.004.

Fraud as a ground for exemplary damages. Fraud, as well as malice, is a ground for recovery of exemplary damages. Tex. Civ. Prac. & Rem. Code § 41.003(a)(1). As a predicate for recovery of exemplary damages, fraud is defined as "fraud other than constructive fraud." Tex. Civ. Prac. & Rem. Code § 41.001(6). In an appropriate case, substitute "fraud" for "malice" in the question proper and insert a definition for "fraud" conforming to the pleadings and evidence of the case, using the definitions for fraud found at PJCs 105.2–.11 as a guide.

Recovery of exemplary damages in a wrongful death case. In a wrongful death case brought by or on behalf of the decedent's spouse or heir of the decedent's body under a statute enacted pursuant to Tex. Const. art. XVI, § 26, exemplary damages may be recovered on a showing that the claimant's damages resulted from willful act, omission, or gross neglect. "Gross neglect" has the same definition as "malice" in Tex. Civ. Prac. & Rem. Code § 41.001(7)(B); that statutory definition is the source of the second definition of "malice" in PJC 110.33. See Tex. Civ. Prac. & Rem. Code § 71.001 *et seq.* for applicable statutes concerning wrongful death, and State Bar of Texas, *Texas Pattern Jury Charges— Malpractice, Premises & Products* ch. 81 (1998), for pattern jury charges in wrongful death cases.

Source of question. Tex. Civ. Prac. & Rem. Code §§ 41.002(b)(6), (7), 41.003.

PJC 110.34   Question and Instruction on Exemplary Damages

[Insert predicate, PJC 110.1.]

QUESTION _____

What sum of money, if any, if paid now in cash, should be assessed against *Don Davis* and awarded to *Paul Payne* as exemplary damages, if any, for the conduct found in response to Question _____ *[question authorizing potential recovery of punitive damages]*?

> "Exemplary damages" means an amount that you may in your discretion award as a penalty or by way of punishment.

Factors to consider in awarding exemplary damages, if any, are—

a.   The nature of the wrong.

b.   The character of the conduct involved.

c.   The degree of culpability of *Don Davis*.

d.   The situation and sensibilities of the parties concerned.

e.   The extent to which such conduct offends a public sense of justice and propriety.

f.   The net worth of *Don Davis*.

> *[Insert additional instructions if appropriate. See, e.g., PJC 110.35.]*

Answer in dollars and cents, if any.

Answer: _____

COMMENT

When to use.   PJC 110.34 is used to submit exemplary damages. It should be predicated on a finding justifying the award of exemplary damages. See comments below. Chapter 41 of the Texas Civil Practice and Remedies Code does not apply to most suits brought under the DTPA, Texas Insurance Code article 21.21, or title 5 of the Texas Labor Code (workers' compensation). Tex. Civ. Prac. & Rem. Code Ann. § 41.002(d) (Vernon 1997). There may be, however, reason to use the "factors to consider" listed in PJC 110.34 in such cases. See PJC 110.11 for the "additional damages" question in DTPA cases, and PJC 110.29 for cases involving retaliation for seeking workers' compensation benefits.

Predicate finding.

A. *Pre-September 1995 cases.* For causes of action accruing before September 1, 1995, the finding required for an award of exemplary damages varies with the individual cause of action. See PJC 103.1 (good faith and fair dealing), 105.1 (common-law fraud), 105.8 combined with 105.11 (statutory fraud), 106.1 (intentional interference with existing contract), 106.2 (interference with prospective contractual relations), or 110.31 (unlawful employment practices) for discussions of the requirements for an award of exemplary damages in these cases.

B. *Post-September 1995 cases.* Chapter 41 of the Civil Practice and Remedies Code governs the requirements for a finding of exemplary damages in causes of action arising on or after September 1, 1995. PJC 110.33 is the predicate question that should be answered affirmatively before the jury answers PJC 110.34. If a defendant has requested a bifurcated trial pursuant to Tex. Civ. Prac. & Rem. Code § 41.009, PJC 110.33 should be answered in the first phase of the trial.

Multiple defendants. There should be a separate question and answer blank for each defendant against whom exemplary damages are sought. Tex. Civ. Prac. & Rem. Code § 41.006; *Norton Refrigerated Express v. Ritter Bros. Co.*, 552 S.W.2d 910, 913 (Tex. Civ. App.—Texarkana 1977, writ ref'd n.r.e.).

Multiple plaintiffs. For multiple plaintiffs, consideration may be given to an additional question asking the jury to apportion the exemplary damages among them. *Burk Royalty Co. v. Walls*, 596 S.W.2d 932, 939 (Tex. Civ. App.—Fort Worth 1980), *aff'd on other grounds*, 616 S.W.2d 911 (Tex. 1981).

Prejudgment interest not recoverable. Prejudgment interest on exemplary damages is not recoverable. Tex. Civ. Prac. & Rem. Code § 41.007; *Cavnar v. Quality Control Parking, Inc.*, 696 S.W.2d 549 (Tex. 1985).

Bifurcation. No predicating instruction is necessary if the court has granted a timely motion to bifurcate trial of the amount of punitive damages. *See Transportation Insurance Co. v. Moriel*, 879 S.W.2d 10, 29–30 (Tex. 1994); Tex. Civ. Prac. & Rem. Code § 41.009. If in the first phase of the trial the jury finds facts establishing a predicate for an award of exemplary damages, then a separate jury charge should be prepared for the second phase of the trial. See the comments above regarding predicate-finding and PJC 110.33.

In such a second-phase jury charge, PJC 110.34 should be submitted with both PJCs 100.3 and .4.

Factors to consider in determining amount of award. The "factors to consider" listed in PJC 110.34 are from Tex. Civ. Prac. & Rem. Code § 41.011(a). Before the 1995 amendments to Civil Practice and Remedies Code chapter 41, a number of U.S. and Texas Supreme Court decisions dealt with factors considered appropriate for the jury to consider in determining the amount of the exemplary damages award. *See TXO Production Corp. v. Alliance Resources Corp.*, 113 S. Ct. 2711 (1993); *Pacific Mutual Life Insurance Co. v. Haslip*, 111 S. Ct. 1032 (1991); *Moriel*, 879 S.W.2d 10; *Hofer v. Lavender*, 679 S.W.2d 470 (Tex. 1984); *Alamo National Bank v. Kraus*, 616 S.W.2d 908 (Tex. 1981).

Limitation on amount of recovery.

A. *Pre-September 1995 cases.* Except in cases of malice or intentional tort, or causes of action accruing before September 1, 1995, exemplary damages may not exceed four times the amount of actual damages or $200,000, whichever is greater. Former Tex. Civ. Prac. & Rem. Code §§ 41.007–.008. Act of June 16, 1987, 70th Leg., 1st C.S., ch. 2, § 2.12, 1987 Tex. Gen. Laws 71, 88, *amended by* Act of April 20, 1995, 74th Leg., R.S., ch. 19, § 1, 1995 Tex. Gen. Laws 108, 111.

B. *Post-September 1995 cases.* For causes of action accruing on or after September 1, 1995, exemplary damages awarded against a defendant ordinarily may not exceed an amount equal to the greater of:

(1)(A)   two times the amount of economic damages, plus

(B)   an amount equal to any noneconomic damages found by the jury not to exceed $750,000; or

(2) $200,000.

Tex. Civ. Prac. & Rem. Code § 41.008(b). "Economic damages" is defined as "compensatory damages for pecuniary loss; [it] does not include exemplary damages or damages for physical pain and mental anguish, loss of consortium, disfigurement, physical impairment, or loss of companionship or society." Tex. Civ. Prac. & Rem. Code § 41.001(4). These limitations will not apply in favor of a defendant found to have "knowingly" or "intentionally" committed conduct described as a felony in specified sections of the Texas Penal Code. *See* Tex. Civ. Prac. & Rem. Code § 41.008(c), (d), and PJCs 110.36–.42.

Source of instructions. Tex. Civ. Prac. & Rem. Code §§ 41.001(5), 41.011(a).

PJC 110.35   **Instructions on Exemplary Damages Assessed against Master for Acts of Servant**

Exemplary damages can be assessed against [*Don Davis*] [*ABC Corporation*] as a principal because of an act by an agent if, but only if,

a.   the principal authorized the doing and the manner of the act, or

b.   the agent was unfit and the principal was reckless in employing him, or

c.   the agent was employed in a managerial capacity and was acting in the scope of employment, or

d.   the employer or a manager of the employer's ratified or approved the act.

COMMENT

When to use.   PJC 110.35 should be used with PJC 110.34 in cases involving fact issues concerning the assessment of exemplary damages against a master for the acts of a servant. The grounds listed in the instruction are alternatives, and any of the listed grounds not at issue in the case should be deleted.

Source of instruction.   Alternative grounds *a* through *d* are derived from the *Restatement (First) of Torts* § 909 (1938), which has been adopted by the Supreme Court of Texas. *See Fisher v. Carrousel Motor Hotel, Inc.*, 424 S.W.2d 627, 630 (Tex. 1967); *see also Fort Worth Elevators Co. v. Russell*, 70 S.W.2d 397, 406 (Tex. 1934), *overruled on other grounds by Wright v. Gifford-Hill & Co.*, 725 S.W.2d 712, 714 (Tex. 1987) (concerning corporate vice-principals); *Restatement (Second) of Torts* § 909 (1977) (containing provisions identical to those set forth in section 909 of the *Restatement (First) of Torts*).

PJC 110.36		**Question and Instructions—Securing Execution of Document by Deception as a Ground for Removing Limitation on Exemplary Damages (Tex. Civ. Prac. & Rem. Code § 41.008(c)(11))**

If you have answered "Yes" to Question _____ [*110.33*], then answer the following question. Otherwise, do not answer the following question.

QUESTION _____

Did *Don Davis* secure the execution of a document by deception [*and was the value of the property affected $1,500 or more*]?

> "Securing the execution of a document by deception" occurs when a person causes another person to *sign* any document affecting *property*, and does so by deception, with the intent to defraud or harm any person.

> A person acts with intent with respect to the nature of *his* conduct or to a result of *his* conduct when it is the conscious objective or desire to engage in the conduct or cause the result.

> "Deception" means creating or confirming by words or conduct a false impression of law or fact that is likely to affect the judgment of another in the transaction, and that the actor does not believe to be true.

> *"Property" means: (a) real property; (b) tangible or intangible personal property, including anything severed from land; or (c) a document, including money, that represents or embodies anything of value.*

Answer "Yes" or "No."

Answer: _____

COMMENT

When to use.   PJC 110.36 should be used in a case where (1) exemplary damages are sought; (2) the harm to the plaintiff resulted from conduct described as a felony in Tex. Pen. Code Ann. § 32.46 (Vernon Supp. 1998); and (3) the jury has previously found that the defendant committed conduct authorizing recovery of exemplary damages as set out in Tex. Civ. Prac. & Rem. Code Ann. § 41.003 (Vernon 1997). *See* Tex. Civ. Prac. & Rem. Code § 41.008(c)(8). This statute applies to causes of action accruing on or after September 1, 1995. If the jury finds conduct that violates Tex. Pen. Code § 32.46, and the conduct rises to the level of a felony, the limitations on exemplary damage awards set out in Tex. Civ. Prac. & Rem. Code § 41.008(b) do not apply. Tex. Civ. Prac. & Rem. Code § 41.008(c).

Bifurcation.   If a defendant has requested a bifurcated trial pursuant to Tex. Civ. Prac. & Rem. Code § 41.009, PJC 110.36 should be answered in the first phase of the trial.

Alternative language for "sign."   In an appropriate case, the word *execute* may be substituted for the word *sign.* Tex. Pen. Code § 32.46(a).

Alternative language for "property."   In an appropriate case, the terms *service* or *the pecuniary interest of any person* may be substituted for the word *property.* Tex. Pen. Code § 32.46(a)(1). If *service* is substituted for *property,* the following definition should be substituted:

> "Service" includes: (a) labor and professional service; (b) telecommunication, public utility, and transportation service; (c) lodging, restaurant service, and entertainment; and (d) the supply of a motor vehicle or other property for use.

Tex. Pen. Code § 32.01(3) (1994).

"Deception."   The definition of "deception" in PJC 110.36 is taken from Tex. Pen. Code § 31.01(1) and *Goldstein v. State,* 803 S.W.2d 777, 790 (Tex. App.—Dallas 1991, pet. ref'd). See Tex. Pen. Code § 31.01(1) for alternative definitions of "deception."

"Value" and requirement that conduct be described as a felony.   Tex. Civ. Prac. & Rem. Code § 41.008(c)(13) requires that the limitation or cap on exemplary damages may only be lifted if the plaintiff's damages are based on conduct "described as a felony" in Tex. Pen. Code § 32.46 (Supp. 1998). The criterion for felony status is that the property or service have a value of $1,500 or higher. Tex. Pen. Code § 32.46(b)(4). The optional language in the basic question in PJC 110.36 establishes whether the defendant's conduct rises to the status of a felony, if there is a dispute about the value of the property in question.

Source of instruction and definition.   The question and instructions are derived from Tex. Pen. Code §§ 1.07(a)(16), 31.01(2), 32.01(2), (3) (1994), § 32.46 (Supp. 1998); Tex. Civ. Prac. & Rem. Code § 41.008.

PJC 110.37   Question and Instruction—Fraudulent Destruction, Removal, Alteration, or Concealment of Writing as a Ground for Removing Limitation on Exemplary Damages (Tex. Civ. Prac. & Rem. Code § 41.008(c)(12))

If you have answered "Yes" to Question _____ [*110.33*], then answer the following question. Otherwise, do not answer the following question.

QUESTION _____

Did *Don Davis* alter [*describe the writing in question, e.g., Terry Testator's will dated February 29, 1992*] with intent to defraud or harm another?

> A person acts with intent with respect to the nature of *his* conduct or to a result of *his* conduct when it is the conscious objective or desire to engage in the conduct or cause the result.

Answer "Yes" or "No."

Answer: _____

COMMENT

When to use.   PJC 110.37 should be used in a case where (1) exemplary damages are sought; (2) the harm to the plaintiff resulted from conduct described as a felony in Tex. Pen. Code Ann. § 32.47 (Vernon 1994); and (3) the jury has previously found that the defendant committed conduct authorizing recovery of exemplary damages as set out in Tex. Civ. Prac. & Rem. Code Ann. § 41.003 (Vernon 1997). *See* Tex. Civ. Prac. & Rem. Code § 41.008(c)(11). This statute applies to causes of action accruing on or after September 1, 1995. If the jury finds conduct that violates Tex. Pen. Code § 32.47, and that conduct rises to the level of a felony, the limitations on exemplary damage awards set out in Tex. Civ. Prac. & Rem. Code § 41.008(b) do not apply. Tex. Civ. Prac. & Rem. Code § 41.008(c). See comment below, "Felonious conduct," for a discussion of the requirements needed to establish that the conduct in question was felonious.

Bifurcation.   If a defendant has requested a bifurcated trial pursuant to Tex. Civ. Prac. & Rem. Code § 41.009, PJC 110.37 should be answered in the first phase of the trial.

Alternative language for "alters."   In an appropriate case, the terms *removes, conceals, destroys, substitutes,* or *impairs the verity (legibility) (availability) of* may be substituted for the word *alters*. Tex. Pen. Code § 32.47(a).

Not applicable to governmental records.   Because Tex. Pen. Code § 32.47 does not apply to writings that are "governmental records," PJC 110.37 is not applicable in a case where the writing in question is such a record. See Tex. Pen. Code § 37.01 (Supp. 1998) for a definition of "governmental record."

Definition of "writing."   In an appropriate case, use a definition of "writing" as provided in Tex. Pen. Code § 32.47(b) (1994).

Felonious conduct.   Tex. Civ. Prac. & Rem. Code § 41.008(c) provides that the limitation or cap on exemplary damages may only be lifted if the plaintiff's damages are based on conduct "described as a felony" in Tex. Pen. Code § 32.47. The criminal conduct described in Tex. Pen. Code § 32.47 rises to felonious conduct only in the following situations:

1.   the writing is a will or codicil of another, whether or not the maker is alive or dead and whether or not it has been admitted to probate; or

2.   the writing is a deed, mortgage, deed of trust, security instrument, security agreement, or other writing for which the law provides public recording or filing, whether or not the writing has been acknowledged.

Tex. Pen. Code § 32.47(d).

Source of instruction and definition.   The question and instructions are derived from Tex. Pen. Code §§ 1.07(a)(16), 6.03, 32.47; Tex. Civ. Prac. & Rem. Code § 41.008.

**PJC 110.38   Question and Instructions—Forgery as a Ground
for Removing Limitation on Exemplary Damages
(Tex. Civ. Prac. & Rem. Code § 41.008(c)(8))**

If you have answered "Yes" to Question _____ [*110.33*], then answer the following question. Otherwise, do not answer the following question.

QUESTION _____

Did *Don Davis* commit forgery with the intent to defraud or harm another?

"Forgery" means that a person *alters, makes, completes, executes, or authenticates* a writing so that it purports to *be the act of another who did not authorize that act.*

A person acts with intent with respect to the nature of *his* conduct or to a result of *his* conduct when it is the conscious objective or desire to engage in the conduct or cause the result.

Answer "Yes" or "No."

Answer: _____

COMMENT

When to use.   PJC 110.38 should be used in a case where (1) exemplary damages are sought; (2) the harm to the plaintiff is alleged to have resulted from conduct described as a felony in Tex. Pen. Code Ann. § 32.21 (Vernon 1994 & Supp. 1998); and (3) the jury has previously found that the defendant committed conduct authorizing recovery of exemplary damages as set out in Tex. Civ. Prac. & Rem. Code Ann. § 41.003 (Vernon 1997). *See* Tex. Civ. Prac. & Rem. Code § 41.008(c)(8). This statute applies to causes of action accruing on or after September 1, 1995. If the jury finds conduct that violates Tex. Pen. Code § 32.21, and that conduct rises to the level of a felony, the limitations on exemplary damage awards set out in Tex. Civ. Prac. & Rem. Code § 41.008(b) do not apply. Tex. Civ. Prac. & Rem. Code § 41.008(c). See comment below, "Felonious conduct," for a discussion of the requirements needed to establish that the conduct in question was felonious.

Bifurcation.   If a defendant has requested a bifurcated trial pursuant to Tex. Civ. Prac. & Rem. Code § 41.009, PJC 110.38 should be answered in the first phase of the trial.

Alternative language for issuance or possession of a forged writing.   Tex. Pen. Code § 32.21(a)(1)(B) (1994) defines "forgery" alternatively as occurring when a person issues, transfers, registers the transfer of, publishes, or otherwise utters a forged writing as defined in Tex. Pen. Code § 32.21(a)(1)(A). Also, Tex. Pen. Code § 32.21(a)(1)(C) gives another alternative definition of "forgery" as occurring when a person possesses a forged writing (as defined in Tex. Pen. Code § 32.21(a)(1)(A)) with the intent to utter it (as defined in Tex. Pen. Code § 32.21(a)(1)(B)). In an appropriate case, an alternative definition of "forgery" may be substituted.

Definition of "writing." In an appropriate case, use an applicable definition of "writing" as found in Tex. Pen. Code § 32.21(a)(2).

Alternative language for "to be the act of another who did not authorize that act." In an appropriate case, the language *have been executed at a time (at a place) (in a numbered sequence) other than was in fact the case,* or *be a copy of an original when no such original existed* may be substituted for the original language of the charge. Tex. Pen. Code § 32.21(a)(1)(A).

Felonious conduct. Tex. Civ. Prac. & Rem. Code § 41.008(c) provides that the limitation or cap on exemplary damages may only be lifted if the plaintiff's damages are based on conduct "described as a felony" in Tex. Pen. Code § 32.21 (1994 & Supp. 1998). The criminal conduct described in Tex. Pen. Code § 32.21 rises to felonious conduct only when the writing—

1. is or purports to be a will, codicil, deed, deed of trust, mortgage, security instrument, security agreement, credit card, check, or similar sight order for payment of money, contract, release, or other commercial instrument;

2. is part of an issue of money, securities, postage, or revenue stamps;

3. is a license, certificate, permit, seal, title, or similar document issued by a government; or

4. is another instrument issued by a state or national government or by a subdivision of either, or part of an issue of stock, bonds, or other instruments representing interests in or claims against another person.

Tex. Pen. Code § 32.21(d), (e).

Source of instruction and definition. The question and instructions are derived from Tex. Pen. Code. §§ 6.03(a), 32.21(a), (b) (1994); Tex. Civ. Prac. & Rem. Code § 41.008.

**PJC 110.39   Question and Instructions—Theft as a Ground for
                   Removing Limitation on Exemplary Damages
                   (Tex. Civ. Prac. & Rem. Code § 41.008(c)(13))**

If you have answered "Yes" to Question _____ [*110.33*], then answer the following question. Otherwise, do not answer the following question.

QUESTION _____

Did *Don Davis* commit theft [*and was the value of the stolen property $20,000 or greater*]?

> "Theft" means that a person unlawfully appropriates *property* with the intent to deprive the owner of property. Appropriating *property* is unlawful if it is without the owner's effective consent.

> A person acts with intent with respect to the nature of *his* conduct or to a result of *his* conduct when it is the conscious objective or desire to engage in the conduct or cause the result.

> "Deprive" means *to withhold property from the owner permanently or for so extended a period of time that a major portion of the value or enjoyment of the property is lost to the owner.*

> "Owner" means a person who has title to the property, possession of the property, whether lawful or not, or a greater right to possession of the property than *Don Davis*.

> "Property" means: (a) real property; (b) tangible or intangible personal property, including anything severed from land; or (c) a document, including money, that represents or embodies anything of value.

> "Consent" means assent in fact, whether express or implied.

> "Effective consent" includes *consent by a person legally authorized to act for the owner. Consent is not effective if induced by deception or coercion.*

Answer "Yes" or "No."

Answer: _____

COMMENT

When to use.   PJC 110.39 should be used in a case where (1) exemplary damages are sought; (2) the harm to the plaintiff is alleged to have resulted from conduct described as a third-degree felony in Tex. Pen. Code Ann. § 31.03 (Vernon 1994 & Supp. 1998); and (3) the jury has previously found that the defendant committed conduct authorizing recovery of exemplary damages as set out in Tex. Civ. Prac. & Rem. Code Ann. § 41.003 (Vernon 1997). *See* Tex. Civ. Prac. & Rem. Code § 41.008(c)(13). This statute applies to causes of action accruing on or after September 1, 1995. If the jury finds conduct that violates Tex. Pen. Code ch. 31, and that conduct rises to the level of a third-degree felony, the limitations on exemplary damages awards set out in Tex. Civ. Prac. & Rem. Code § 41.008(b) do not apply. Tex. Civ. Prac. & Rem. Code § 41.008(c). See comment below, " 'Value' and re-quirement that conduct be described as a third-degree felony," for a discussion of the requirements needed to establish that the conduct in question was felonious.

Bifurcation.   If a defendant has requested a bifurcated trial pursuant to Tex. Civ. Prac. & Rem. Code § 41.009, PJC 110.39 should be answered in the first phase of the trial.

Alternative definition for "unlawful appropriation of property."   "Unlawful ap-propriation of property" also occurs when the property is stolen and the actor appropriates the property knowing it was stolen by another. Tex. Pen. Code § 31.03(b)(2) (1994). In an appropriate case, this definition should be substituted for the one shown above, and the Pe-nal Code's definition of "knowing conduct," found at Tex. Pen. Code § 6.03(b), should be given as well.

Alternative definitions for "deprive."   In an appropriate case, one or more of the fol-lowing definitions of "deprive" may be substituted for the one shown above.

> to restore property only upon payment of reward or other compensation.

or—

> to dispose of property in a manner that makes recovery of the property by the owner unlikely.

Tex. Pen. Code § 31.01(2)(B), (C).

Effective consent.   In an appropriate case, the language *Consent is not effective if in-duced by deception or coercion* may be replaced with any of the following alternatives:

> [Consent is not effective if]
>
> (a)   given by a person *Don Davis* knows is not legally authorized to act for the owner;
>
> (b)   given by a person who by reason of youth, mental disease or defect, or intoxication is known by *Don Davis* to be unable to make reasonable property dispositions; or
>
> (c)   given solely to detect the commission of an offense.

Tex. Pen. Code § 31.01(3). If the defendant's knowledge of a fact is in issue (as in option (a) above), the definition of "knowing conduct" found at Tex. Pen. Code § 6.03(b) should be given.

Theft of services and trade secrets. Tex. Pen. Code § 31.04 (1994 & Supp. 1998) should be consulted if the alleged theft was of services rather than of property, and Tex. Pen. Code § 31.05 (1994) should be consulted if the alleged theft was of a trade secret.

"Value" and requirement that conduct be described as a third-degree felony. Tex. Civ. Prac. & Rem. Code § 41.008(c)(13) requires that the theft be at a level of a third-degree felony or higher in order to lift the limitation or cap on exemplary damages awards. The general criterion for a third-degree felony is that the property or service have a value of $20,000 or higher. Tex. Pen. Code § 31.03(e)(5) (Supp. 1998). The optional language in the basic question in PJC 110.39 makes this inquiry, if there is a dispute about the value of what was stolen. Tex. Pen. Code § 31.08 (1994) contains additional criteria for ascertaining value to determine the level of the offense, and Tex. Pen. Code § 31.03 (1994 & Supp. 1998) contains additional, nonmonetary criteria for ascertaining the level of punishment.

Source of instruction and definition. The question and instructions are derived from Tex. Pen. Code §§ 1.07(a)(9), (24), 2.05, 6.03, 31.01(4), (5), (6) (1994), § 31.03 (1994 & Supp. 1998), § 31.08 (1994); Tex. Civ. Prac. & Rem. Code § 41.008.

PJC 110.40   **Question and Instruction—Commercial (Fiduciary) Bribery as a Ground for Removing Limitation on Exemplary Damages (Tex. Civ. Prac. & Rem. Code § 41.008(c)(9))**

If you have answered "Yes" to Question _____ [*110.33*], then answer the following question. Otherwise, do not answer the following question.

QUESTION _____

Did *Don Davis*, without *Paul Payne*'s consent, intentionally solicit, accept, or agree to accept any benefit from another person on the agreement or understanding that the benefit would influence *his* conduct in relation to the affairs of *Paul Payne*?

> A person acts with intent with respect to the nature of *his* conduct or to a result of *his* conduct when it is the conscious objective or desire to engage in the conduct or cause the result.

Answer "Yes" or "No."

Answer: _____

COMMENT

When to use.   PJC 110.40 should be used in a case where (1) exemplary damages are sought; (2) the harm to the plaintiff is alleged to have resulted from conduct described in Tex. Pen. Code Ann. § 32.43 (Vernon 1994); and (3) the jury has previously found that the defendant committed conduct authorizing recovery of exemplary damages as set out in Tex. Civ. Prac. & Rem. Code Ann. § 41.003 (Vernon 1997). *See* Tex. Civ. Prac. & Rem. Code § 41.008(c)(9). This statute applies to causes of action accruing on or after September 1, 1995. If the jury finds conduct that violates Tex. Pen. Code § 32.43, the limitations on exemplary damages awards set out in Tex. Civ. Prac. & Rem. Code § 41.008(b) do not apply. Tex. Civ. Prac. & Rem. Code § 41.008(c).

Bifurcation.   If a defendant has requested a bifurcated trial pursuant to Tex. Civ. Prac. & Rem. Code § 41.009, PJC 110.40 should be answered in the first phase of the trial.

Consent.   If a definition of "consent" is required, use the following:

"Consent" means assent in fact, whether express or apparent.

Tex. Pen. Code § 1.07(a)(11).

Benefit.   If a definition of "benefit" is required, use the following:

"Benefit" means anything reasonably regarded as economic gain or advantage, including benefit to any other person in whose welfare the beneficiary is interested.

Tex. Pen. Code § 1.07(a)(7).

Knowing standard of conduct.   Tex. Civ. Prac. & Rem. Code § 41.008(c) authorizes elimination of the limitation on exemplary damages awards if the conduct described in the applicable Penal Code section was committed either knowingly or intentionally. If knowing instead of intentional conduct is alleged, use the following definition:

> A person acts knowingly with respect to the nature of *his* conduct or to circumstances surrounding *his* conduct when *he* is aware of the nature of *his* conduct or that the circumstances exist. A person acts knowingly with respect to a result of *his* conduct when *he* is aware that *his* conduct is reasonably certain to cause the result.

Tex. Pen. Code § 6.03(b).

Offering bribe also criminal conduct.   A person who, for an improper purpose, intentionally offers, confers, or agrees to confer a benefit to a fiduciary also commits commercial bribery. Tex. Pen. Code § 32.43(d). In an appropriate case, the question should read:

> Did *Don Davis* intentionally offer, confer, or agree to confer a benefit on *Fred Fiduciary* on the agreement that the benefit would influence *Fred Fiduciary*'s conduct in relation to the affairs of *Paul Payne*?

Fiduciary.   The defendant must be a fiduciary for the conduct described in Tex. Pen. Code § 32.43 to apply. "Fiduciary" is defined there as (a) an agent or employee; (b) a trustee, guardian, custodian, administrator, executor, conservator, receiver, or similar fiduciary; (c) a lawyer, physician, accountant, appraiser, or other professional advisor; or (d) an officer, director, partner, manager, or other participant in the direction of the affairs of a corporation or association. Tex. Pen. Code § 32.43(a). If the existence of such a fiduciary relationship is disputed, a preliminary question should be submitted, and PJC 110.40 should be made conditional on a "Yes" answer to that question. *See Schiller v. Elick*, 240 S.W.2d 997, 999 (Tex. 1951) (dispute whether defendant was plaintiff's agent). See chapter 104 of this volume regarding fiduciary and confidential relationships.

Beneficiary.   For purposes of the commercial bribery statute, a "beneficiary" is the person for whom a fiduciary acts. Tex. Pen. Code § 32.43(a)(1). PJC 110.40 assumes that the plaintiff is the beneficiary.

Source of instruction and definition.   Tex. Pen. Code § 32.43; Tex. Civ. Prac. & Rem. Code § 41.008.

PJC 110.41   Question and Instructions—Misapplication of Fiduciary Property as a Ground for Removing Limitation on Exemplary Damages (Tex. Civ. Prac. & Rem. Code § 41.008(c)(10))

If you have answered "Yes" to Question _____ [*110.33*], then answer the following question. Otherwise, do not answer the following question.

QUESTION _____

Did *Don Davis* intentionally misapply [*identify property defendant held as a fiduciary, e.g., 300 shares of ABC Corporation common stock*] in a manner that involved substantial risk of loss to *Paul Payne* [*and was the value of the property $1,500 or greater*]?

> "Misapply" means a person deals with property [*or money*] contrary to *an agreement under which the person holds the property* [*or money*].

> "Substantial risk of loss" means it is more likely than not that loss will occur.

> A person acts with intent with respect to the nature of *his* conduct or to a result of *his* conduct when it is the conscious objective or desire to engage in the conduct or cause the result.

Answer "Yes" or "No."

Answer: _____

COMMENT

When to use.   PJC 110.41 should be used in a case where (1) exemplary damages are sought; (2) the harm to the plaintiff is alleged to have resulted from conduct described in Tex. Pen. Code Ann. § 32.45 (Vernon 1994 & Supp. 1998); and (3) the jury has previously found that the defendant committed conduct authorizing recovery of exemplary damages as set out in Tex. Civ. Prac. & Rem. Code Ann. § 41.003 (Vernon 1997). *See* Tex. Civ. Prac. & Rem. Code § 41.008(c)(10). This statute applies to causes of action accruing on or after September 1, 1995. If the jury finds conduct that violates Tex. Pen. Code § 32.45, the limitations on exemplary damages awards set out in Tex. Civ. Prac. & Rem. Code § 41.008(b) do not apply. Tex. Civ. Prac. & Rem. Code § 41.008(c).

Bifurcation.   If a defendant has requested a bifurcated trial pursuant to Tex. Civ. Prac. & Rem. Code § 41.009, PJC 110.41 should be answered in the first phase of the trial.

Knowing standard of conduct. Tex. Civ. Prac. & Rem. Code § 41.008(c) authorizes elimination of the limitation on exemplary damages awards if the conduct described in the applicable Penal Code section was committed either knowingly or intentionally. If knowing instead of intentional conduct is alleged, use the following definition:

> A person acts knowingly with respect to the nature of *his* conduct or to circumstances surrounding *his* conduct when *he* is aware of the nature of *his* conduct or that the circumstances exist. A person acts knowingly with respect to a result of *his* conduct when *he* is aware that *his* conduct is reasonably certain to cause the result.

Tex. Pen. Code § 6.03(b) (1994).

Agreement. If a definition of "agreement" is required, use the following:

> "Agreement" means the act of agreement or coming to an agreement; a harmonious understanding; or an arrangement as to a course of action.

Bynum v. State, 711 S.W.2d 321, 323 (Tex. App.—Amarillo 1986), *aff'd*, 767 S.W.2d 769 (Tex. Crim. App. 1989) (applying ordinary, dictionary definition of "agreement").

Property. Tex. Pen. Code § 32.01(2) defines "property" broadly to include tangible or intangible property as well as money. Because the jury may not understand money to be "property," the word "money" should be used if money is involved in the case.

Acting contrary to a law governing disposition of property. In an appropriate case, the phrase *a law prescribing the custody or disposition of the property* may be substituted for, or added to, the phrase *an agreement under which the person holds the property.* Tex. Pen. Code § 32.45(a)(2).

Fiduciary. The defendant must be a fiduciary for the conduct described in Tex. Pen. Code § 32.45 (1994 & Supp. 1998) to apply. "Fiduciary" is defined there as including (a) a trustee, guardian, administrator, executor, conservator, or receiver; (b) any other person acting in a fiduciary capacity, but not a commercial bailee unless the commercial bailee is a party in a motor fuel sales agreement with a distributor or supplier, as those terms are defined in Tex. Tax Code Ann. § 153.001 (Vernon Supp. 1998); and (c) an officer, manager, employee, or agent carrying on fiduciary functions on behalf of a fiduciary. Tex. Pen. Code § 32.45(a)(1) (Supp. 1998). "Any other person acting in a fiduciary capacity" embraces all fiduciaries, not just the categories of fiduciaries enumerated in Tex. Pen. Code § 32.45(a)(1). *Coplin v. State*, 585 S.W.2d 734, 735 (Tex. Crim. App. 1979); *Showery v. State*, 678 S.W.2d 103, 107-08 (Tex. App.—El Paso 1984, pet. ref'd).

If the existence of such a fiduciary relationship is disputed, a preliminary question should be submitted, and PJC 110.41 should be made conditional on a "Yes" answer to that question. *See Schiller v. Elick*, 240 S.W.2d 997, 999 (Tex. 1951) (dispute whether defendant was plaintiff's agent). See chapter 104 of this volume regarding fiduciary and confidential relationships.

Substantial risk of loss. The definition of "substantial risk of loss" is derived from *Bynum*, 767 S.W.2d at 774–75; *Casillas v. State*, 733 S.W.2d 158, 163–64 (Tex. Crim. App. 1986), *appeal dismissed*, 108 S. Ct. 277 (1987).

Misapplication of property of financial institution. If the defendant is alleged to have misapplied property of a financial institution instead of fiduciary property, the question should be amended to read as follows:

QUESTION _____

Did *Don Davis* intentionally misapply property of *ABC Bank* in a manner that involved substantial risk of loss to *ABC Bank* [*and was the value of the misapplied property $1,500 or greater*]?

"Misapply" means to deal with property contrary to a law prescribing the custody or disposition of the property.

"Substantial risk of loss" means it is more likely than not that loss will occur.

A person acts with intent with respect to the nature of *his* conduct or to a result of *his* conduct when it is the conscious objective or desire to engage in the conduct or cause the result.

"Value" and requirement that conduct be described as a felony. Tex. Civ. Prac. & Rem. Code § 41.008(c) provides that the limitation or cap on exemplary damages may only be lifted if the plaintiff's damages are based on conduct "described as a felony" in Tex. Pen. Code § 32.45 (1994 & Supp. 1998). The criminal conduct described in Tex. Pen. Code § 32.45 rises to felonious conduct only when the value of the property misapplied is $1,500 or higher. Tex. Pen. Code § 32.45(c) (1994). The optional language in the basic question in PJC 110.41 establishes whether the defendant's conduct rises to the status of a felony, if there is a dispute about the value of the misapplied property.

Source of instruction and definition. Tex. Pen. Code § 31.08 (1994), § 32.45 (1994 & Supp. 1998); Tex. Civ. Prac. & Rem. Code § 41.008.

PJC 110.42   Other Conduct of Defendant Authorizing Removal of Limitation on Exemplary Damages Award (Comment)

In addition to the actions described in PJCs 110.36–.41, nine other instances of the defendant's conduct, listed in Tex. Civ. Prac. & Rem. Code Ann. § 41.008(c) (Vernon 1997), will support a removal of the limitation on exemplary damages awards set out in Tex. Civ. Prac. & Rem. Code § 41.008(b). They are:

- murder (Tex. Pen. Code Ann. § 19.02 (Vernon 1994));

- capital murder (Tex. Pen. Code § 19.03);

- aggravated kidnapping (Tex. Pen. Code § 20.04 (Supp. 1998));

- aggravated assault (Tex. Pen. Code § 22.02 (1994));

- sexual assault (Tex. Pen. Code § 22.011 (1994 & Supp. 1998));

- aggravated sexual assault (Tex. Pen. Code § 22.021);

- injury to a child, elderly individual, or disabled individual (Tex. Pen. Code § 22.04);

- intoxication assault (Tex. Pen. Code § 49.07 (1994)); and

- intoxication manslaughter (Tex. Pen. Code § 49.08).

When to use.   A question asking whether the defendant engaged in the conduct described in the Penal Code provisions set out above should be used in a case where (1) exemplary damages are sought; (2) the harm to the plaintiff is alleged to have resulted from the felonious conduct described in the Penal Code provision; and (3) the jury has previously found that the defendant committed conduct authorizing recovery of exemplary damages as set out in Tex. Civ. Prac. & Rem. Code § 41.003. *See* Tex. Civ. Prac. & Rem. Code § 41.008(c). This statute applies to causes of action accruing on or after September 1, 1995. If the jury answers "Yes" to such a question, the limitations on exemplary damages awards set out in Tex. Civ. Prac. & Rem. Code § 41.008(b) do not apply. Tex. Civ. Prac. & Rem. Code § 41.008(c).

Drafting of question.   A jury question regarding one or more of the acts set out in the Penal Code sections listed above should follow the pattern set out in PJCs 110.36–.41. See also Paul J. McClung, *Jury Charges for Texas Criminal Practice* (rev. ed. 1995).

Standard of conduct—"intentionally" or "knowingly."   Tex. Civ. Prac. & Rem. Code § 41.008(c) authorizes elimination of the limitation on exemplary damages awards if the conduct described in the applicable Penal Code section was committed either knowingly or intentionally. "Knowingly" is defined as follows:

> A person acts knowingly, or with knowledge, with respect to the nature of his conduct or to circumstances surrounding his conduct when he is aware of the nature of his conduct or that the circumstances exist. A person acts knowingly, or with knowledge, with respect to a result of his conduct when he is aware that his conduct is reasonably certain to cause the result.

Tex. Pen. Code § 6.03(b).

"Intentionally" is defined as follows:

A person acts intentionally, or with intent, with respect to the nature of his conduct or to a result of his conduct when it is his conscious objective or desire to engage in the conduct or cause the result.

Tex. Pen. Code § 6.03(a).

Felonious conduct.   Tex. Civ. Prac. & Rem. Code § 41.008(c) provides that the limitation or cap on exemplary damages may only be lifted if the plaintiff's damages are based on conduct "described as a felony" in the applicable Penal Code section, unless the conduct is intoxication assault or intoxication manslaughter.

PJC 110.43   Question on Attorney's Fees

If you have answered "Yes" to Question _____ [*the liability question, e.g., 101.2, 103.1, 105.1, or 106.1*], then answer the following question. Otherwise, do not answer the following question.

QUESTION _____

What is a reasonable fee for the necessary services of *Paul Payne*'s attorney in this case, stated in dollars and cents?

Answer with an amount for each of the following:

a.   For preparation and trial.

Answer: _____

b.   For an appeal to the Court of Appeals.

Answer: _____

c.   For an appeal to the Supreme Court of Texas.

Answer: _____

COMMENT

When to use.   Attorney's fees are recoverable in contracts, DTPA, Insurance Code, Texas Whistleblower Act, and Texas Commission on Human Rights Act (TCHRA) claims. Tex. Civ. Prac. & Rem. Code Ann. § 38.001 (Vernon 1997); Tex. Bus. & Com. Code Ann. § 17.50(d) (Vernon Supp. 1998) (DTPA); Tex. Ins. Code Ann. art. 21.21, § 16(b)(1) (Vernon Supp. 1998); Tex. Gov't Code Ann. § 554.003(a) (Vernon Supp. 1998); Tex. Lab. Code Ann. § 21.259 (Vernon 1996). PJC 110.43 is to be used regardless of the terms of the fee agreement.

In *Arthur Andersen & Co. v. Perry Equipment Corp.*, 945 S.W.2d 812, 817-18 (Tex. 1997), the supreme court held that a percentage award question should not be used; *see also Lubbock County v. Strube*, 953 S.W.2d 847, 858 (Tex. App.—Austin 1997, no writ) (Whistleblower Act case). Although a contingent fee is proper, the jury's award must be stated in dollars and cents.

Factors to consider.   In *Arthur Andersen & Co.*, the supreme court held that the following factors must be considered in determining the reasonableness of an attorney's fee award:

* the time and labor involved, the novelty and difficulty of the questions involved, and the skill required to perform the legal services properly;

- the likelihood that the acceptance of the particular employment will preclude other employment by the lawyer;

- the fee customarily charged in the locality for similar legal services;

- the amount involved and the results obtained;

- the time limitations imposed by the client or the circumstances;

- the nature and length of the professional relationship with the client;

- the experience, reputation, and ability of the lawyer or lawyers performing the services; and

- whether the fee is fixed or contingent on results obtained or uncertainty of collection before the legal services have been rendered.

Arthur Andersen & Co., 945 S.W.2d at 818. *See also* Tex. Disciplinary R. Prof'l Conduct 1.04, *reprinted in* Tex. Gov't Code, tit. 2, subtit. G app. A (1998) (Tex. State Bar R. art. X, § 9).

In an appropriate case, one or more of these factors may be included as additional jury instructions.

Attorney's fees mandatory if plaintiff prevails.   The phrase *if any* should not be included in the questions for fees. The jury determines the amount of reasonable and necessary fees, not whether fees should be recovered. Attorney's fees in some amount are required to be awarded to a prevailing consumer. *See Satellite Earth Stations East, Inc. v. Davis*, 756 S.W.2d 385 (Tex. App.—Eastland 1988, writ denied); *Doerfler v. Espensen Co.*, 659 S.W.2d 929 (Tex. App.—Corpus Christi 1983, no writ). The same rule applies to appellate fees. *Great State Petroleum, Inc. v. Arrow Rig Service*, 706 S.W.2d 803, 812 (Tex. App.—Fort Worth 1986) (opinion on rehearing, 714 S.W.2d 429, no writ); *see also McKinley v. Drozd*, 685 S.W.2d 7 (Tex. 1985) (net recovery not required to obtain attorney's fees under article 2226 (now chapter 38 of the Texas Civil Practice and Remedies Code) or DTPA).

Segregating claims.   Though the general rule is that attorney's fees claims must be segregated, most DTPA cases will be governed by the exception to the rule, which states that if the statutory and nonstatutory claims are dependent on the same set of facts, segregation is not required. *Paramount National Life Insurance Co. v. Williams*, 772 S.W.2d 255, 266 (Tex. App.—Houston [14th Dist.] 1989, writ denied); *see also Village Mobile Homes, Inc. v. Porter*, 716 S.W.2d 543, 552 (Tex. App.—Austin 1986, writ ref'd n.r.e.) (DTPA claim); *Hruska v. First State Bank*, 747 S.W.2d 783, 785 (Tex. 1988) (erroneous broad submission of attorney's fees waived by defendant's failure to specifically object to nonsegregated question).

Defendant's attorney's fees.   This question may be modified to submit the defendant's attorney's fees as well, if recoverable under contract law or under DTPA §§ 17.50(c) or 17.506 (1987 & Supp. 1998).

STATUTES AND RULES CITED

[Decimal references are to PJC numbers.]

Texas Constitution

Art. XVI, § 26 . . . . 110.33

Texas Revised Civil Statutes

Texas Administrative Code

Title 28

Texas Business & Commerce Code

Texas Election Code

Texas Family Code

Texas Finance Code

Texas Government Code

Texas Health & Safety Code

Texas Insurance Code

Texas Labor Code

Texas Penal Code

Texas Property Code

Texas Tax Code

Texas Rules of Civil Procedure

State Bar Rules
Texas Disciplinary Rules of Professional Conduct

United States Code

Code of Federal Regulations

Miscellaneous

Age Discrimination in Employment Act (ADEA): *see* title 29, §§ 621– 634, of United States Code

Americans with Disabilities Act (ADA): *see* title 42, §§ 12101–12213, of United States Code

Civil Rights Act of 1964: *see* title 42, §§ 2000e to e-17, of United States Code

Civil Rights Act of 1991: *see* title 42, § 2000e, of United States Code

Deceptive Trade Practices–Consumer Protection Act (DTPA): *see* §§ 17.41–.63 of Texas Business & Commerce Code

Rehabilitation Act of 1973: *see* title 29, § 31, of United States Code

Texas Commisson on Human Rights Act (TCHRA): *see* §§ 21.001–.306 of Texas Labor Code

Texas Whistleblower Act: *see* §§ 554.001–.010 of Texas Government Code

CASES CITED

[Decimal references are to PJC numbers.]

A

ACS Investors, Inc. v. McLaughlin, 106.1

Adams v. Petrade International, Inc., 101.3

Adams v. Valley Federal Credit Union, 107.6

Adolph Coors Co. v. Rodriguez, 101.2, 103.1

Aetna Casualty & Surety Co. v. Marshall, 102.15, 110.13

Airborne Freight Corp. v. C.R. Lee Enterprises, 110.19-.20

Akin v. Dahl, 109.1

Alamo National Bank v. Kraus, 110.34

Albemarle Paper Co. v. Moody, 107.6

Alexander v. Handley, 101.32

Alexander & Alexander, Inc. v. Bacchus Industries, Inc., 110.7

A.L.G. Enterprises v. Huffman, 101.28

Allison v. Harrison, 110.15

Allstate Insurance Co. v. Watson, 102.15

Alvarado v. Bolton, 102.22

American Bank v. Thompson, 110.3

Ames v. Great Southern Bank, 101.4

Anderson v. Griffith, 110.17

Anderson Development Corp. v. Coastal States Crude Gathering Co., 110.3

Anthony Pools v. Charles & David, Inc., 110.23

Antwine v. Reed, 101.12

Aranda v. Insurance Co. of North America, 103.1

Arce v. Burrow, 110.17

Archer v. Griffith, 104.2, 108.2-.7, 110.17

Armendariz v. Mora, 110.23

Armstrong v. O'Brien, 110.17

Arnold v. National County Mutual Fire Insurance Co., 103.1

Arthur Andersen & Co. v. Perry Equipment Corp., 110.43

Atkinson v. Jackson Bros., 101.46

Austin Lake Estates, Inc. v. Meyer, 101.22

Azar Nut Co. v. Caille, 107.5, 110.26

B

Bach v. Hudson, 101.33

B.A.L. v. Edna Gladney Home, 101.27

Bankston (W.O.) Nissan, Inc. v. Walters, 110.9

Barfield v. Howard M. Smith Co., 101.25

Bashara v. Baptist Memorial Hospital System, 101.42

Beaston v. State Farm Life Insurance Co., 110.13

Beeman v. Worrell, 101.42, 101.46

Bell v. Bradshaw, 105.3

Bell v. Manning, 105.16

Benavides v. Moore, 107.20

Bendalin v. Delgado, 101.8, 101.13

Berry v. Golden Light Coffee Co., 109.1

Bexar County Sheriff's Civil Service Commission v. Davis, 107.1

Black Lake Pipe Line Co. v. Union Construction Co., 101.26, 101.42

Blalack v. Johnson, 110.6

Blue Bell, Inc. v. Peat, Marwick, Mitchell & Co., 105.16

Blue Island, Inc. v. Taylor, 110.11

Bocanegra v. Aetna Life Insurance Co., 101.25

Bowles v. Fickas, 101.12

Boyles v. Kerr, 110.9

Brandy v. City of Cedar Hill, 107.1

I

Import Motors, Inc. v. Matthews, 102.22

International Bankers Life Insurance Co. v.
Holloway, 104.2, 109.1, 110.15-.16

International Brotherhood of Teamsters v.
United States, 107.6

International Security Life Insurance Co. v.
Finck, 105.4

International Union UAW v. Johnson
Controls, Inc., 106.1

Investors, Inc. v. Hadley, 110.9

Island Recreational Development Corp. v.
Republic of Texas Savings Ass'n,
101.21, 101.24

J

Jack v. Texaco Research Center, 107.9

Jackson v. Fontaine's Clinics, Inc., 110.2,
110.8-.9, 110.13-.14, 110.19-.22

Jacobs v. Danny Darby Real Estate, Inc.,
110.9

James Stewart & Co. v. Law, 101.8

James T. Taylor & Son v. Arlington
Independent School District, 101.28

Jenkins v. Henry C. Beck Co., 101.32

Jett v. Dallas Independent School District,
107.10

Jim Walter Homes, Inc. v. Valencia, 110.11

Johnson v. Peckham, 104.2

Johnson v. Zurich General Accident &
Liability Insurance Co., 100.8

Jones v. Flagship International, 107.21-.23

Jon-T Farms, Inc. v. Goodpasture, Inc.,
101.2

Jordan Drilling Co. v. Starr, 101.22

Juliette Fowler Homes, Inc. v. Welch
Associates, 106.2

K

Kamarath v. Bennett, 102.13

Kelleher v. Flawn, 107.10

Keller Industries, Inc. v. Reeves, 110.10

Kerrville HRH, Inc. v. City of Kerrville,
105.8

Kingsbery v. Phillips Petroleum Co., 109.1

King Title Co. v. Croft, 101.22

Kinzbach Tool Co. v. Corbett-Wallace
Corp., 104.2, 110.15, 110.17

Kirkwood & Morgan, Inc. v. Roach, 101.1

Kish v. Van Note, 110.8-.9

Koral Industries v. Security-Connecticut
Life Insurance Co., 105.2

Kuehne v. Denson, 101.25

L

LaChance v. Hollenbeck, 110.3

LaChance v. McKown, 102.24

Lake (P.G.), Inc. v. Sheffield, 110.3

Lakeway Land Co. v. Kizer, 107.6

Lambert v. H. Molsen & Co., 101.9

Land Title Co. v. F.M. Stigler, Inc., 101.5

Laredo Hides Co. v. H & H Meat Products
Co., 101.10

Larson v. Ellison, 100.8

La Sara Grain Co. v. First National Bank,
102.8-.9

Lee-Wright, Inc. v. Hall, 107.2, 110.25

Lemos v. Montez, Introduction (4)(c)

Leonard Duckworth, Inc. v. Michael L.
Field & Co., 106.2

Leyendecker & Associates v. Wechter, 110.9

Lone Star Steel Co. v. Scott, 101.1

Lone Star Steel Co. v. Wahl, 107.2, 110.24

Lovell v. Western National Life Insurance
Co., 103.1

LSR Joint Venture No. 2 v. Callewart,
110.19

Lubbock County v. Strube, 110.43

Ludt v. McCollum, 110.9

T

U

V

W

SUBJECT INDEX

[Decimal references are to PJC numbers.]